THE CREATIVE BUSINESS GUIDE TO MARKETING

Selling and Branding Design, Advertising, Interactive, and Editorial Services

CAMERON S. FOOTE

W. W. Norton
London • New York

For information about permission to reproduce selections from this book, write to Permissions, W. W. Norton & Company, Inc., 500 Fifth Avenue, New York, NY 10110

For information about special discounts for bulk purchases, please contact W. W. Norton Special Sales at specialsales@wwnorton.com or 800-233-4830

Manufacturing by Edwards Brothers
Book design by Jonathan Lippincott
Composition by Ken Gross
Production manager: Leeann Graham

Library of Congress Cataloging-in-Publication Data

Foote, Cameron S.
    The creative business guide to marketing : selling and branding design, advertising, interactive, and editorial services / Cameron S. Foote. — 1st ed.
        p.   cm.
    Includes index.
    ISBN 978-0-393-73347-1 (hardcover)
    1. Marketing. 2. Strategic planning. 3. Branding (Marketing) I. Title.

    HF5415.F5656 2012
    658.8—dc23   2011021989

    ISBN: 978-0-393-73347-1
    ISBN: 978-0-393-73373-0 pbk

W. W. Norton & Company, Inc., 500 Fifth Avenue, New York, N.Y. 10110
www.wwnorton.com
W. W. Norton & Company Ltd., Castle House, 75/76 Wells Street, London W1T 3QT

0 9 8 7 6 5 4 3 2 1

CONTENTS

PREFACE

Marketing is the biggest problem that affects the long-term success of creative services businesses, both single-person and multi-person. More businesses fail to achieve success (or go out of business) because of marketing than because of any other cause. The other reasons cited—bad luck, insufficient finances, difficult clients, weak employees, and so on—all pale by comparison.

The reason is simple: the old standbys of word-of-mouth, referrals, and occasional promotions are no longer enough in today's increasingly commoditized and competitive environment. Without regular and consistent marketing, a business can find itself on a feast-or-famine roller coaster at best; at worst, struggling for its very existence.

Today more than ever, there's a strong correlation between the success of a creative business and the effectiveness of its marketing efforts.

It is ironic that creatives don't embrace marketing more enthusiastically, or that they think of it only in terms of occasional selling. After all, whether their focus is design, advertising, interactive, copy, public relations, or a combination of these and more, they are all primarily in the marketing business. It is their bread and butter. Yet they have difficulty practicing what they so enthusiastically preach to others.

A justifiable reason for this behavior is that creative businesses are unusual: they require marketing techniques and programs that are different from the ones their clients commonly apply. Not justifiable, however, is the other major reason: hubris. It is the belief that creative individuals shouldn't have to stoop to marketing, that doing so somehow belittles their talent.

This is a book for you if you are interested in running a profitable creative organization, whether you work alone or as a larger firm's principal or manager. This book will tell you why marketing is important regardless of your firm's size and no matter whether your firm is already a stable organization with a depth of talent and good, steady clients. The book will also inform you about which techniques work most often for most organizations. It is a book for anyone who is unsure of the need for marketing, has had difficulty prospecting for clients, needs to know more about hiring and motivating business development (sales) personnel, or has been less than successful in converting presentations into projects, and concepts into client-approved work.

Note that the subject here is marketing—not just selling, which represents only a portion of the problem and the solution. Those who run single-person firms should also note that the book is not just about self-promotion. Rather, it is about how to market the services of a distinctive type of business to other businesses.

Much of this book's content comes from my decades of experience in Fortune 500 marketing organizations and from running my own creative businesses. Even more, however, comes from attendees at Creative Business workshops, seminars, and roundtables, and from subscribers to the *Creative Business* newsletter, the only publication devoted exclusively to addressing the business needs of creative organizations. Their feedback—what actually works and doesn't work in the real world—is the primary source of content. Moreover, since much of the content has previously been published in the *Creative Business* newsletter, it has passed the tests of relevance and accuracy through extensive peer review.

The Creative Business Guide to Marketing is the third in a series of books covering important aspects of the creative services business. *The Business Side of Creativity* (2006) treats freelancing and setting up a small communications business. *The Creative Business Guide to Running a Graphic Design Business* (2009) addresses managing a design organization. Each of these companion volumes also contains marketing information in a different and complementary context.

SECTION ONE

STRATEGIES AND TACTICS

This first section lays the foundation for marketing success by covering four subjects. Chapter 1 addresses the misconceptions that creative professionals often have about marketing, and it explains the several reasons why marketing is a crucial element in the long-term success of any commercial endeavor. Chapter 2 discusses the many strategic considerations that should go into marketing. Chapter 3 presents the basics of tactics, who should be involved, and how much to spend. Chapter 4 explores the essentials of implementation, including developing a plan.

1

WHY MARKETING IS IMPORTANT

One of the ironies of the creative services business is that we who make our living addressing the marketing needs of others are often inept marketers of what we ourselves do. We recognize its importance—except, that is, when it comes to spending our own money. Sometimes we don't do any marketing, relying instead on word-of-mouth to sustain our businesses. Sometimes we do it only after discovering that the project pipeline is drying out. And sometimes we invest our money in all the wrong places.

THE CREATIVE PSYCHE

These problems have roots deep in the psyche, and they flower in the everyday world of working with clients. As creatively gifted individuals, we expect success to be primarily a function of our talent. In our hearts, most of us would prefer to operate a "practice" supported by needy and appreciative clients who seek us out for the benefits of our talent and wisdom. This desire seems vindicated whenever our talent, as evidenced by the work we produce, wins praise from current clients or leads us to new ones. It is the creative skill, not the marketing, that gets all the credit.

To a large extent, this is justified. As in any industry, the better the product, the greater its sales, and the more successful a business will probably be. But also, as in any other industry, there is a lot more to success, especially long-term success. This is particularly so when success is defined in terms of growth, profitability, and owner satisfaction.

As important as the quality of their products is, businesses in other industries largely accept the fact that quality is seldom enough for growth or stability. Marketing is also necessary. If businesses don't constantly market their products, many potential customers will never know of them, or only the wrong types of customers will know of them, or they won't be able to generate enough volume to price competitively. It is ironic that the creative community does not accept this point more widely. After all, marketing for clients supports that community.

Several decades of following the fortunes of creative firms both large and small leads me to the inescapable conclusion that there is a nearly perfect correlation between a creative organization's profitability and longevity, and its embrace of consistent marketing activity.

THE FOUR FUNCTIONS OF ALL ORGANIZATIONS

As unique in many ways as creative service organizations are, in one important respect they are just like all others. Every commercial entity—regardless of its industry, field, product, or profit or not-for-profit status—is organized around four major functions:

- *Procuring.* In its most elementary form, procuring involves getting enough business to stay in business. This is the function of marketing, a specialized type of which is the subject of this book.
- *Producing.* In most organizations, this function would be called operations or manufacturing. In service organizations, it is the production function, including the creative process.
- *Delivering.* This is the distribution function, which for most commercial organizations includes ordering channels, warehouses, wholesalers, and dealers. For service organizations, it means delivering what pleases the client and managing client relations.
- *Financing.* Regardless of the product or service produced, costs must be kept in line with income. Watching the bottom line, or "balancing the checkbook," is the financial function.

By temperament, creative individuals tend to concentrate on the second and third functions listed above. After all, producing (creating) and delivering are what we find most enjoyable and what we've been trained to do. We also reluctantly pay attention to finances because we know that ignoring them can kill any business very quickly. That leaves marketing—the function least appreciated and most easily ignored, for the reasons that follow. (For a review of common marketing mistakes, see Appendix I.)

THE MISCONCEPTIONS PROBLEM

Marketing suffers from several basic misconceptions that are rife among creative individuals. One involves doubting the necessity for marketing. The other involves considering it too narrowly. Let's deconstruct both.

NOT BELIEVING. There is, one could posit, something of an ethical disconnect in individuals who recommend marketing activities to their clients but won't practice the same in their own organizations. That aside, there is a common belief among artistically talented individuals that marketing shouldn't be necessary. If an individual or organization is good enough, the world should beat a path to their door. In other words, any marketing activity is considered a negative reflection on their creative talent. So to the extent that there is any marketing activity, the individual or organization conducts it reluctantly, usually as a temporary solution to a business downturn. When situations improve, the activity stops.

If you need proof, consider asking this of any principal or freelancer at a gathering of creatives: "Does your firm do much marketing?" Chances are the answer will be something like this: "Not really. Our business comes by referral. Oh, last year, when times were tough, we did a little, but that was an exception." Such a response is a good representation of reality, and it also indicates a common reluctance to admit to marketing even where it does occur. Most creative organizations expect to get their business from referrals and consider anything else a compromise. (For more on why this is not a healthy viewpoint, see the discussion later in this chapter.)

THINKING TOO NARROWLY. Although the primary purpose of marketing is to bring in business, it does not necessarily have to be the immediate purpose. Indeed, selling, the most recognized aspect of marketing, is only one of its functions. There are several other advantages as well. The danger of considering marketing strictly in a business-generating (sales) context is that it keeps an organization from reaping these supplementary benefits.

When marketing is initiated only when necessary to generate new business, it is less effective and more costly. There are none of the scale economies and benefits from the awareness that accompanies consistent activity. Tellingly, inconsistency also exacerbates the business roller coaster effect: marketing when there is little business brings in more, which then encourages cutting back on marketing, which ultimately results in a drop in business, which then encourages renewed marketing. And so on. Consistent marketing activity is the only way to minimize the workflow peaks and valleys that are inherent in any service business.

THE BENEFITS OF MARKETING: MORE THAN GETTING WORK

Essentially, marketing is nothing more than the process of making a firm better known. The many benefits of doing this are too lengthy to catalog here, but the following five stand out.

FINDS NEW KINDS OF CLIENTS AND PROJECTS. When an organization merely relies on current clients or referrals, chances are it will get mostly more of the same type of work. The only way to break the pattern, to get out of the "same-old, same-old" rut and land different types of projects and clients, is to promote the organization's capabilities to a new, wider audience. Relying solely on referrals takes the direction of an organization out of its own hands and places it into the hands of others.

POSITIONS AN ORGANIZATION. In the absence of marketing activity, others will draw their own conclusions regarding an organization's strengths and capabilities. Only through directed marketing activity is it possible to redefine an organization and break out of the category that clients tend to place it in. Doing so enables an organization to create its own business image, its positioning, rather than sitting by while clients do it by default. Better yet, more accurate positioning has the business benefit of encouraging new types of referrals. In addition, it can enhance an organization's staff morale, make recruiting talented staff easier, and intimidate competition. (See also "Positioning" in Chapter 2, and Appendix II on branding, a close relative to positioning.)

AVOIDS BUSINESS "SPIRALING DOWN." Long-time clients often take familiar suppliers for granted, which can result in unreasonable demands, lack of pricing flexibility, or categorization. Such clients' referrals are mostly to others who have similar or lower-level assignments; they rarely lead to higher-level clients or yield higher-level opportunities. In short, projects and clients seldom get better over time without a marketing effort. You can think of it in terms of evolution: new blood is necessary to stay healthy and grow.

AVOIDS TOO MUCH FROM TOO FEW. One of the leading causes of creative firm failure is the loss of one or more clients who are responsible for a large chunk of business. Further, when a few clients dominate a firm's income, it can easily be held hostage—financially and creatively—to their unreasonable demands. Only by soliciting new clients and projects—via marketing—can a firm protect itself against these dangers. From both a financial and a creative standpoint, it is far better to have a few projects from many clients than to have many projects from a few clients.

ENHANCES SATISFACTION AND PROFITABILITY. This is the most significant, and often unappreciated, benefit of marketing. The greater the predictability and stability of an organization's workflow, the higher its profit and principals' satisfaction will be. By helping to promote workflow predictability and stability, marketing makes planning easier, makes deploying resources more efficient, and allows the amortizing of fixed costs to cover a broader base. For any organization to be successful in the long run, it must ensure that its workflow occurs in a consistent, predictable manner.

THE MULTIPLIER EFFECT OF CONSISTENCY

Speaking of consistency, this is another mistake that creative individuals often make when considering marketing: they think of it only in the context of getting immediate work. The tendency is to market when they aren't busy and to relax their efforts when they are. As understandable as this is, especially for freelancers and small, resource-thin shops, it is hardly the way to build a stable business. It may at first seem counterintuitive, but marketing when you're busy is as important as when you aren't. Consider the following reasons.

MEMORY IS SHORT-LIVED. Many clients purchase creative services only occasionally. Other clients only occasionally change or add suppliers. When the time comes to find a new supplier or award a project, clients remember those who have been in frequent contact. Most others have been long forgotten.

THE BETTER THE JOB, THE LONGER THE PROCESS. Landing good projects and clients typically requires multiple contacts over several months. Delaying marketing until you are not busy usually produces either a workflow drought or the need to accept lesser jobs and clients to maintain cash flow.

IT'S EASIER AND COSTS LESS. The more consistent your activities, the more routine they become and the less they cost. Promotional costs decline with frequency, and administrative efficiencies accrue when procedures become routine. The most difficult and expensive marketing always happens under the pressures of immediate necessity.

WHY REFERRALS AREN'T ENOUGH

Here is one of the great paradoxes of building a creative business: referrals are the least expensive, most productive way to get good clients, yet referrals are among the major reasons for lack of profitability and business failure. Both statements are correct. How can this be? We'll look at the positive aspects of referrals and why they should be part of any marketing program later in Chapter 4. For now, though, let's look at why no firm should rely solely on them.

The most obvious and potentially significant reason is the hit-or-miss nature of referrals. To put it in simple terms, you can't count on referral business. This not only poses a cash flow concern (bills are regular even when income isn't), but it can raise havoc with workflow and scheduling, the disruption of which increases both specific project and general overhead costs. In contrast, active marketing provides more project consistency and raises profitability.

Another problem is that referrals typically bring in more of the same types of clients and projects. Since individual clients provide referrals to others at their own level or lower, and usually for familiar types of work, over time a firm's referral business tends to move down the desirability ladder. (See "Avoids Business 'Spiraling Down'" above.) Moreover, doing the same types of projects for similar clients pigeonholes a firm and negatively affects its staff's creativity. The only way to ensure good new clients and projects and to move up the ladder is with an active marketing program. In fact, an active program can actually increase referrals by reminding past clients of a firm's breadth of capabilities.

Referrals often result in less pricing and scheduling latitude, too. Referral clients tend to expect preferred treatment. Even if they don't, there's a tendency for firms to make pricing and scheduling concessions to stay in the good graces of a referring client. Given this phenomenon, any savings that a firm gains by not marketing actively can easily disappear through lower profits.

For all the above and many other reasons, a creative business should never be totally dependent on referrals. At best, it will lead to erratic workflow and reduced profitability while diminishing a principal's control. At worst, it will lead to failure, either through too little work or because of cash flow problems. Again, there's more on how referrals should fit into a firm's marketing program in Chapter 4.

2

DEVELOPING STRATEGIES

Perhaps the most significant aspect of marketing strategies for creative firms is the way that principals tend to think about them: "What can we do to generate more work and more income?" Generating work and income should, of course, play a major role in strategic thinking for the simple reason that no business can survive without them. But a good marketing strategy requires thought that goes a little deeper than just how to keep the pipeline full. What should be the elements of a good marketing strategy for your firm? (If your response is little more than "getting more sales," then take a moment to go back and reread Chapter 1.)

THE 3PS OF CREATIVE FIRM MARKETING

In many industries, marketing strategy is often explained in terms of four essential components known as the 4Ps—product, price, promotion, and place. Different marketing techniques are applied in each. Although this approach has some relevance for service firms, a more accurate way of explaining the marketing process is to think of 3Ps instead—positioning, promotion, and presentation. That's because a service firm's products are less tangible, *pricing* is different from *price*, promotion has a different focus, and place has little relevance.

The first of the 3Ps, positioning, involves how prospects and clients perceive a firm. The second, promotion, relates to ways of making client contact. The third, presentation, covers the personal interaction that is almost always necessary to make a sale. Subsequent chapters in this book will discuss how to implement each of these three fundamentals. Before that, though, a summary is in order.

POSITIONING: WHAT DO YOU WANT TO BE? Prospects' and clients' perceptions of your firm are formed by a combination of factors, some of which, such as reputation, are beyond anyone's direct control. But many others can be strongly influenced by deliberate actions, as I will discuss below in the second of the 3Ps, promotion. Although it is true that a business cannot will itself to be something it is not, it is equally true that the market will define a business that does not define itself. In other words, a business ends up being perceived not as what it believes it is, but as what prospects and clients believe it is. Good positioning (a self-branding strategy, if you will) takes into account what a firm wants to be, what is practical for it to be, and what it can credibly claim to be. (For more on branding generally, see Appendix II.)

Will your firm be a generalist or a specialist? There are ample opportunities for all shades of both, and there will be even more in the future as the creative services industry continues to evolve. A firm can opt to be a generalist that offers a variety of creative services across several markets, or a specialist focusing on a specific service within a specific market. Or it can choose to be anything in between. For instance, a design firm might handle a mix of collateral, Internet, and branding work for all types of clients, or it might focus only on branding. An advertising agency might take on all comers or specialize in a given industry, such as retail. The point is that how general or specific a firm's business is should not be left to happenstance. It should be a conscious decision made by the principal(s). Such decisions are not permanent; they can always be changed later as circumstances warrant. Thus the risk is not in considering how a firm should position itself, but in *not* considering it.

Deciding how much or how little specialized work to pursue should involve consideration of the potential upsides and downsides. For instance, more generalized, less specialized firms are less affected by trends and economic fluctuations, have a broader field of clients to choose from, needn't be as concerned about possible client conflicts, and are more likely to stay fresh creatively. In contrast, more specialized, less generalized firms can charge higher fees, face fewer competitors, serve a greatly expanded geographic market, and have lower marketing expenses.

Where are you located? Location is an important consideration because local clients usually account for most of a firm's opportunities. Not counting specialists and firms that have a national reputation, that's because it is difficult to price competitively and still be profitable when servicing clients involves traveling a long distance. So the composition of the local economy can be a crucial factor, especially in markets with concentrations around a few types of industry. As an example, a firm that stresses its consumer package goods expertise would find little resonance in a market dominated by

B2B (business to business) technology. Even though most markets have a variety of opportunity types, the best ones are usually among those organizations most prominent in the local economy. This is not to suggest that it's impossible to be successful by following your own muse; it is just a reminder that you'll always be more successful when your firm orients its services around what local clients want to buy, as opposed to what you want to sell.

What should you emphasize? This is the actionable element of positioning. It takes place through, first, surveying all the things that make your firm in any way distinctive—talent, experience, service, dependability, expertise, pricing, and so on. Next, decide which of these will have the most appeal to targeted clients. Then, prepare a short positioning statement for internal use that summarizes your firm's uniqueness. For example: "Fifteen years helping academic institutions develop and sustain brand awareness through a uniquely experienced staff developing novel solutions. National reputation." Finally, make sure henceforth that all promotional activity relates to and reinforces this statement. Don't deviate from it. Stay on the message.

PROMOTION: WHAT TO CONSIDER? The second stage of marketing strategy involves complementing positioning with implementation—that is, applying a firm's positioning to its promotions. Chapter 5 will cover the specifics, including which activities and media are the most productive and why. But first it will help to look at promotion planning from a strategic viewpoint and to point out what firms often misunderstand.

Short term versus long term. A firm's marketing, and more specifically its promotional activities, are most effective when they happen on two complementary levels—short term and long term. Short-term activities are used for soliciting an immediate client response, such as seeking an appointment or an order. Long-term activities are used to raise client awareness and by so doing create the environment that makes short-term efforts less costly and more productive. In other words, the long term builds the brand and the short term does the selling. Working together, they produce a multiplier effect.

Planning for both long-term and short-term activities is not as common as it should be. Rather, there's a tendency to think only in the context of filling the project pipeline—a singular, short-term strategy. The result is marketing activity that fluctuates, increases or decreases, with the immediate need, or lack of it, to bring in more new business. This short-term fixation is a major reason why some firms never break though to the next level of better clients and steadier work. A good marketing strategy requires a plan that encompasses both long- and short-term objectives, as Chapter 4 will discuss.

Frequency versus impact. A central element of a firm's long-term marketing strategy should be to ensure that prospects and clients never have a chance to forget about the firm's capabilities. The reason is that their need for creative services is only occasional, their memory is short-lived, and the firms they remember are the ones that recently contacted them. Whatever the size of a firm's marketing budget, this reality argues for dribbling it out over many small efforts rather than spending it on a few novel and more expensive ones. In advertising lingo, this is called opting for frequency over impact. Novel promotions are creatively exciting, often win awards, and do get noticed. Yet their effect is short-lived. Even though the widespread availability of electronic media has made regular promotional contact less time consuming and less expensive (for more on this, see Chapter 5), there is still a tendency to do occasional "creative" promotions rather than to do regular promotions that are less exciting but more effective.

PRESENTATIONS: HOW TO HANDLE? Few sales of creative services happen without being preceded by a personal presentation, the show-and-tell of a firm's capabilities. Positioning and promotion are by and large just lead-ins to this, the main act. Nothing, therefore, is more crucial. Section Three of this book covers the many aspects of making effective presentations. Before that, though, it helps to understand what's strategically feasible.

Who presents? For organizations that have fewer than four creative employees, presentations are normally handled by principal(s) because the firm is too small to afford professional sales (business development, or BDP) persons. Using other employees and part-time salespeople for new business pitches seldom pans out for reasons that Chapter 7 will cover. Larger firms usually have professionals handle the presentations, with principals still required at new business pitches to add credibility and to act as a closer.

What are the responsibilities? In addition to having excellent presentation skills and knowledge of the firm and its capabilities, salespeople should contribute to a firm's marketing strategy and be responsible for cold-calling and setting up appointments. Account service should also be a responsibility for firms having clients with extensive ongoing work, such as agencies. But for those doing mostly project-to-project work, as is the case with most design firms, the emphasis should be on generating new business, with minimal account responsibility. (A good ratio for design firm salespersons is 3 to 1, sales over servicing.)

THE ACTIVE/PASSIVE MIX

Another strategy consideration is that there are two complementary marketing modes for creative services firms. One, the focus of most of this book, is active marketing—that is, all those activities involved with positioning, promoting, and presenting. Active marketing constitutes most of the focus here because it is the more difficult consideration for creative individuals to come to grips with. It also has its own, sometimes obscure, processes and techniques. And most important, it gives the fastest and most predictable results.

This said, the other type—passive marketing—shouldn't be overlooked. It is the indirect, behind-the-scenes activity that leads to contacts, reputation building, referrals, and new clients and projects. It consists of such things as generating publicity, social networking (both electronic and in-person), doing pro-bono work, and entering award shows. Although longer term and less prescriptive and predictive, it, too, is crucial. From a strategic perspective, nothing more than a recognition of the need has to be made now. For a discussion of where, when, and how passive marketing is appropriate, see Chapter 4.

THE CLIENT ELEMENT

When purchasing products, customers are usually able to compare several models or alternatives before they buy. In such cases, seller-buyer interaction is minimal and usually short-lived. Moreover, predictable manufacturing and distribution costs give a seller predictable profit margins. Now compare this to purchasing services, wherein clients agree to buy something before it is even made, essentially buying into a promise of satisfaction. Seller-buyer interaction in these cases is more intense and longer-lived. And most important from our perspective, how smoothly things proceed affects the seller's profitability. Quick approval followed by few changes increases profit; slow approval and many changes decrease it.

The above comments illustrate why seeking the *right type* of clients, as opposed to just more clients, must be a crucial component of strategic thinking. The satisfaction of both parties depends on a good fit, because profit hinges on mutual satisfaction. Additionally, whom a firm works with and what it works on affect principals' satisfaction and employee morale, an important quality consideration. The nature of any creative business is such that individuals on staff need to be constantly refreshed with novel challenges and new opportunities. Without this, they can easily fall into a rut and lose their edge. The work begins to suffer, and the firm's ability to attract good clients and projects suffers along with it. Equally significant in the long term, the clients that a firm attracts today affect those it will attract tomorrow. Flying with eagles attracts more eagles.

So in general terms, the purpose of a marketing strategy is to allow a firm to have more control over whom it does business with. Thinking about positioning, as previously described, should start this process. Later will come the transforming of general strategy into specific marketing objectives—developing a plan (see Chapter 4). Before that, though, it helps to recognize several considerations that should always be part of a creative firm's marketing strategy.

MOVING IN THE RIGHT DIRECTION. Not every client and project does this. And sometimes it is not possible to be selective. But whenever possible, you should be careful to refrain from soliciting or accepting too much of what doesn't fit with your goals. Doing too much of the wrong stuff might keep you from being considered for what you want and are qualified to do, or it might mean you are considered only for certain types of work (i.e., you become pigeon-holed).

STEPPING UP THE LADDER. Whether your ultimate goal is growth or stability (see the next section), set your sights on work that is a rung higher up the ladder than where you are today. This is a small enough step-up to be credible to prospects and still be easily achievable. Yet it is large enough so that over time your situation will continually improve—creatively, financially, and in personal satisfaction. This is the way to achieve your personal and business best.

NO CLIENT SHOULD BE OFF LIMITS. No matter what your talent and firm's size, some work will always be inappropriate. However, no client should ever be considered inappropriate because of size alone. Even corporate giants having major agencies hire smaller firms for some projects. In fact, many have a mandate to work with smaller firms, particularly local ones. So never be reluctant to contact any potential client.

NO EDUCATING NEEDED. Avoid going after clients who are inexperienced and don't understand the process, or who don't appreciate the commercial value (return on investment) of what your firm provides. Be careful not to fall into the trap of thinking that one of your goals is to bring great creativity and understanding to places where it doesn't presently exist. Clients who have to be educated or convinced of the value of your work do so at your expense. Make it your strategy to go after those who know how the game is played and what professional services cost.

CONSIDERING GROWTH, SIZE, AND STABILITY

One of the distinguishing factors of service businesses, and creative services businesses in particular, is that growth and size are not requisites for financial success. In many other types of businesses, they can be important because they often lead to scale economies—the savings that come from mass volume and repetitive tasks. Given that large organizations can generally outperform small organizations, ways of growing are a strategic consideration.

Growth for this reason alone is not important for service businesses because there are few opportunities for scale economies. The size, scope, and effort required for every project are different, so there are no savings through mass volume. And it takes almost as long to perform most tasks the hundredth time as the first time, so there are no savings through repetition either. What this means is that even though growth might be desirable for other reasons, it has little effect on survival. (There is no need to "grow or wither," as is often the case in other industries.) In fact, many creative firms have remained more or less the same size for years without apparent ill effect. Others have grown and shrunk as clients have come and gone. A firm can be financially successful at two persons or a hundred. In business-school terms, most creative businesses are scalable: they can operate well at any size.

THE RIGHT SIZE. Still, size does matter. One reason is that creative firms are unique small businesses whose success is inextricably tied to their principals' visions and enthusiasm. Being the right size, the one that provides the most comfort and happiness, also produces the greatest possibility of success. Conversely, firms are less successful and more prone to failure when they exceed their principals' interests and capabilities. Trying to be what one is not cut out to be is a frequent cause of burnout and firm failure.

Thus another purpose of a marketing strategy is to think about what size firm you would be most comfortable running, for it will have a major influence on your, and the firm's, future. The following points summarize the general personality traits of principals who successfully run firms of four different sizes. See how each one matches your own desires and idiosyncrasies.

Single-person firm—enjoys working alone . . . is self-disciplined . . . is moderately competitive . . . would rather not supervise others . . . is not always well organized . . . prefers or needs to work at home . . . is somewhat but not primarily motivated by money . . . has slight interest in business details . . . is uncomfortable with investing in business.

Small (2–5 person) firm—is uncomfortable with structure . . . is somewhat comfortable delegating. . . is moderately well organized . . . would rather do than manage . . . feels uncomfortable with marketing . . . is motivated by money . . . has moderate interest in business . . . understands investment concepts.

Mid-size (6–11 person) firm—prefers a structured environment . . . enjoys organizing as much as doing . . . is comfortable delegating . . . is very well organized . . . enjoys training and educating . . . appreciates the role of marketing . . . feels comfortable with planning . . . believes that personal style and ego are secondary . . . enjoys the challenge of personnel management . . . is obsessive about clients . . . is highly motivated by money . . . has strong interest in business detail . . . is interested in investing.

Large (12+ person) firm—enjoys business-building activity . . . enjoys setting direction for others . . . feels very comfortable delegating . . . enjoys long-term planning . . . considers marketing crucial . . . considers size an attribute . . . enjoys the challenge of personnel management . . . is philosophical about occasionally losing jobs . . . enjoys high-level client interaction . . . is somewhat motivated by money . . . has moderate interest in business detail . . . is very interested in investing.

A STABLE SIZE. However big or small a firm is or becomes, maintaining stability must also be a major goal of its marketing strategy. From a financial perspective, the steadier the workflow, the more profitable it becomes; orderly growth is almost always more profitable than rapid growth. From a principal's personal perspective, workflow ups and downs are worrisome and stressful. For employees, instability often translates into concerns about their jobs and negatively affects their morale. And since choosing to work with a creative firm is based more on subjective than objective factors, any hint of instability causes clients to think twice about working with that firm.

THE PSYCHOLOGY OF SIZE

Regardless of the actual size of your business, it usually helps when clients perceive it as somewhat greater than it really is. The only universal exception is for solo artists, such as illustrators, for whom a solitary work style (laboring away in the fictional garret) is seen as beneficial. For most other creative businesses—from freelance writers to large design shops— it is usually better to be perceived as larger, more established, and more accomplished than may actually be the case.

There are three major reasons why bigger is usually viewed as better. (1) *Backup*: the larger the project, the more is at stake and the more clients will worry about getting it done on time and on budget. (2) *Stability*: since creative vendors come and go, size and longevity imply stability, which makes clients more comfortable. (3) *Reassurance*: because creative work is often esoteric and always subjectively evaluated, a history of working successfully with many other clients provides a dose of confidence for clients who are less than secure.

This is not to suggest being dishonest in the ways you talk about your business. Rather, it suggests taking pains to minimize possible client concerns. This can be essential for single-person and small- to mid-size shops pitching large clients, and it can also be important for large shops pitching very significant assignments. Creating an impression of greater size usually, albeit not always, makes it easier to attract larger, better clients. And it almost always makes it easier to charge higher fees.

YOU OR YOUR FIRM? Principals of single-person businesses should be particularly sensitive about how they describe their firm. For instance, the word "freelancer" can connote a lack of professionalism and reliability to many corporate clients. A name like "John Smith Freelance Copywriter" is just not as professional or impressive as "Smith & Company, Business Writing Services." And it is better to use phrases such as "Since the founding of (company) in . . ." rather than "Since I started freelancing." Small-firm principals often fall into the trap of describing everything their company does in personal terms—for example, "I'll be able to make those changes for you by next Tuesday." It's much better to get in the habit of using plural pronouns— "we," not "I" —anytime appropriate. This practice conveys a subtle, but important, sense of being in charge of a larger organization.

110%, BUT SELDOM MORE. Half of a creative services business is service— which means doing everything reasonable to satisfy a client's desires. But it should not include regularly acquiescing to the unreasonable. Those who consistently jump through hoops to satisfy client demands lose respect. They define themselves as small and hungry, which devalues their services and keeps them out of contention for larger, more professional, and more creatively challenging projects.

PRICE AND CREDIBILITY GO TOGETHER. Every firm has lost jobs because of an estimate higher than competitors'. Although not as common, many have also lost jobs because their estimate was lower and the client didn't want to risk quality just to save a bit. A price estimate in the same ballpark as one's competitors is usually necessary for credibility. Low-balling to get business often backfires, too. It is no guarantee of success, and there is a strong correlation between clients who demand low prices and those who turn out to be difficult to work with.

WHAT THEY SEE IS WHAT YOU BECOME. It is, of course, impossible to be something you aren't. But you can punch higher than your weight implies. Frequent promotional activities convey a sense of competence and sophistication that enable a small firm to compete on more equal terms for larger assignments. General impressions count, too. Sophisticated clients like to work with sophisticated vendors. Appearance, the quality of presentations, social and business skills, the location and style of a place of business, the friendliness of staff—all contribute to an overall impression. The more positive it is, the better the chances of working with sophisticated clients on challenging and profitable assignments.

PROSPERITY BEGETS PROSPERITY. Everyone loves a winner. Regardless of a firm's size, the more successful and prosperous it appears to be, the more clients will be inclined to work with it. Discuss your firm's business and activities in a positive way whenever suitable, taking care not to exaggerate or be phony. Always appear confident and upbeat. For example, reply to conversation openers such as "How's business?" with a cheerful and engaging response: "Actually, it has been quite strong lately. We have recently been . . ."

REACTING TO THE COMMODITIZATION PERIL

Commoditization (or commodification) is the process whereby products appear so similar to customers that price, not features or benefits, becomes the deciding factor in purchasing. Although this phenomenon is usually associated with consumer expendables (think bread, gasoline, or dry cleaning), it can also be a threat to creative services. This previously small, insular, and esoteric industry is becoming large and more commonplace. The good side is that client needs and appreciation for good work have risen: there's more around today than ever before. The bad side is that there's also more competition, clients are more demanding, and some previously arcane (and profitable) processes can now be handled by anyone with a computer. All of these factors contribute to commoditization.

For better or worse, the business environment for creative services continues to evolve toward commoditization. This does not mean, however, that it is every firm's destiny. How a firm responds—whether single- or multi-person—can have a major impact on its future. Principals need to ensure that their firms don't turn into easy commoditization targets.

WHAT'S HAPPENING. The drift toward commoditizing comes from several sources. One is the fact that universal computer access, along with inexpensive, do-it-yourself software, have dumbed-down some markets, such as producing newsletters or logo designs. Another is greatly increased competition, particularly at lower levels, caused by more graduates from more communications and design programs. A third source is the transfer of organizational purchasing away from function managers and toward centralized purchasing departments.

The result is that clients who are more likely to understand the creative process and recognize incremental value have been replaced by ones who don't. These new clients are more likely to view creative services as just another commodity purchase. Despite this fact, it is not necessary to play the commoditization game. Rather, by learning to spotlight the additional value a firm brings to each project, you can hold commoditization at bay. Ten strategies follow. Each is a different way for a firm to differentiate—to "un-commoditize"—its services. You can combine them as suitable to justify your value pricing.

#1 THE IMPRESSIONS STRATEGY. Although true value resides in results, apparent value resides in client impressions. There's no guarantee that even a firm sensitive to their importance won't face commoditization pressure. But it is almost certain that an insensitive firm will.

Client impressions are formed in dozens of different ways. One is through a firm's branding efforts, of which there's more discussion below. But other ways include how a firm's principals and employees appear and act when meeting with clients. Clients who get downscale impressions anticipate and will accept only low prices (call this the Walmart effect). Conversely, those who get upscale impressions are much more likely to accept higher prices (the Neiman Marcus effect). Small firms needing to overcome a credibility or experience deficit should be particularly attentive to impressions. As a rule of thumb, a firm's representatives should appear to be at least as professional, in demeanor and dress, as whomever they are calling upon.

Personal impressions, especially first ones, can easily categorize a firm— whether it's a commodity supplier or a value supplier.

#2 THE BRANDING STRATEGY. This is a page right out of the playbook of brand marketers. They know through long and extensive experience that by far the most effective way to resist commoditization is through brand building. Essentially, customers are willing to pay more for anything that's easily identifiable and familiar. This occurs even when there is otherwise little or no perceived difference between products.

Customers assume that better-known products are of higher quality, and they therefore are willing to pay more for those products. This truism explains why national marketers spend heavily not just on touting their products' benefits but also, often, on nothing more than brand reinforcement. In addition to juicing demand (higher sales), a highly promoted brand can command a higher price (higher margins). It is ironic, then, that creative firms, particularly those that advise clients on branding, often seem unaware of this when it comes to their own marketing. As crucial as promotions can be in scoring new clients and projects, of equal importance is brand building. Regular promotions, which raise the level of brand awareness, affect both what a firm can charge its new clients and its pricing latitude with current clients. (For more on branding, see Appendix II.)

Branded products and services are always the least susceptible to commoditization. Anything not well branded is vulnerable.

#3 THE POSITIONING STRATEGY. This is an extension of the branding strategy described above. As effective as greater name awareness alone can be in avoiding commoditization, it is even more so when the name (brand) stands for something easily distinctive.

How a firm chooses to differentiate itself (its brand) from competitors is, of course, central to all its business development activity. Several of the approaches covered below—partnering, quality/expertise, soft benefits, low cost (versus low price), and so on—could be suitable, depending on a firm's background, location, competition, and ambitions. In terms of battling commoditization, however, a firm's approach to differentiation is less important than its long-term regularity and consistency. As challenging as arriving at the right positioning can be, usually even more so is sticking with it (or its derivations), month after month or (preferably) year after year. Firms tend to get tired of their positioning strategy long before it becomes ineffective in the marketplace. Establishing strong market positioning—that is, getting a client to associate certain visual or mental "triggers" with a firm—can often take years of consistent activity.

Positioning—which is all about differentiation—can effectively combat commoditization—which is all about sameness, or lack of differentiation.

#4 THE VOLUME STRATEGY. In addition to branding and positioning, two other benefits of regular and consistent marketing are often overlooked. One is the fact that marketing increases higher-level opportunities because it makes a firm appear more significant. This attracts more clients a level or two above ones who are commodity oriented.

Regular marketing also has the potential of creating excess demand, which enables a firm to be more selective in whom it does business with or what conditions it will accept. Many firms make the mistake of viewing marketing only in the context of generating immediate business. Too often, they cut back or cease activity as soon as they have achieved this objective. Although doing so results in short-term savings, in the long term it can be false economy. Continuing marketing with the goal of creating excess demand can be more economical. When a firm ends up with more business than it can comfortably handle, it faces new options: (1) selecting only the better projects or clients, (2) raising prices to restrict future demand without affecting income, or (3) expanding staff and facilities to handle the extra business. Care should be taken, too, to avoid the trap of trying to accommodate every new client that marketing generates. Keep in mind that marketing is simply a means of adjusting demand.

The more new business options a firm has, the less susceptible it will be to accepting commoditized work.

#5 THE PARTNERING STRATEGY. This could also be called the relationship-building strategy. That's because a well-established relationship makes it easier for a client to think of an outsider (your firm) as a member of its team—that is, a "partner" with specialized expertise.

But how can a firm make a partnering relationship happen? There are many aspects, most of which are too personal, numerous, and complex to cover here. One way to begin, though, is right up front with a new business pitch. Nothing worthwhile ever gets accomplished in a service business in the absence of interaction. Therefore, projecting an ability to understand clients' needs and work hand-in-hand with them has to be a major component of every presentation. It is always equal in importance to what's in a portfolio. And for some clients and projects, particularly large ones, a firm's process—how it works with clients—is far more important. For these clients, examples of outstanding creativity—the contents of a firm's portfolio—are just the price of consideration. Decision-making, including price negotiation, is based on comfort with the process a firm uses. (For more on process versus portfolio presentations, see Chapter 11.)

The promise of a partnering relationship, as opposed to merely handling a client's project, dramatically decreases the pressure for commodity pricing.

#6 THE PREFERRED SUPPLIER STRATEGY. When working with many mid-size to large organizations, this is the next step up from the partnering strategy (relationship building) discussed above. Many such clients have lists of officially sanctioned suppliers. In some cases, any firm not on a list will be totally excluded from working with that client; in other cases, the client will only work with certain types of business or under certain circumstances.

The process of becoming a preferred supplier typically involves an internal recommendation (e.g., from the marketing department) and, often, the submission of references, financial history, and similar information to a purchasing department. The process can be informal in smaller organizations or formal in larger ones, especially if there are several purchasing operations. Whatever the process, no firm should be deterred. Many organizations establish programs specifically to provide work to small or local suppliers. To check whether a regular client has a preferred supplier list, ask the usual contact person to look into it. For a potential new client, call the purchasing department and inquire about how your firm (never you personally) can be added.

A firm that's on a client's preferred supplier list seldom faces commoditization pricing pressure.

#7 THE SURPRISE STRATEGY. This seldom works with bottom-feeding clients, but it often does with others. And even where it doesn't, there's a "pushing back" aspect to it that's empowering and conducive to self-esteem. So it's worth a try.

Whenever a client presents an unrealistic budget or aggressively challenges a realistic price, act very surprised. Comment that unfortunately the client's expectation is well below normal industry pricing. Further, point out that firms agreeing to work at that price would be inexperienced, or forced to cut corners, or count on later "changes" to boost billing. If not, they'd lose money. This path is neither in the client's nor your best interests. Your firm, just like theirs, must make a modest profit. Otherwise, your firm would not be able to offer the talent, resources, and service that result in satisfied clients. Nothing less than your firm's outstanding reputation relies on it.

Then, whenever possible, illustrate how the difference the client will pay is very small in the larger context of effectiveness—for instance, only a few cents more per brochure, or perhaps twenty-five dollars per ad insertion amortized over its projected life. Whatever the price, be particularly careful not to apologize. Remember that it, not a client's expectation, is the norm. Clients worth having will understand; the ones that don't, aren't.

When faced with commodity pricing, "push back" by stating that it is unrealistic without making unacceptable sacrifices.

#8 THE QUALITY/EXPERTISE STRATEGY. Think of this as the "no-free-lunch" approach. However wishful clients' thinking may be, effective work doesn't come at fire-sale prices. As in most aspects of life, clients will pretty much get what they're willing to pay for.

Most of a creative firm's pricing is determined by its labor costs. The more talented and experienced its employees, the higher these costs will be. And vice versa. So rock-bottom pricing is only feasible when a firm's labor costs are low (offering less talent and experience) or when it opts to forego profitability. Less experience often leads to costly, misdirected efforts. Less talent can lead to less creative impact, less bang for the buck. Question to ask the client: how much more will settling for less end up costing?

As for expecting a modest profit, there's no reason to be defensive. Again, profit enables a firm to employ above-average individuals and maintain a high level of service. More to a client's direct benefit, when there's little or no profit, there's an open invitation for a firm to cut corners everywhere possible; there's little incentive to go the extra mile to encourage repeat business. Question to ask the client: would it expect to work for its customers at little or no profit? (Or for a not-for-profit, would it expect not to balance its books?)

Commodity pricing usually indicates that minimally talented or experienced individuals will work on the business.

#9 THE SOFT-BENEFIT STRATEGY. A "soft benefit" is one that, unlike price, can't be easily quantified. So clients often ignore these benefits when making pricing decisions. Yet they can be just as important over the length of a project because their absence can be costly.

For instance, by its very nature, bare-bones pricing makes no allowance for the changes that inevitably occur between receiving a job and completing it. Even the most thorough RFQs (Requests For Quote) can never foresee everything. Things that derail projects happen, and they happen unexpectedly. When a project changes or goes astray, as most do, the costs—in money, time, and inconvenience—mount up quickly. More often than not, bargain-seeking clients find themselves stuck in the midst of a suddenly complex project being mismanaged by a firm that's in over its depth. It will probably end up seeking additional compensation as well.

How much would getting things done right the first time have saved in expensive client time? What about the value of easy working relationships? Or, when handling complex changes, the lack of hassle that comes from having already "been there, done that"? There are no easy answers. But the soft benefits of a firm's efficiency can easily save more over the course of a project than any small savings in its initial price. Say this to your client: "Our prices are indeed higher. But our clients find that much, sometimes all, of the difference is recouped by our more efficient procedures in working with them."

Commodity pricing never anticipates the additional cost to clients of inefficiencies in workflow and handling changes.

#10 THE LOWEST-REAL-COST STRATEGY. Regardless of a client's wishes or a firm's pricing, the bottom line involves delivering the greatest value for the money spent. In a service business, this is almost always a combination of quality, effectiveness, and service.

Quality establishes a communication's tone and environment as well as affecting a client's image and reputation. Anything less can be ineffective at best; at worst, it can be damaging to the client's business interests. Effectiveness—being able to meet or exceed objectives—is nothing less than the very purpose of any project. Anything less provides an unacceptably low return on a client's investment. Service involves getting what's expected when it's expected, and more. It speeds the production process and makes the client's life easier. Anything less than attentive service can waste time and result in costly errors.

With creative services, as with most businesses (usually including a client's), a rock-bottom price never includes all the above factors. Something has to be sacrificed. Using one or more of the strategies described above, you should make commodity-pricing clients aware of the difference between price and value. Many will understand and entertain realistic pricing. Others will not and will stick to their objective of getting the lowest possible price. Walk away from the latter. Let another, less savvy firm take these clients' money-losing and reputation-damaging business. With commodity pricing, as with any other unrealistic client demands, caving is ultimately self-defeating.

The lowest real cost is determined by the value received, not by the initial price. Clients who can't understand this are usually "penny wise and pound foolish" and too expensive to do business with.

3

DEVELOPING TACTICS

In classic marketing terms, strategy defines what a firm wants to accomplish. Tactics, then, defines what needs to be done to make it all happen. Colloquially speaking, strategy is the roadmap; tactics is the vehicle that gets you there. In this sense, much of the rest of this book is about tactics in that it discusses operational techniques. But before we explore them, it is first necessary to consider some general issues: the effect marketing can have on an owner's (your) future, how much money should be allocated for marketing, who should be involved, why marketing needs to become part of a firm's culture, and what role it plays in client relations. Without these considerations, planning (covered in the following chapter) would be premature.

THE PERSONAL FACTOR

Creative firms are not started by investors who are seeking business opportunities with growth potential. Rather, they're started by individuals who have a passion for creativity but also want the freedom and economic potential of doing it on their own terms. This means that creative firms are almost always started by a single or two or three individuals and built from the ground up, often by trial and error.

This reality has many ramifications, not the least of which is a history of skimping on marketing. When starting out, it is understandably difficult to invest scarce money in activities that often do not show immediate rewards. Some firms even start off with enough business from friends and contacts to lead them to question whether it makes sense to spend any money on marketing. Then, too, when the firm is nothing more than an individual working out of a home office, not much business is needed to stay alive and perhaps even prosper.

Whatever a start-up's size and whether it's blessed with early success or continuing to struggle, the first few years take place in an artificial environment that is in no way predictive of its or the owners' future. Sooner (probably) or later, some marketing effort will be necessary if the firm is to become a place that can reliably provide a good living. The individual working from home might discover that the low fees that have attracted her or his clients are inadequate to cover the expenses of a real, not a hobby, business. Yet higher fees will cause bargain-shopping clients to depart. The two-person firm that was initially blessed with work from friends and contacts will likely find that over time the workflow peters out. In both these cases, replacement business is needed to stay even. And if a firm and its owners' income are to grow, something beyond this will be needed as well.

Whether the underlying cause is lack of money or lack of appreciation for the need, without a regular influx of new business many start-ups fail by their third anniversary. They become weaker and weaker until they finally wither away, with their owners reentering the employment market. Those that manage to make it through the start-up years sometimes experience a spike in the failure curve a few years down the road when owners fall victim to their own hubris. They find their firms doing well with lots of business from just a few clients who love their work. The money pours in, and confidence and happiness abound, so the firm expands. Then, suddenly, the few clients cut back or go somewhere else. There's nothing to replace them, and the bills pile up, often to the point of threatening a business.

Experience and maturity are no guarantee of long-term security, either. The market for creative services is constantly changing. The potential among some industries and clients is falling; among others, it's rising. Also, there are always restless clients seeking something different, a new look or approach. Without the knowledge that comes from regularly soliciting business, a firm's and its owner's future is at risk. It is not unusual to hear of firms folding that have been around for more than a decade because their owners lost touch with the changing market.

Then, too, there are the general economic conditions that every business in every industry must accommodate. While these are impossible to predict, what *is* predictable is that firms that have a visible presence in the market are always far better off in times of economic stress than those that don't.

In short, marketing is not just about growth or even survival. It is also about protecting and enhancing the lifestyle of a firm's owner(s) and that of the employees who depend on it. Yes, it is possible for a firm to be successful and its owners prosperous with little recourse to marketing. But there's lots of evidence that it's a poor bet to make.

BUDGETING GUIDELINES

The preceding discussion points to some of the often-hidden and often-delayed costs when firms ignore or under-spend on marketing. But it also raises a question: how much should businesses spend on marketing? There is no right answer because marketing budgets must take many factors into account. For instance, and generally speaking: marketing usually costs less for a well-known brand than for a lesser-known one; less for low-price or commodity products than for high-price or specialty ones; less to sustain mature products than to introduce or build awareness in new ones; less for those that are widely available than for those that are hard to locate; less for those with little competition than for those with much. Then, too, there are the costs of promotional media and marketing infrastructure, which vary from industry to industry and product to product. Thus there is no single marketing budget number that will fit all businesses.

For many corporations, marketing expenses fall into the SGA, or Selling General and Administrative, expense category. It consists of all salaries and expenses involved in merchandising. This category can be well over 50 percent of annual sales for some luxury consumer expendables, such as perfumes and cosmetics, or well under 10 percent for heavy industrial machinery. The average, though, is usually between 15 and 20 percent of sales.

Because income for many creative firms is of two main types (fee-for-services and pass-through for the purchase of client printing and media), budgeting as a percentage of sales can be misleading. It is better, therefore, to consider marketing costs as a percentage of expenses, and my experience is that the right number is roughly 20 percent of the yearly total. This figure includes not only obvious expenses (Web site, promotional mailings, etc.) but also, and more significant, the salaries of individuals while performing marketing functions—the value of a principal's hours spent on selling and client hand-holding, and the salaries and commissions of sales and account personnel. Account personnel are included because they perform the important marketing function of making sure clients remain happy.

An estimate of 20 percent of expenses compares favorably to 15 to 20 percent of sales because it excludes profit. It is supported by the experience of many multi-person firms with a healthy mix of clients and projects that roughly one individual needs to be devoted full-time to "feeding" every three or four creative employees. (One out of four salaried employees would be 25 percent of payroll, and personnel costs are typically about 70 percent of a firm's expenses.) The estimate is also supported by the experience of many single-person firms that sustaining their business requires devoting about eight hours (one day) each week to drumming up new projects. For firms starting out that need to build a presence in the market, this percentage will be somewhat low; it will be somewhat high for a firm that is well known and has a stable of repeat clients. (Caution: although having more repeat clients reduces the immediate need for marketing, it can be a risky trade-off in the long term by making a firm more dependent, and thus more vulnerable.)

The 20 percent of annual expenses figure is for firms doing mostly project-based work where there's a constant need to replace finished projects with new ones. The percentage will be somewhat lower to the extent a firm is involved in process-based work, such as advertising, public relations, and Internet servicing.

Marketing expenses fall essentially into two categories: the cost of labor as represented by salaries and commissions, and the cost of activities, such as promotional mailings. Of the 20 percent of annual expenses recommended, about 15 percent is usually devoted to covering personnel costs, and 5 percent or less for other needs. For more detail on personnel costs and what should be expected from them, see Chapter 6. For more detail on promotional options and their costs, see Chapter 5.

WHO SHOULD BE INVOLVED

For most small firms, marketing is a principal's responsibility, and one that cannot be delegated. It is too important inasmuch as it sets the direction in which the firm is headed—what business to go after and how. When there are several principals, the primary responsibility should fall to just one, rotated yearly if suitable. When a firm reaches the size at which employing sales or new business development persons is appropriate, they should play a major role in marketing decisions. But decision-making should still rest with a principal. Only when a firm reaches several dozen employees and has a marketing department can a principal step away, although he or she should still provide oversight.

Actually, making marketing decisions is seldom a concern, and when it is, the concern is usually over putting aside enough time to think about it. The issue is normally the selling aspect of marketing—specifically, having to go out and prospect for new clients. It is by far the part of marketing that principals dislike most—partly because individuals everywhere are uneasy about selling, but partly also because it involves the creative psyche. As discussed in Chapter 1, many of us only begrudgingly acknowledge the need to sell, and we certainly don't want to have to do it ourselves.

Unfortunately or perhaps fortunately, principals of most small firms do have to sell. It is part and parcel of the job; it comes with the territory. The reason is twofold. First, as we have touched on already and will continue to explore, regular sales efforts are necessary for a firm to become stable and profitable, never mind grow. Second, it is seldom practical to hire anyone else to do marketing until a firm has a creative staff of at least three. The economics of employing sales help, full- or part-time, salaried or commissioned, is covered in detail in Chapter 6.

Even when there is sales help, principals still need to be involved in "closing" some orders and in pitching for major new business. Clients of small firms and major clients of large firms often expect a principal's personal involvement, sometimes including acting as their account person. Again, it is only when a firm has several dozen employees and a marketing department that a principal can walk away from selling if he or she so desires.

A MARKETING CULTURE

Most firms don't have a marketing culture, which is understandable given creatives' traditional ambivalence toward marketing. Nonetheless, it is a prerequisite for long-term marketing success. And developing one can actually improve a firm's creative product. How so? Because most creatives do their best work when it is appreciated and in demand, which is the very purpose of marketing. In addition, the chances of losing their jobs or not getting a raise due to lack of work diminish in direct relation to the aggressiveness of marketing efforts.

The creation of a marketing culture can only be accomplished by a firm's principal(s). Direction has to come from the top down because that's the manner in which any small organization operates. Its priorities, procedures, and style always reflect the preferences of the principal(s). Even large organizations often carry in their DNA the predilections and idiosyncrasies of the founder(s) long into the future. There's nothing wrong with this. It is, after all, why the boss is the boss. But it does point to the fact that a marketing culture won't just happen unless or until the boss embraces it.

For firms without sales help, the extent of their marketing culture shows in a principal's priorities: how high is business development on the list? For firms with sales help, it shows in their rank, stature, and compensation: are they on a par with those of senior staff? It's also apparent in the extent to which employees are kept informed and understand marketing's importance to their jobs. An occasional report on long-term plans should be shared with them. And a report on activities—who has been called on, who is being considered, what the chances are of obtaining new business, and feedback received from current clients—should be a regular presentation at weekly staff meetings by whoever handles sales. Also, it's a good idea to solicit employees' suggestions on possible sales opportunities. Employees at a firm with a strong marketing culture are informed and supportive.

PASSIVE MARKETING

Most of this chapter, and the rest of the book, is about active marketing (proactive tactics) because it is the only type that can be counted on to deliver. There is, though, the other type previously mentioned in Chapter 2: passive marketing. Three activities partially or wholly undertaken for other purposes affect a firm's reputation and awareness, and thus they have a spillover effect on its marketing.

GENERATING PUBLICITY. The more mention a firm gets in the business (and sometimes the creative) press, the more successful it will appear to be; the more successful it appears, the more others will want to work with it and refer it. An article about some unique aspect of a firm is often easy to arrange in the local press. And even the smallest firm can find several reasons each year to issue a press release: landing an important new client, appointing new staff, or winning an award. (See Appendix III for a sample press release.)

VOLUNTEERING AND DOING PRO-BONO WORK. In smaller communities especially, volunteering and doing pro-bono work can substantially increase a firm's visibility and, in turn, referrals. Serving side-by-side with prominent local leaders in a charitable organization can generate the "working together" comfort and respect that can easily develop into future business. This activity also has the psychic and social benefit of giving something back to the community. Keep in mind, however, that when the main purpose is to build your firm's reputation, you should choose these opportunities primarily for their business benefits.

HIGHLIGHTING AWARDS. It is easy to overstate the commercial value of awards, but they can help build or reinforce a firm's reputation. In this regard they are most effective for young, small, and less-well-known firms. They are also effective in markets where creative impact and innovation are highly valued, such as advertising and PR work, and where client personnel are, themselves, creative individuals. The referral effectiveness of awards, however, often relies on publicizing them.

4

PLANNING IMPLEMENTATION

Planning—laying out the path to ensure that marketing strategies and tactics are achievable—can be easier in theory than in practice. The world of most creatives, principals included, is defined more by instinct and emotion than by forecasting and preparation. Add to this the pressures of creating, meeting deadlines, dealing with suppliers and employees, and keeping the books, and it's easy to see why planning can have a priority so low that it never gets done. Yet investing in planning can save much more than it costs by making marketing activities significantly more efficient, especially when a plan is simple and straightforward. That's what this chapter covers.

FORMALIZING THE PROCESS

Some firms (wisely) have business plans that include a specific marketing section. When this is the case, the marketing section should be reviewed and brought up to date annually. For most single-person and two- or three-person firms, a business plan and marketing plan are synonymous because there is little need for much else.

Business plan or not, there's no reason not to have a marketing plan. It can stand on its own, and the time required to prepare it is not all that significant. Putting a plan together is appropriate at any time, and it will be immediately productive—if not in increased sales right away, at least in knowing that it will be helpful in controlling the direction of your business. (For sample business/marketing plans showing how they are integrated, see Appendix III.)

Although a plan hastily put together because of sudden need is better than none, it is unlikely to be as effective as one that has been well thought through. Less likely still is a plan that's only carried around in your head. Without the discipline of reflection, organization, and writing down, it is easy for a plan to turn into nothing more than a collection of ideas that end up squandering valuable resources or never being acted upon. Making a plan formal—writing it down—not only helps ensure that the planning process is deliberative and taken seriously, but it also provides benchmarks against which to measure progress and refine ideas as time passes.

Marketing plans should be prepared annually, typically at the end of each calendar year. With the year's results at hand, this is the logical time to assess which activities will be most needed and effective in the year to come. Year-end is also a period when there is traditionally a lull in business activity, allowing more development time. A review of the year's plan should then take place quarterly, followed by changes and updates to improve it. This routine enables each yearly plan to build on the previous one, making each one easier to prepare and more effective. The process applies to all firms regardless of size, location, or services offered. The only difference between planning in large versus small operations is the extent of the effort and its degree of formality.

SHORT-TERM VERSUS LONG-TERM OBJECTIVES

Both types of objectives need to be considered when planning. Success depends on both long-term activities to build market awareness and short-term ones for contacting and motivating specific prospects. Long-term objectives build the brand; short-term ones sell the product. As an example, classic marketing models for consumer brands employ mass media advertising, a long-term strategy, to create awareness and build demand. This is supplemented by local retailer promotions, a short-term strategy, to promote price and availability. Large marketers do, of course, have the advantage of ample budgets and many options. Yet the same principle applies to marketing creative services. The only major difference is scale.

Understanding the importance of both short- and long-term marketing is important because too much concentration one way or the other diminishes overall effectiveness. Without the marketplace awareness that long-term activities build, sales calls and presentation appointments become substantially more difficult to arrange. Conversely, marketing campaigns that lack sales follow-up and presentations produce few orders. An effective marketing plan contains a mix of both short- and long-term activities.

PLANNING FOR THE SHORT TERM. Because short-term marketing is, well, short-term, it is often neglected. But without planning, the activities of prospecting and making sales calls are too easily considered only in the context of addressing a current drought of business. One frequent result of the absence of regular, planned sales activity is a workflow roller coaster that keeps a firm fluctuating between being busy and not busy: lack of work encourages sales, which diminishes when orders come in, which necessitates the need to ramp up again, and so on. Another result is a tendency to go after similar types of work (the default), a reason why some firms never break though to the next level of better clients and projects. For these reasons, a plan of regular sales-generating activities—cold-calling and sending out solicitation letters leading to presentations—should be scheduled. Short-term marketing shouldn't be just a reaction to current conditions.

PLANNING FOR THE LONG TERM. The tendency here is to under-fund or neglect long-term marketing activity because, unlike short-term activity, there's rarely a direct link between cause and effect. What is done today may produce results months from now, but the cause could be unknown. Having a plan, even a highly informal one, helps to keep this from happening. It enables you to overcome the sales obstacle of prospects having never heard of you or knowing little about you. The smaller your business, the more important this is. In addition, long-term marketing prevents the erosion of any awareness that does exist. The less often clients and prospects hear from you, the less likely they will be to think of you when they have a project. Many clients purchase creative services only occasionally. Others only rarely change or add suppliers. When the time comes to find someone, they choose whomever they are most likely to remember.

Moreover, long-term marketing is the only non-personal way a firm has to influence how the market perceives it (positioning). These perceptions become an important aspect of how the market interprets everything from the firm's capabilities to the quality of its products and its pricing. (For more on this issue, see "Positioning" in Chapter 2.)

DEVELOPING A PLAN

Compared to a business plan, which must cover resources, capital, staffing, and forecasts of income, expenses, and growth, a marketing plan is simple. Yet it can be easily ignored or hastily prepared, perhaps because it's unlikely that faulty planning, even the lack of planning, will have immediate consequences. Bad or no planning seldom sinks a firm. Nonetheless, damage can occur though the continued inefficiency and business atrophy that often accompany inaction. On a more positive note, there is no better antidote for creative ennui or sagging morale than bringing in new projects with new clients, which is the objective of every marketing plan. Making more money helps, too.

REVIEW YOUR STRATEGY. A marketing plan is just a way to put a voice—an actionable voice—to a previously considered marketing strategy. So the first step is to review the personal and business factors that need to be considered for a plan to be effective. As outlined in Chapter 2, these include a firm's positioning, location, talent, resources, and experiences. Add to this the equally important preferences of principals.

PREPARE YOUR OBJECTIVES. Now develop and write down roughly half a dozen business objectives, or goals, for the period of the marketing plan, usually one year. (More are seldom realistic.) It should be possible to do this in several hours. Defining objectives provides a blueprint for the marketing plan that will follow, and establishing clear rationales for future action reduces the chances of wasting time and seeing money go off in the wrong direction.

Develop a short paragraph on each objective explaining what desire or need it addresses. Put emphasis on those that will move your business another step up the ladder, either through income growth or through better clients and projects. Take the time to think each objective through, and be as descriptive as possible. Then put the list aside, and come back in a week for reconsideration and modifications. As marketing experts often say, "When you can describe the need, you're already halfway to achieving it." (For a sample marketing plan worksheet, see Appendix III.)

BRAINSTORM IDEAS. Using the possibilities and limitations of your marketing objectives as the framework, begin brainstorming. Recall and consider any past marketing thoughts that you never fleshed out and acted upon. Are there still untapped opportunities in areas of previous success? In which fields are you strongest relative to competitors? What about contacting past clients about the possibilities of an introduction to other units or divisions of their organizations? In what direction does the market appear to be headed, and do you need to strengthen your presence there?

INVOLVE EMPLOYEES. Unlike business planning, which is proprietary, marketing planning should encourage employee participation. Evidence that there's a plan to market their good work is both morale building and reassuring to creative staff. For employees whose responsibilities include sales, it's a good idea to include input into marketing objectives as part of their job description. Ideas and suggestions should be solicited from all, and key employees and sales staff should be directly involved in the vetting of ideas as well as in plan development.

WRITE IT DOWN. Take the list of ideas and suggestions, and toss out those that don't further your firm's objectives. Rewrite the ones that remain, indicating how they fit your firm's objectives and adding the investment required in time and money. (See Chapter 3 for budgeting guidelines.) Then rank each activity by attractiveness—its feasibility and probable return on investment. Finally, put down how each can be practically accomplished, and divide them among the year's four quarters. For example, the plan for one quarter might include the following: eight presentation solicitation letters and cold-call follow-ups (two a week), four e-mail newsletters or Facebook postings describing recent projects and activities (one monthly), and one direct mail piece showcasing a recently completed project. (Again, see Appendix III for sample business/marketing plans.)

ENSURE YOUR PLAN'S EFFECTIVENESS. Once completed, keep the plan where it is easy to consult, either electronically or on paper. Too far out of sight is out of effectiveness. Take out the plan and refer to it at least once each quarter. Evaluate how well you are doing compared to it, and what changes are necessary if you are to meet its goals. The best plans are those that are active documents, constantly modified. The time spent on making revisions will almost certainly be among your most productive. Don't make the mistake of being too busy. Otherwise, there might not be any future business left to plan. And don't be concerned or discouraged if the plan falls short of its objectives. It is better to plan to reach the stars and get only halfway there, than not to plan at all. As you update and revise your plan from year to year, learning as you go along, you'll find that the process gets easier and more effective. You will likely come to view it as indispensable to a more productive and enjoyable business.

REFERRALS MANAGEMENT

In some respects, referrals are the bane of marketing because for ill-advised firms they can make marketing seem unnecessary. The many reasons why *relying* on referrals is a bad business practice are covered in Chapter 1. There is, though, no denying that having some referrals is good business: there are no marketing expenses (saving up to 20 percent), referred clients are probably already aware of your skills and are predisposed to working with you, and they tend to be less critical during a job. There is no right ratio of referrals to generated business, but having more than 50 percent of a firm's income dependent on them is risky because they are so unreliable, especially for multi-person firms with substantial fixed obligations.

For firms well below the risky level, generating more referrals should be part of the marketing plan. This is not quite the oxymoron it seems to be. Generating more referrals is possible through "viral marketing" or "word-of-mouth" advertising. It is also possible by taking the initiative and asking those with whom you've had a pleasant business relationship to refer you to their friends and associates. (See also "Passive Marketing" in Chapter 3 for its contribution in generating referrals.)

NETWORKING. The essence of referral generation is that business people are most comfortable recommending those whom they know personally. And the best way for non-client business people to get to know you is to occasionally socialize with them. Productive networking requires considering business social needs separately from personal or creative ones. Creative club meetings, where the ratio is usually a few clients to many competitors, are seldom productive. In contrast, local business organizations, such as the American Marketing Association, Kiwanis, or the Jaycees, usually are. These groups can be especially productive in smaller communities. Aside from regular attendance at meetings and social functions, look for opportunities to become an official, to chair special functions, or to speak on subjects of member interest, such as "How to Get More Impact from Your Web Site." Along the same lines, business-oriented networking Web sites such as LinkedIn.com provide an opportunity to interact with an even broader circle of contacts.

ASKING. This is often all it takes. There are two points to keep in mind, though. First, choose carefully whom and why; some referrals aren't worth the spending of "good-will capital." Second, don't be shy about it. Think of asking as a compliment offered only to a select few. The implication is this: "I like you so well that I want to do business with others like you." Happy clients, suppliers (e.g., printers), other business people (e.g., your accountant), non-creative friends, even non-competitive creatives will be surprisingly happy to help out. Individuals most likely to follow through are those who like you personally, not necessarily those who have most benefited from your services. Also keep in mind that the more important an individual is, the more likely a referral will pay off.

The reason for asking should never be that your firm could use more work or that it doesn't do other marketing. On the contrary, imply that your firm is busy and successful. Asking is nothing more than a way to improve your firm's business mix. A higher percentage of pre-qualified clients or a better project mix enables your firm to hold down marketing costs and prices. Besides, you prefer to work with a happy "family" of clients on a diverse mix of projects. Recognize, too, that occasionally someone will agree to make a referral, but then nothing will come of it. They'll forget, or they prefer not to give referrals but aren't comfortable saying so. One or two gentle reminders is okay, but don't go beyond this. As described below, there are two ways of asking: informally and formally. (Because e-mails and social media are not formal and their informality is also not personal, they are seldom a good choice.)

Informal requests. These are best made in a relaxed social environment when discussing business. An ideal setting is a friendly lunch. For example: "One of the things I've recently rediscovered is that referrals have become a very good source of new business. So I've decided to make them a bigger part of our future marketing mix. Can you recommend anyone I can call? I'm particularly interested in developing more (type) work." In particular, be sure to ask individuals working within large organizations whether they know anyone in other offices, divisions, or functions who might benefit from your services. When names are forthcoming, confirm that it is okay to use the referrer's name in making the contact.

Formal requests. The best time to make formal requests is after finishing a particularly good project for a client with whom you will have minimal future contact. Wait a few weeks, and then send a referral request letter such the one shown in Appendix III. Follow up with a phone call a week or so later.

PAYING. This is the last resort in generating referral business, but one that's occasionally appropriate. Typically, a colleague knows someone who could use your services and is willing to introduce you. But the colleague wants a "finder's fee." Although trading referrals is always preferable, and there should be no hesitation to call in a past favor, payment is occasionally warranted. How much depends on the quality of the lead and the involvement of the referrer. Typical finder's fees are 5 to 10 percent of fee income during the first six months, nothing or something less than 5 percent for up to a year thereafter. Payment to the referrer always takes place after the new client has paid you. Never offer or agree to a discount on future work for a client who provides referrals. It is unethical and unnecessary with good clients. Be wary of those who ask.

PROSPECTING AND CONTACTING

Having discussed logic and planning in Section One, now we turn to the externally visible aspects of creative firm marketing: finding and contacting prospects. Chapter 5 explains the media options that are available, including which ones produce the best results. Chapter 6 examines the process of prospecting for new clients and reconnecting with old ones. Chapter 7 covers expectations, hiring, and compensation of sales or business development (BDP) persons. Chapter 8 explores prospects' budgets and their relationship to pricing.

TODAY'S PROMOTIONAL LANDSCAPE

Orders for creative services almost always occur at or following a presentation showing a firm's work and explaining its capabilities. Promotional activity—direct mailers, ads, e-mail blasts, e-zines, social media, Web sites, keywords, and so on—seldom results directly in a sale. It performs two functions. The primary one, and the subject of this chapter, is long term: creating the awareness that positions a firm positively in prospects' minds, which in turn makes setting up appointments easier and predisposes prospects to be comfortable with what they will see and hear. The other function, more short term and covered in Chapter 6, is direct contact.

This chapter addresses two main questions: Which activities work best in creating awareness of a firm's capabilities, given today's evolving media opportunities? Which activities do so most cost effectively?

THE CHANGING ENVIRONMENT

Just as electronics changed production, so has it changed promotion—specifically, through the Internet. We'll get to the importance of online messaging shortly, but the real marketing game changer is the universality of Web sites. Today every prospective client has the opportunity to check out a possible supplier without the supplier even knowing it. Many prospective clients do so before agreeing to entertain a sales call or presentation. Not only are a Web site's content and design crucial for this reason, but they also impact other functions. There is, for instance, less need for the capability brochures and samples that firms used to prepare. And since most prospective clients have probably already viewed at least some of a firm's work on its site, that fact changes the dynamic of presentations.

Before looking further at today's promotional environment, let's put things in perspective by looking at the recent past. Despite the crucial role that promotion can play in the marketing mix, it has always been somewhat limited, inconsistent, and ineffective in many firms. One major reason has been cost. Traditional efforts typically involved the expenses of printing, mailing, and media, and the payback was not always immediately apparent. In contrast, more direct, sales-related efforts, such as cold-calling and sending out appointment-soliciting letters, are practically free and generate immediately apparent responses, as we will see in Chapter 6.

Another reason for ineffectiveness is one's personal preferences overruling proven promotional principles. This is evident in the inclination among many creatives to spend their limited promotional budget on occasional showcasing and attention-getting efforts. Creatives do this largely because it is more creatively challenging and personally satisfying, but also because it involves less scheduling. The ubiquitous year-end promotions, a staple of many firms, are a case in point. As much as they might demonstrate a firm's creative muscle, even the best don't contribute much to long-term awareness; they are soon forgotten.

This tendency violates the "threshold effect" that is central to promotional effectiveness—namely, that a certain level of activity is needed before it will register. Further, the more activity a firm engages in, the more effective each succeeding effort will be. For instance, when all factors are equal, the second of two ads usually outscores the first, the third outscores the second, the fourth outscores the third, and so on. This is because it takes a certain amount of repetition to overcome individuals' varying "thresholds" of interest. Put another way, the effectiveness of increasing activity is usually geometric, not arithmetic.

The threshold effect is particularly important for direct sales contact, as is covered in Chapter 6. The lower the threshold of awareness, the greater the chances of having a prospect take a phone call or agree to a presentation.

Getting back to today, there's no longer any reason not to have a regular and effective promotional program. The major drawback, the high cost, is virtually nonexistent for promotions over the Internet. Falling printing costs, including the possibility of using in-house office printers, makes small runs of targeted mailers feasible. Regular contact with "new media" advertising (used here in the generic sense) has become, if not exactly free, eminently affordable.

This doesn't mean that traditional media are obsolete or even passé. Just as TV hasn't replaced radio and DVDs haven't replaced movie theaters, there is a place for both traditional and new media. New technology hasn't changed what needs to be done; it has merely expanded the options and opportunities for doing it. A particular example is the ongoing need for a printed brochure to summarize a firm's capabilities and experiences.

Although the role of Web sites has reduced the need (and expense) of having one to show examples, a "capability" brochure continues to play an important role in responding to inquiries and as a leave-behind after presentations.

TRADITIONAL MEDIA OPTIONS

Since the use of traditional media is more expensive than new media, let's start by looking at traditional media's role in keeping a firm in front of prospective clients. Although there are occasional opportunities as diverse as billboards, event sponsorships, and even public radio spots, the two principal forms are direct postal mailings and magazine ads.

DIRECT MAIL. This has long been the primary and preferred medium, and with good reason. From an effectiveness standpoint, direct mail has maximum flexibility because there are few size and format constraints. Mailers provide a good canvas on which to display a firm's work, and they offer easy readability for telling its story. A means for response, a business reply card, can be included. Mailers almost always get delivered to the addressee, which is not a small consideration when compared to their electronic counterparts (no deletes or spam filtering). When well designed and sent to the right individuals, the message, both visual and verbal, will almost certainly register. And the simple act of the addressee picking a mailer out of a stack of mail involves the tactile sense that's important in creating or reinforcing awareness, even if the mailer immediately goes into the wastebasket.

From a cost-effectiveness standpoint, mailers can be precisely targeted; so as long as there's a good mailing list, there's no waste circulation. Mailers can also be produced quickly and inexpensively today in small quantities, even in-house on office printers. Not only does use of a business mailing company (mail house) for distribution provide many customization options, but its postal permit allows mailing at bulk rates in the United States when quantities exceed two hundred pieces.

The major limitation (also shared with e-mail, as we will see shortly) is the need for a good mailing list. Developing and maintaining a database that can be used for mailings is crucial, not only for this purpose but also for making cold calls and for keeping a history of prospect contacts. Compiling a database that includes at least a few hundred names is something that even single-person operations can accomplish. If used several times a year for mailings, it will create more than enough awareness and interest in a firm's capabilities to provide a steady stream of inquiries. (For more on developing prospect/contact lists, see Chapter 6.)

Mailing lists can also be rented for one-time mailings to reach specific market segments, such as marcom (marketing communications) managers in a certain industry. An Internet search under "mailing lists for marketing" will turn up dozens of list brokers. Local list brokers can also be found under "Mailing Lists" in the local Yellow Pages. And local business organizations and regional magazines often rent their member/subscriber lists as well. The charge will likely be in the range of a $150 per thousand names with a minimum of a few hundred dollars.

In short, even in the age of electronic alternatives, no other medium has as much going for it as direct mail. Whether or how much a firm chooses to use it is a personal choice with many considerations, but it should always be considered.

ADVERTISING. Ads can produce a lot of exposure at a low per-reader cost, can make a firm appear more substantial than it might actually be, and once prepared can be rerun with little additional effort. But since advertising of services that are needed only occasionally must be cumulative to be effective, it typically requires running a series (campaign) of insertions before the message sinks in enough to warrant the cost. Other factors that come into play in overcoming the awareness threshold are placement, consistency, and advertiser recognizability. Then too, format restrictions limit how much can be communicated, and readership is limited to a publication's circulation, which seldom is as specific ("vertical") as desired.

Classified ads can be a cost-effective way to keep a firm's name in front of prospective clients and should be considered when there are appropriate media. Display advertising, though, is rarely cost-effective unless a firm has $2 million or more in fee income and unless space can be obtained at attractive rates in a publication targeted at the desired audience. For these firms, ads can be an effective way to position a firm, particularly to a specialized audience. Whether classified or display, the key to making any advertising investment pay off is frequency. At least six months or a year in a publication is normally required.

NEW MEDIA OPTIONS

Online marketing has been around since the beginning of the Internet. Although many firms have used it over the years, they often selected this approach more on the basis of low cost and personal preference than effectiveness. This no longer need be the case; online marketing can now be effective, too. Today there's wide acceptance by prospective clients who use it in their own businesses. There's also less concern about spam, and broadband coverage is universal among businesses. In short, online marketing does offer up new opportunities. But let's also be clear: it is not the answer to a creative firm's prayers because of its low cost. Traditional media still are more productive in many instances.

The major advantage of online marketing is its low cost, especially when combined with better accountability. Every promotional medium, whether traditional or electronic, has waste. Addresses change, and some recipients ignore or trash anything they receive. But two things make online waste less of a concern. First, the cost of waste is a tiny fraction of what can be expected in traditional media, such as mailings or ads. For most readers, it will be so low as to be a non-issue. Second, viewer statistics are available to show just how much, or little, waste there actually is—for instance, how many e-mail messages are received and how many are opened. In addition, automatic tallying of responses is an option.

Except for certain formatting restrictions, an online PDF brochure can include everything that's in a printed one. However, what's possible electronically is not always possible on paper: instant delivery, linking to other material and Web sites, and the inclusion of motion, sound, and video. Indeed, these capabilities, coupled with low production costs, provide temptations that can easily lead to gratuitous creativity and gimmickry.

The attributes of electronic media open up totally new marketing avenues, varying from initial contact to relationship management to just keeping in touch. Some, like e-mail blasts, offer a new way to reach the same end—the promotion of a product. And some, like business networking, provide a means of making connections in more relaxed and informal contexts. Let's look in more detail at the expanding range of options.

WEB SITES. We'll start here because it is the oldest form of online marketing, albeit a largely passive one. A Web site is crucial in that when hearing of a firm, most prospects look at its site before going any farther. This makes the site the source of early and often lasting impressions. It not only showcases a firm's style but also functions as a portfolio and a conduit for information on experience, procedures, and contacting. And it can provide the portal for entering a firm's social networking pages or blog. Overall, a firm's Web site does nothing less than communicate the degree to which it possesses professionalism and business sophistication.

The look, feel, and wire framing of a site are not only well beyond the scope of this text but should have minimal outside input anyway. A Web site needs to be a highly individualistic expression of what a firm wishes to communicate about its capabilities. Therefore, it must be self-directed. This said, care should be taken not to go overboard on style or techniques that might indicate self-indulgence or more interest in demonstrating craft than in conveying the firm's ability to address clients' communications needs. A site should be built to impress prospective clients, not peers. Given the impressionable impact of a site, it is particularly important to make sure it is quick to load, easy to navigate, and requires only the most common plug-ins. Also, keep in mind compatibility with mobile devices, which viewers use increasingly these days.

E-MAIL MARKETING. Bulk e-mailing, the oldest form of active online marketing, has gradually become better accepted and more effective. Anti-spam laws, firewalls, and filters have greatly diminished offensive and irrelevant messages. Moreover, many prospects and clients use this approach for their own marketing, and unsubscribe or opt-out links (required by law in the United States) are readily available. All these factors provide e-mail marketing with the legitimacy it previously lacked.

Bulk messaging software and services make mass transmissions easier and more effective, and they overcome the limitations of regular e-mailer clients (i.e., e-mail software). Two types, standalone programs and Web-based subscription services, are available. Pricing ranges from free to several hundred dollars depending on feature sets and the number of messages sent monthly from subscription services. It is a good idea to check with your Internet service provider (ISP) first if messages are to be sent using standalone software. To control spamming, many ISPs have limits on the number of messages they allow to be sent in a given period without special dispensation. (For home-based firms, sending bulk e-mails might require a commercial versus a residential service contract.)

Much more than with postal mailings, the major limitation to bulk e-mailings is the address list. Unlike postal addresses, which are public record, e-mail addresses are private and thus more difficult to come by legitimately. Lists are available to purchase and are inexpensive, but seldom are they the high-quality, targeted ones a firm desires. Organizations that freely sell members' postal addresses rarely do the same for e-mail addresses. The upshot, at least for now, is that about the only way to get a good e-mail address list is to compile your own (opt-in) from clients and prospects who have contacted you.

As for what to include and when to send e-mailings, anything that shows or summarizes what a firm has recently been up to is appropriate—new projects, clients, personnel, awards, activities, and the like. So is any information or tips recipients would find useful. Probably the best strategy is to create an "e-newsletter" or "e-zine" containing interesting and informative material presented in a distinctive style and sent out on a regular basis, ideally every month.

WEB LISTINGS. An Internet search for "freelance job sites" will turn up a number of sites devoted to bringing together firms looking for work with clients that have it. Registration is usually free, and the site generally collects a small commission (e.g., 10 percent) on payment. Other "directory" sites provide a place for firms to list and show their capabilities, usually for a fee. Potential clients do free searches to find firms that best meet their needs. In both instances, such sites appeal to bargain-seeking clients, often with small projects, and to occasional freelancers. Sites that encourage bidding typically have project and hourly prices well below what is necessary to run a stable and successful business.

KEYWORD ADVERTISING. The short messages that appear next to the results of an Internet search involving keywords (e.g., AdWords) are something of a hybrid. That is, they are not active in the sense of an e-mail blast, but they are not passive in the sense of a static message to a wide audience. The viewer has self-selected through the search request, and there is interactivity by clicking through to the advertiser's site. The advertiser only pays for actual viewer impressions (not raw circulation), as well as for any clicks-through. Pricing is not arbitrary; it is determined by bidding based on the specificity of the keyword and the search criteria.

Keep in mind, however, that even where the cost per contact is small, the number of contacts and link-throughs add up very quickly. Keyword advertising is seldom inexpensive. The effect will be short term, which does make it possible to continuously evaluate its cost effectiveness, though. Advertise as long as doing so produces more in income than it costs, but be ready to stop as soon as it doesn't. There is no benefit otherwise because impact is not cumulative. Keyword advertising is not a medium for awareness building.

BUSINESS NETWORKING. Contacts—who you know and who knows you—have always been important business generators for service firms. Online business networking (e.g., LinkedIn) can vastly expand traditional contacts by dozens, perhaps hundreds. It provides a way to contact those with similar business interests and to reconnect with former business colleagues, college chums, and others who might put you on to opportunity. It could lead to a source of direct sales contacts (see Chapter 6). Moreover, it is free and less time-consuming than traditional networking. So there is little reason not to participate.

Yet for all its advantages, online networking cannot match shaking someone's hand while looking them in the eye. The traditional networking that happens at business organizations and meetings (e.g., local chambers of commerce) hasn't become any less effective since the birth of the Internet. A common mistake, with both traditional networking and online networking, is participating only in groups with a personal rather than a business interest.

SOCIAL NETWORKING. The introduction of these sites (e.g., Facebook) dramatically expanded marketing opportunities for many businesses, including many clients'. For this reason alone, every reader should be aware of such sites' possibilities. In consumer markets, for example, having a social networking page that customers follow is an inexpensive and novel way to engage them with a brand's products, activities, and promotions. This not only builds loyalty but also—and more important—is a low-cost way to drive impulse purchasing of the consumables featured. For many B2B (business-to-business) organizations, the attraction comprises a more efficient and less expensive way to communicate with dealers, customers, and stakeholders on everything from announcements of price changes and sales promotions to reports of quarterly earnings.

None of these situations, though, apply to creative firms, which rarely make such promotions and have limited need for frequent communication. While not critical to marketing, especially for smaller firms, a social networking page for the firm (separate from the principal) is important nonetheless. It demonstrates familiarity with social media and can function as a mini Web site, communicating which projects and clients a firm is currently working on, highlighting recent awards and staff activities, and sharing information and contacts that could be helpful to client followers. The larger the firm and its client and prospect list, the greater the potential.

MICRO-BLOGGING. This has even greater limitations for creative firm marketing. By design, micro-blogging (e.g., Twitter) has less promotional flexibility. The attraction is in its ability to pass along short comments or links to information that will be helpful to business followers. Doing so can impress and build loyalty among current clients, as well as introduce a firm to new prospects. The downside, in addition to the time involved, is that useful and valued messaging requires interests similar to those of clients (mostly business topics). This is not a strength for many creative firms, and messaging that clients might view as frivolous can do more harm than good. Assuming, however, that the time and appropriateness criteria can be met, microblogging could be an important addition to a firm's long-term marketing. But it is not essential.

BLOGS AND PODCASTS. These outlets give firm principals a forum in which to express their viewpoints and to show work not necessarily related to their normal business, or even business in general. They can be powerful long-term marketing tools because of their unique ability to differentiate by impressing clients and prospects with the breadth of a principal's communications skills and insights. However, the bar for successful blogging and podcasting is high. Preparation can be time-consuming and requires writing skills, not to mention engaging content. There is also the risk of being self-indulgent, controversial, or overtly promotional—three sure turn-offs. And a blog or a podcast has to appear regularly to hold an audience's attention.

6

LOCATING PROSPECTS

As good and consistent as a firm's promotional activity might be, it is often not enough to provide a steady stream of new business. Typically needed as well are prospecting for new clients—known as cold-calling—and occasionally mining a firm's database of previous contacts. Because these activities involve direct contact and selling, they are among the least inviting functions of marketing, and the most often put off. Creatives who have little concern about making a presentation (it is, after all, just talking about how good their work is) clutch up when it comes to picking up the phone and cold-calling a prospect. Avoiding these calls is a major reason why principals seek professional sales help. (For a discussion of hiring sales help, see Chapter 7.)

Personal reluctance aside, direct sales contact can be very productive. It is the marketing effort that offers the shortest time between making contact and receiving income, which is a key consideration when business is lagging. And when only a principal's time is involved, it is by far the least expensive way to generate sales.

BUILDING CONFIDENCE

Despite the advantages of direct sales contact, the distaste for doing it is easy to understand. In general, creative individuals tend to be a little less outgoing than others. Many also feel that overt sales efforts are demeaning, and soliciting is the most overt of all. Then, too, telemarketing has something less than a sterling reputation. We're often not sure whom to call or what to say. And, of course, there's the fear of outright rejection. While it might not be possible to turn dread into enthusiasm, it is possible for almost anyone to do a passable job.

ADOPTING THE RIGHT ATTITUDE. Anyone who does direct selling needs to recognize from the outset that this is a numbers game. That is, it can take many calls before securing a single presentation appointment, even for firms that are well known. Rejection is part of the process, and it can't be taken personally or as a comment on the firm or its work. Yet if a personable caller with a persuasive message makes enough contacts to the right prospects, the effort will pay off handsomely in sales. And that is all that really matters.

When they put their minds to it, principals as well as salespersons can do well at prospecting. It's a job requirement for anyone involved with sales—including reluctant principals, who should consider it a do-or-die necessity. Although it is occasionally possible to hire someone to handle prospecting part-time, either internally or outside through telemarketing, this can be difficult to arrange. (For an explanation of why this is so, see Chapter 7.)

PICKING THE RIGHT TARGETS. This is a no-brainer: the better qualified the prospects, the greater the chances of success. Also, lack of success causes discouragement and premature abandonment of otherwise viable efforts. Prospects need, therefore, to be a good fit with the firm's business development strategy, as discussed in Chapter 2. While sometimes any business can be better than none, long-term success (at least as defined by better and more profitable work) requires chasing the right types of projects and clients, particularly those you're most likely to land. Never forget that it can take as long to sell your firm to a bad prospect as to a good one.

You can improve your success rate by prioritizing your prospecting against the following criteria: *The projects are a good match to your talent and skills*—the better the match, the better the chances of securing the client. *They'll move your business in the right direction*—major projects will affect the future course of your business. *There's a good possibility of an ongoing stream*—multiple projects amortize prospecting costs. *The projects will have high visibility*—the higher the profile, the more they will pay and the higher your profit potential will be. *The clients don't need educating*—those that do always learn at your expense. *They won't be spending out of their own pockets*—professional managers are easier to deal with than owner/entrepreneurs. (For a sample client backgrounder form, see Appendix III.)

HAVING THE RIGHT TOOLS. Business contact lists can be purchased. An online search will turn up several sources. Note, however, that there's a difference between *mailing lists*, which provide just names and addresses, and *contact lists*, which also provide details on the prospect's business, names of who handles what, and telephone numbers. Contact lists can cost up to several dollars a name, often with a minimum of several hundred names.

Although the detail they provide can be helpful, particularly when pursuing larger clients, for most purposes it will be adequate to compile your own list by watching personnel change notices in the local business press or by calling prospective organizations and asking. (See "Calling the 'switchboard' when you don't have a name" below.) However your contact list is compiled, be sure to enter the names in a contact database that will allow tracking of all contacts and activity. (See "Contact Mining" below.)

An isolated, comfortable, and quiet office is essential for calling. Any noise in the background is not only unprofessional but might give an impression of a "boiler room" call center. Calls should always be made over a business landline for clarity and caller identification, never on a cell phone.

BEING PREPARED. Because calling is a personal form of business solicitation, preparation and comfort level are crucial. Uneasiness, fear of embarrassment, and bumbling efforts can doom any attempt to failure. Approaches to take, scripts to use, and ways to counter objections are covered later in this chapter.

It's also very helpful if the prospect being contacted is already aware of your firm. This is why callers from larger, established firms have a considerably higher success rate. (Having professional salespersons helps, too.) In simple terms, the more a prospect knows, the more receptive he or she will be, which makes the process less intimidating.

TAKING THE RIGHT APPROACH

There are four direct contact sales techniques that are appropriate—knocking on doors, telemarketing, contacting social and business network "friends," and sending letters with a telephone follow-up. Each is suitable in certain situations.

KNOCKING ON DOORS. Although appearing unannounced and hoping for an appointment is usually unproductive, it shouldn't be entirely dismissed. Occasionally it makes sense, such as when making several calls in an industrial park or when already seeing another client or prospect in the neighborhood.

Here's what to say to a potential prospect's gatekeeper (receptionist) after first introducing yourself and your business: "I wonder if you could help me out? I was just calling on (name another company) down the street, and it occurred to me that someone here at (prospect organization) probably also uses (type) services. Can you tell me who the person in charge of your (sales materials, advertising, public relations, Web site, etc.) might be? I'd like to see if there's a chance that he or she might be available so I could very quickly introduce my firm."

If you're successful in getting a name, ask to use a house phone to make the call. Repeat the relevant sections of the above message to the person who answers. Promise that you will only stop long enough to say hello and leave information about your services: five or ten minutes, nothing more. (For negative responses, see "Countering Negatives" below.)

If you're granted an audience, have a sample or two and your capability brochure in a briefcase, but do not attempt to do a portfolio showing. Showing your work on another day will provide time to put together a presentation that's suited to the client's interests and will minimize any appearance of "trolling for business."

If you make contact and the prospect is busy, try to set up an appointment. If you do not make personal contact, leave a short voice mail preceded by "Sorry I missed you." At very least, try to get the prospect's full name, title, and e-mail address from the gatekeeper for calling later or adding to your mailing list. If you are stonewalled, ask the gatekeeper to pass your business card and information (capability brochure) along to the right person, say thanks, and move on.

TELEMARKETING. Perhaps you find telemarketing a great annoyance at home (dinner-time calls) and even occasionally disrupting at the office. But don't let personal reactions affect a business decision. Telemarketing can be very cost effective, especially for introducing business-to-business services. ("Do not call" lists don't apply to business calls.) Calling referrals from current clients can be especially productive. (See "Referrals Management" in Chapter 4.)

The upside. You already have everything you need—a voice, a telephone, and probably an idea of whom to call. Time is the only expense, so just a few appointments are necessary to generate a handsome payoff. Creative services are something most businesses need, but many don't know how to get. Others will be receptive to alternatives to whatever services they are presently using. Although getting through to the right contact person is no less a problem, he or she is far more likely to be receptive to your pitch for a service the company already uses than to pitches for other products and services.

The downside. Most significant is a low success rate and the discouragement that can accompany it. Also, telemarketing is typically less effective for a small firm than for a large one because prospects are more likely to accept a call from someone they've heard of. And anyone who only occasionally does telemarketing isn't usually as good at it someone who does it regularly.

Scripting. The initial objective should be to make an appointment, not to sell. That comes later in a face-to-face meeting and presentation. A call will often be an interruption to the recipient, so it should be short and to the point. Much telemarketing isn't successful because of the caller's poor telephone skills—unfriendly voice, unclear diction, unfocused message, overly pushy manner. Scripting, practice, and more practice can eliminate or minimize them all.

As important as scripting can be, it's important that the call never sound that way. Telemarketing succeeds best when the caller sounds friendly and spontaneous. Several scripts are presented below, and they can be modified as circumstances require. For suggestions on responding to the inevitable negative replies, see "Countering Negatives" below.

Calling specific individuals. "Good morning, (prospect name). This is Joe Artiste of (firm). Thank you for taking my call. (Sara Goodfriend of [organization] suggested I give you a call.) My firm provides (type of services). We've never had the pleasure of working together, so I'm calling to introduce myself and see whether it might be possible to come by and show you, very quickly, what we've done for organizations similar to (prospect's organization). Some of our recent clients have included (two or three names). I plan to be in your area early next week. Would you be available then, or would another time be more convenient?"

Should a personal gatekeeper (secretary) answer, say the following: "Good morning. This is Joe Artiste of (firm). Is (first name) available?"

If not, say you will call back and ask when would be the best time. If questioned about the reason for the call, adapt the above script as needed. Should someone else answer, say who you are and ask when the prospect will return. Should an answering machine answer, see below.

Leaving a message. Use the same script as above, adding "Sorry I missed you" and replacing the last paragraph above with the following: "If you could give me a call at (telephone number) at your convenience so we could set something up, I believe it would be beneficial to both of us. Also, you might want to check out what we do at (your firm's Web site URL)."

Immediately after the call, send the prospect an introductory letter with your capability brochure. Don't use e-mail and PDFs, as they carry less impact. Say that you are sorry you missed her or him and will call again. Meanwhile, emphasize that the enclosed material will provide a short introduction.

Of course, few calls will be returned. So call back in a week or so. Mention sending the material, and ask whether it shows the type of services that the prospect occasionally has need for. Make one more call a week later, and another two weeks after that. If there's still no connection, give up and move on. But keep the name on your mail/e-mail lists for regular contact.

Calling the "switchboard" when you don't have a name. "Good morning. This is Joe Artiste of (firm). I'd like to speak with (send introductory material to) the individual responsible for (materials). Can you tell me who that might be (and connect me, please)?"

Future calls. Make a point to call every major prospect at least once a year, preferably twice. You are almost certainly more sensitive to calling too frequently than your prospects are. Situations change, memories fade, and persistence pays off. Say you are just checking in to see if there is anything you can help them with.

EXPLOITING NETWORK CONNECTIONS. Chapter 5 explained the role of social and business networking in a promotional context. Now it is time to put it in a direct sales context. Just as you might ask personal friends for a business connection within their workplace (either with or without using them as a reference), it is appropriate to do the same with some of your electronic networking "friends." Select carefully, but don't be shy about it, particularly with business networking sites. It is expected. Indeed, help in making connections is their stated purpose, especially with business networking sites.

SENDING A LETTER FOLLOWED BY A CALL. This, the fourth method of direct contact, should be a business-generating staple for all firms. Not only is it effective, but it is easier for most of us than knocking on doors or tele-marketing. It is also acceptable to most prospects. The only disadvantage vis-à-vis telemarketing is that it takes longer to make the contact.

First, the letter. The purpose is to get an appointment, not to sell, so the letter should be a short, personal, one-page introduction to your firm, its capabilities, recent clients, and relevance to the prospect's needs. Use the final paragraph to state that you will be calling soon to ask about set-ting up an appointment. Use the post, not e-mail, and don't enclose any samples or promotional material (they lessen the need to see you). Enclosing a stamped or postpaid reply card can increase the chances for success, but it does not obviate the need for a follow-up call. (A sample prospecting letter is in Appendix III.)

Then, the call. When thus primed, prospects tend to be more receptive to a phone call. Make the follow-up call a week or so after they have received the letter. Ask if they received it, whether they are the right person to talk to, and if they have any questions. Then ask when would be a good time to set up an appointment. See the section below for how to answer negative responses. If you are unsuccessful in getting through, see "Leaving a message" above.

COUNTERING NEGATIVES

No matter which direct contact method you use, you can expect a variety of negative responses. See below for a selection of the most common ones and suggestions on how to reply. Note that most replies turn the prospect's response into another question. The purpose of this is to continue the conversation, to draw out the prospect's concern and address it. It is impossible to provide responses for all the ways each concern might play out beyond this, but a good place to start an extended conversation is by asking another question, such as "Is that because of (reason intuited from the conversation)?"

"WE'RE NOT INTERESTED." "I appreciate your candor. Tell me, is this because you already have a supplier you're happy with, or is there another reason?" (See other relevant responses below.)

"I'M NOT THE RIGHT PERSON." "I'm sorry to have bothered you. Can you direct me to whoever is? Also, would you happen to know his or her e-mail address? It might be a quicker way to make contact and avoid playing telephone tag."

"I'M VERY BUSY (RIGHT NOW)." "I know the feeling. Let me call back later. When would be a good time? Would early or late in the day be better?"

"I DON'T REMEMBER YOUR LETTER." "It's possible I might have had the wrong address. Anyway, (adapt the "Calling specific individuals" script, above)."

"SHE'S NOT AVAILABLE RIGHT NOW." "Would you tell her that (name) called and that I'll call back? When do you think would be a good time to catch her? Also, would you happen to know her e-mail address? It might keep us from playing telephone tag."

"WE'RE HAPPY WITH THE FIRM WE CURRENTLY USE." "No problem. Actually, many (most) of our clients use others as their primary (agency) (design firm). We pinch-hit for them when necessary, and they've also found that it helps sometimes to see alternative creative solutions and prices. Then, too, no one can predict what might happen in the future, so it's always good to know what other suppliers and resources are available. Our introductory presentation takes only (a half hour), and I can schedule it for the beginning or end of the day if you'd like. Would you be free anytime next (day or day) morning?"

"DO YOU HAVE EXPERIENCE IN (SPECIALIZED AREA)?" "I'm afraid we don't, but we consider that a competitive advantage. It allows us to approach a new client's work with fresh ideas and without any preconceived notions. We've successfully handled (projects) (accounts) in unfamiliar industries for a variety of clients in the past, such as (one or two examples). Would you like me to show you some of the innovative ways we've produced outstanding results for them?"

"HOW MUCH DO YOU CHARGE?" "Well, I wish I could tell you specifically. But every project is different. I can tell you, though, that (type of job) typically runs from ($X to $Y). Does this sound like the range you would be comfortable with?"

When the response is positive, try to set up an appointment. When negative, forget the prospective client and move on.

"SEND ME SOME SAMPLES / DROP OFF YOUR PORTFOLIO." "My experience is that it would be better if you could spare me (a half hour) to show them (it). I'm very proud of the quality of our work, but samples only show half of what's made our firm so successful in working with clients (such as . . .). What samples never show—what can only be conveyed in a personal meeting—is what the objectives of each client were, how we worked with each one to strategize and meet their objectives, and how efficient and economical the whole process was.

"Also, anyone looking at our work for the first time always has a few questions about why we did things a certain way, what things cost, and— perhaps most important of all—how effective a piece was. In other words, whether it met all the client's objectives. I promise our meeting won't take longer than a half an hour, and I can schedule it at the beginning or end of your workday. Is there a time next week that's convenient?"

"GIVE ME YOUR WEB SITE, AND I'LL CHECK IT OUT FIRST." (Same basic response as above.)

"SORRY, I'M TOO BUSY. YOU'LL HAVE TO SEND SAMPLES." There are two alternatives to this response. One, as follows, is to decline. Although this might seem self-defeating, samples and drop-offs have a poor record of leading to significant projects. Implying that your firm is sufficiently successful that it doesn't have to waste time playing the "Don't call me, I'll call you" game just might change the prospect's mind.

"Frankly, there are lots of (type) firms out there that do great creative work. But what really sets us apart is what we do that makes working with us more efficient and creates high value in what we produce. Unfortunately, this takes explanation. So I'm afraid I will pass at this time. In the meantime, you can look at our portfolio on our Web site at (www.oursite). I'll call you again in a month or so when perhaps you'll be less busy."

What follows is the other response, often more appropriate for freelancers, particularly when pitching agencies or other creative firms: "I understand. I'll do it right away. Is there anything in particular you would be most interested in? After you get them, I'll give you another call. My experience is that they always raise questions on pricing and client needs that can only be answered in person. Will you be in around this time next week so we can discuss your reactions and perhaps set up a future meeting?"

Put together a half dozen (seldom more) samples relevant to the client's interests. Attach a transmittal letter or note indicating a return date within two weeks, a business card, and your firm's brochure. Because samples often get mislaid and sometimes misattributed, make sure that each is clearly identified (stamped) with something similar to the following: "Evaluation sample from (firm). More examples of our work are online at (www.oursite). Please return to (firm address)."

To emphasize their importance, don't simply drop off samples or a portfolio. Instead, send them by a means that requires a signed receipt —overnight express (e.g., FedEx) for samples, a taxi or messenger for a portfolio or reel. Provide a pre-addressed express envelope with account number for their return by express, or a voucher for return by taxi or messenger.

Call a week or so after the client receives what you've sent, ask if there are any questions, and see whether an appointment to discuss the client's needs would be appropriate at this time. Or inquire, if perhaps, would later be better?

CONTACT MINING

There is a tendency to take previous clients and contacts for granted. They are seldom solicited with the same zeal as new prospects. ("They already know about us. They'll call if they have work.") And the advantage enjoyed over perhaps lesser-known competitors is seldom exploited. Compounding this is clients' tendency to pigeonhole a firm or individual: some are only considered for printed literature, others for Web sites, still others only for packaging. Many clients associate certain agencies with an industry or approach: for example, a freelance writer might be known as "a direct mail guy." And in many clients' eyes, design firms are differentiated more by their creative style than by their business sophistication. In other words, for some clients it's likely that you will come to mind only when they have a project of the type they already associate with you. That is, unless you work to change their perceptions.

Running a promotional campaign to broaden a firm's positioning is one way to do this (see Chapter 5). Another way is by mining the firm's database. Every firm should have one that contains detailed information on every prospect and client. This database should provide not only a record of contacts and sales, but also information on each company's business and products, as well as personal information such as likes and dislikes. Database entries can be sorted by organization, or by individual names so that you can follow them through their career moves. General database software (e.g., FileMaker) works well. Even better is Customer Relationship Management (CRM) software (e.g., ACT), which offers additional features such as calendars, to-do lists, scheduling, expense recording, and reporting functions—all of which are valuable to dedicated salespersons. The name, job title, address, and organization on each record should be verified by telephone yearly. (For a sample of a typical contact database record, see Appendix III.)

Successful salespeople know that the way to turn a contact into a client is through more contact. In addition to normal promotional mailings and e-mailings, do the following for those you've assigned a high priority.

CHECKING IN. Every first-time contact and all presentations that don't lead to immediate work should end with a request: "Do you mind if I call and check in with you every so often?" Few prospects will say no, which should help dispense with any later concern about "bugging" them. How often? For those with good potential, up to three times a year—enough to sustain awareness, not so often as to be irritating. For clients with lesser potential, one or two times a year.

Don't be shy. Most clients, particularly those holding marketing positions, respect suppliers who are moderately aggressive. Chances are you're more sensitive than they are. Even if you can't get through, a voice-mail message will be a reminder of your interest. Don't give up too soon, either. Continue calling as long as the client doesn't seem irritated. If, however, there is no encouragement after four or so calls, try the following and then move on.

SCHEDULING PRESENTATION UPDATES. Anytime it's been a year or more since you've shown your work to a prospect, call to try to set up an "updater" appointment. Stress that the meeting will only take around fifteen minutes and that its purpose is to show new things that you believe he or she will want to see, given the interests expressed at your last presentation.

SENDING SAMPLES. Purchase samples of high-profile jobs you've worked on from the printer or past client, and mail them to a few good prospects, selected by priority and probable interest. Or send screen shots of an impressive Web site by mail or e-mail along with a short, personal note: "I thought you'd be interested in seeing this." Nothing more is required.

RESPONDING TO UNSOLICITED INQUIRIES

This scenario seems ideal at first glance: an unknown prospect contacts you by phone or e-mail to ask about meeting and discussing some work. You don't want to offend a potentially good prospect by asking if he or she is serious. But you also don't want to be wasting your efforts on the under-budgeted, the clueless, and the tire-kickers. Unfortunately, there is no sure way to make certain that you only invest time on real opportunities. Some wasted effort is part of any sales process. Qualifying a prospect before scheduling a visit and presentation can minimize it, though. The busier you are, the more important how you respond becomes. (See also "Picking the Right Targets" above.)

SETTING THE TONE. Even when the inquiry is by phone, your firm's Web site plays an important role in qualifying prospects because most will visit the site before making contact. What they experience affects their expectations. Don't expect that portfolio samples showing quality (expensive) work will put off less sophisticated and low-budget visitors. It doesn't seem to work that way, probably because some inquiries come from those who either are unaware of what creative work costs or are hoping to score quality work at bargain-basement prices.

What *can* be effective in qualifying prospects is posting hourly rates or representative prices. But because doing this can also limit marketing and pricing flexibility, it is not generally recommended. An exception, however, is for certain single- and two-person firms that feel a need to define the quality circles in which their business operates. (When posting prices, use a 100 percent minimum-to-maximum range for typical projects: high enough to discourage the undesirables, low enough not to discourage others.)

Another important consideration is what appears on the "About Us" pages on many sites. Copy that plays up a firm's smallness or unconventional nature plays directly to the interests of small and less conventional clients. Copy that stresses strategic thinking and partnering will be discouraging to them. And be aware that what you say and post in social media pages can have an effect on inquiries. While they can open up new levels of business contacts, they are also part of an Internet culture that fosters informal communications and shopping around. The more personal the postings, the more they will encourage this type of informal contact.

FIRST RESPONSE. Of course, the Internet works the other way, too. In the case of social media, it is often possible to get profile information that will give an indication of an inquirer's background and potential for business. And just as most prospects, whether making contact by phone or e-mail, have likely checked out your site, you can check out theirs. What you see might give an indication of their size (budget?) and tastes.

Regardless of the impressions you come away with—"great opportunity," "no way," or someplace in between—they are only impressions and can be misleading. A good site doesn't necessarily vouch for the individual or group that made contact. And a bad site and materials, or their absence, could be the very reason for the inquiry. More information is still needed to assess true potential.

MAKING CONTACT. Every inquiry is a sales lead, and it should be followed up despite its origin or its apparent potential. Even when the inquiry asks the improbable (e.g., "Would you like to bid on a logo? Our budget is $300."), you never know an inquirer's connections or what positions she or he might occupy in the future. Follow-up normally means responding with a telephone call—not an e-mail, which is too impersonal. Also, e-mails eliminate any ability to further assess the potential of the prospect, or to persuade or negotiate.

THE INTRODUCTION. Thank the inquirer for contacting you. Ask where she or he heard about your firm, how much she knows about it, and what her interest is. Then give a brief summary noting former clients, work, and experience—your "elevator pitch." This summary will reinforce what is already known or will enlighten new prospects. In the latter case, ask if your summary describes the type of firm the inquirer is looking for. Do not mention pricing at this point unless asked. If asked, respond this way: "The type of work you are interested in normally runs from a low of ($X) to as much as ($Y), depending on complexity. Is this more or less what you had in mind?"

THE TURNDOWN. When the inquirer's background or pricing indicates an inquiry not worth pursuing, tactfully turn it down by saying something like this: "As you can see from what I've just described, I'm afraid we are not the right firm to handle your work. But I do thank you for the opportunity." If suitable, also add something along the lines of: "You might want to try (name of a local smaller firm or franchise copy chain), which is better suited to handle needs like yours."

THE POSSIBLE. When prospects pass the potential test, you can move to set up a presentation meeting, ideally a week or more out. This scheduling will allow time for the prospect to receive information on your working procedures, which constitute the second level of qualification. Send a copy of your firm's capability brochure, working procedures, and any other relevant material under a "thanks for the opportunity" confirmation letter. Here, too, the postal service is preferable to e-mail in that it makes a more professional impression. If your firm does not have a printed piece explaining your working procedures, it should. (See the sample "How We Work Together" form in Appendix III.)

A day or two before the appointment, call to confirm and to ask if your mailing raised any questions. This follow-up helps to ensure that the prospect hasn't forgotten. More important, it keeps you from making a wasted call if there is concern about your procedures, such as the expectation of progress payments. If so, it is better to face up to the issue sooner rather than later.

OTHER CONSIDERATIONS. Adopting the above strategies will minimize time squandered on inquiries that are destined to go nowhere. At the same time, for serious prospects it creates an impression of professionalism and of a firm that welcomes new opportunities but is not hungry. This makes scheduling and pricing less subject to pressure.

7

SALES RESPONSIBILITIES

The nature of the creative services business is such that landing most clients and projects requires a personal effort. Someone has to make a cold call or follow up a lead, schedule an appointment, make a presentation, address any prospect concerns, and close the sale. In small firms, that person will likely be a principal; in large firms, usually a combination of sales professional and principal. Whoever handles it, though, selling is one of the more important functions in a firm, ranking below only ownership responsibilities and creative direction. A firm can be awash in talent and still fail if there isn't someone who can generate sufficient sales. And in the long run, any sizeable firm's market value is strongly affected by the degree to which sales (and also creative) can be produced independently of a principal's direct involvement.

A PRINCIPAL'S ROLE

Sales is an integral part of an owner's job description, an unavoidable aspect of being an entrepreneur in a service business. For smaller operations, this means direct involvement; for larger ones, involvement at the management level. Either way, an owner is a firm's chief sales executive, at least until size exceeds a dozen or more employees. No one else knows as much about the business or has as much riding on its success. Those who understand this and approach sales responsibilities enthusiastically will likely prosper; it's a toss-up whether those who approach them reluctantly can be successful over the long term.

Due to economic considerations (explained later in this chapter), principals of firms with a creative staff fewer than four typically have to shoulder the sales burden among their other tasks. Alternatives might be possible, but most are compromises—and usually unsatisfactory ones. (See "Looking at Sales Staffing Alternatives" below.)

When firms are large enough to employ four creative individuals, usually a full-time person needs to be assigned to keeping the workflow pipeline full. (I say "usually" because it depends somewhat on the type of work and how much of it comes from a few clients.) Even after hiring a salesperson (sometimes called a business development person, or BDP) for this purpose, a principal is still typically involved in providing credibility and confirmation at many presentations. When desired, however, a principal can continue to perform the role of full-time salesperson—if (and it is a big if) he or she can successfully delegate most management and creative functions.

It is a good idea for principals of growing operations to consider this decision point before it becomes necessary. Why? Because there's a natural tendency when the time comes to put it off and try to continue handling everything—sales, management, and creative direction—often with the result that there's not time enough to do everything well. Where there are two principals, reaching a creative staff of three or four is also a good time to split management responsibilities if that has not occurred already: one individual responsible for external functions such as sales and finances, and one responsible for internal functions such as creative and management.

Firms reaching a creative staff of six full-time employees typically need a professional, full-time salesperson. At this size and larger, a principal's management responsibilities are too extensive to be delegated. Additional salespersons then normally need to be hired for every six or so creative employees, although it is difficult to generalize, given the diversity of larger operations. Only after a firm reaches a dozen or more employees can a principal step totally away from active sales involvement, if desired. Until then, she or he is usually still required to close new sales or serve as the point person with repeat clients. And one important responsibility that always remains is setting a firm's marketing and sales strategies—what types of clients and projects to go after, and how to best do it.

THE AFFORDABILITY EQUATION

All employees are human resources investments. To put it simply and somewhat callously, their role is to produce products or services worth more than the combined costs of their salaries, benefits, and overhead. This is no less true of those who generate sales. So let's see what it takes for an investment in full-time sales help to pay off. We'll look at compensation in three ways: salary, commission, and salary-plus-commission. (For a full discussion of compensation arrangements, see "Arranging Compensation" below.)

For example purposes, we'll use a hypothetical design firm with a staff of one full-time employee and a principal. Gross revenue is $215,000, with a gross margin (sometimes referred to as agency gross income, or AGI) of $180,000. (The difference between gross revenue and gross margin here is the money collected for client media and printing, which is just sent on to the publication or printer.) The margin figure ($180,000) is low ($220,000+ would be better), a fact the principal attributes to time diverted to selling. Her desire is to hire a full-time salesperson to prospect for business. This will enable her to focus more on the firm's creative product and also have a higher percentage of billable time.

SALARY COMPENSATION. Let's say our principal hires a new full-time sales-person at a salary of $55,000. Assuming a conservative $10,000 (roughly 20 percent of salary) to cover benefits and overhead, and $6,000 ($500 monthly) for direct sales expenses, this will run the firm around $71,000 annually, which we will round off at $6,000 a month.

To cover this cost, two things have to happen. One, the obvious, is that the salesperson will have to produce at least $6,000 a month (gross margin) in brand-new business. The second, less obvious, is that the new business would have to be handled without otherwise increasing the firm's overhead. In other words, it must be accommodated either through existing excess capacity or through the new capacity created by freeing up the principal's time. If, as is more probable, additional staff will be needed to handle the new business, the additional overhead costs (hiring expenses, salaries, benefits, workstations, etc.) must be added to the salesperson's costs for a true picture of the impact generated by the new business.

COMMISSION COMPENSATION. As will be explained in more detail later in this chapter, the standard sales commission on fee billings (gross margin) when there's no base or partial salary is 15 percent. Using this figure, a sales-person would need to land new business worth around $27,775 (gross margin) a month ($333,300 yearly) to earn a commission of $50,000. This would mean an average of around $110,000 in fee billings for each of the firm's (now) three employees. Moreover, even this level of performance does not include covering the firm's costs of benefits, overhead, and sales expenses.

In short, a salesperson limited to the production capacity of a two-creative firm could not make enough commission to make this a full-time job. Looking at this situation in another way, a productive salesperson working on commission will produce enough work to keep at least three billable employees busy, depending on their speed and efficiency.

SALARY-PLUS-COMMISSION COMPENSATION. For an example of this arrangement, we will use a typical salary-plus-commission mix: $30,000 base, with a commission of 10 percent of fee billings for new work and 8 percent on repeat work.

Using only new projects for our example, the salesperson will have to bring in $200,000 worth of projects to earn $50,000 annually ($30,000 base plus $20,000). In doing so, however, he or she will have raised the firm's payroll costs by around $50,000—salary, benefits (same as for higher-paid employees), and sales expenses. Not to mention the commission payments. There are too many firm-specific variables to predict profitability in a salary-plus-commission arrangement, but it is unlikely that it would be cost effective for a firm with a billable staff of just two.

LOOKING AT SALES STAFFING ALTERNATIVES

As the above discussion illustrates, the sales conundrum for small firms is that it takes time away from creative and management functions when principals handle sales, yet the cost of having a dedicated salesperson is too high. And even when a firm is of sufficient size to afford professional sales help, there are still hiring, employment, and expense costs with no guarantee that the individual will produce enough to pay off. It's little wonder, then, that principals look for other ways to fulfill the sales need.

Is there an alternative? Is it possible for a small firm to find someone to take on the most difficult and frustrating aspects of sales—the prospecting and cold-calling that everyone hates? Asked another way, is it possible for a principal to handle only the relatively pleasant sales tasks—providing credibility, pricing and closing, even doing occasional portfolio showings and presentations?

WHAT ABOUT PART-TIME SALES HELP? This seems like the logical option to consider when full-time sales help isn't feasible. Unfortunately, what's good in theory is difficult to put into practice. Unlike other functions that are more or less adaptable to flexible work hours, calling on clients and servicing accounts require being available during most business hours. As we will see later in this chapter, finding capable full-time sales help is a major challenge. It is even greater when looking for a part-time individual. She or he should not only possess a sales background or talent but also be capable of representing creative products and interpreting client needs. All this said, part-time help could work out if you can find the right person.

WHAT ABOUT SHARING A SALESPERSON? It's usually impractical. Firms that share should not be competitors, so it is difficult for someone with industry expertise to represent a group diverse enough for a profitable business. Even if sharing were possible, chances are there would be destructive competitive pressures when the sharing firms have conflicting priorities. Further, clients usually want to entrust their business to an insider—an employee—whom they can call on when needed.

WHAT ABOUT HIRING SOMEONE TO MAKE CALLS? This approach has been successful for some firms. But it is crucial that he or she represent the firm professionally and be well enough versed in the firm's capabilities to answer prospective clients' questions and concerns. These requirements, along with good telephone skills and the willingness to work on an as-needed basis, make it a difficult position to fill well. In addition, two other factors make hiring a good telemarketing company a long shot: lack of background knowledge, and the fact that the needs of a small firm are often not enough to interest professionals.

WHAT ABOUT USING EMPLOYEES PART-TIME? It seldom works out because the personal qualities that are helpful in selling—extroverted, insistent, impulsive, persistent, undaunted—are polar opposites from those of most creatives. Also, additionally compensating non-sales employees to motivate them to bring in new business sends the wrong signal. Passing along sales leads and tips should be expected of all employees because doing so constitutes nothing more than protecting a firm's workflow and everyone's jobs.

WHAT ABOUT PAYING FINDER'S FEES? Paying outsiders for referrals is occasionally productive, although it is preferable to arrange it on a "you do a favor for me now, I'll do a favor for you later" basis. There are, however, situations when you are not in a position to return a favor or when someone has invested considerable effort on your behalf. In such cases, a fee of between 5 and 10 percent of fee income, and 25 percent of markup income (e.g., 25 percent of 20 percent), is appropriate one time. After this, you have earned the account. In making such arrangements, be careful not to cross the lines of business ethics and conflicts of interest. Never pay a client for a recommendation, and keep in mind that it is better not to pay anyone with whom you do business. The former is prohibited by most clients and may be illegal; the latter can easily be interpreted as a kickback.

WHAT ABOUT TALENT REPS? They're an outside long shot unless your business involves illustration, photography, animation, filmmaking, or the like. Most reps don't handle providers of other creative services. The reason is that their business—representing a stable of talents in return for sales commissions of 25 to 40 percent—is financially remunerative only in selected circumstances. The client universe has to be easy to identify, relatively small, and having frequent needs, such as agencies and publications. Projects have to be easy to define, pricing has to be easy to quote, and there has to be little need for client-creative interaction. The focus of a rep's clients is on filling a specific artistic need, not on working to solve a client's broader communications need. For more on how talent reps work, visit the Web site of the Society of Photographic and Artists Representatives, www.spar.org.

CONSIDERATIONS BEFORE HIRING A RAINMAKER

Okay, your business has now reached the point at which it probably needs a professional salesperson. We'll get to hiring shortly. Before that, though, there are a few more things to consider.

YOU WILL NEED A SALES STRATEGY. What is it specifically that you want a professional salesperson to accomplish: Simply assume the sales activity you now handle? Go after certain types of new clients or work? Increase sales by some percentage? Shift the project/account mix from low-profit to higher-profit? Without thinking this through, you could well end up looking for the wrong type of person. Or you might find the right person, who ends up calling on the wrong prospects at the wrong time. After all, even world-class sales talent can't help achieve what can't first be defined.

If you don't already have a business development plan (sales strategy), it is best to develop one before going any further (see Chapter 4). Ultimately, it is important for salespeople to contribute to it, and doing so should be part of their job description. But initially, and for better or for worse, that person will have to rely on what you already have in place.

YOU WILL NEED TO PROVIDE ADEQUATE COMPENSATION. More than for creative employees, the motivation of most salespeople is money. The opportunity to be involved with great creative projects or work in a "cool" shop is secondary, if present at all. You must be willing to accept that the size of the salesperson's paycheck is immaterial as long as the result is higher profit for the business. It is even okay if she or he makes more than you do, assuming the equity in your business grows. Scrimping on the compensation of salespeople is a shortsighted and common situation among small to mid-size firms. Most large firms have learned not to make this mistake.

YOU WILL NEED TO OFFER RANK AND STATURE. Salespeople need to have the same prestige and clout as the most senior creative persons in a firm—in other words, just one or at most two levels down from you. Furthermore, since most clients need reassurance that everyone they deal with is important, salespeople should have impressive titles—Senior Vice President of Marketing, or Executive Vice President of New Business Development.

YOU WILL NEED TO PROVIDE THE NECESSARY TOOLS. Salespeople can spend a lot of time on the telephone, so they require isolated, quiet offices. They also need a dedicated laptop loaded with contact relationship management (CRM) software and an impressive PowerPoint presentation on the firm's capabilities. Clerical needs (preparing proposals, etc.) should take top priority, and a high-quality leave-behind (capability brochure) for sales calls is essential.

HIRING A RAINMAKER

No hiring decision should ever be taken lightly, but hiring a salesperson, particularly the first one, calls for special consideration. Unlike the hiring of creative staff, there is no portfolio from which to judge an individual's talent. With only a resumé and your impressions to go on, it is hard to tell just how much substance lies behind the polish.

THE RISK FACTORS. When hiring a salesperson, it's important to recognize that financial and other risks are easily double those of hiring most other employees. Other hiring decisions are almost always production driven. That is, they are based on work that already exists. So the up-front costs of a new employee are quickly offset by his or her billed time. In contrast, hiring a new salesperson is often based on projections of new business. Even when such projections are accurate (and these are as likely to be off as on), there will be weeks, perhaps months, before business increases enough to compensate.

Furthermore, sales time is not billable. A slow-to-produce hire becomes a financial sinkhole, even when paid on commission. In contrast, the salaries of less-than-great creatives are at least partially covered by their billable activity.

Salespeople also become a prospective client's first impression of a firm's sophistication and capabilities. Moreover, much of what they do occurs outside the firm where there is little or no opportunity for management intervention or oversight. Salespeople are on their own, yet what they say and do have a profound impact on the firm's business. The quality of repeat clients may be in the hands of the creative staff, but the quality of prospective new clients is mostly in the hands of the sales staff.

THE RIGHT TYPE OF INDIVIDUAL. Differences in the ways project-based firms (such as design) operate versus those of process-based firms (such as agencies) are especially significant in terms of sales. Project-based firms need continuous new sales and relatively little client servicing activity, whereas process-based firms require continuous client servicing and relatively little new sales activity. So a firm's business mix influences the appropriate type of individual to look for. Unless a firm operates primarily as an agency, the emphasis should be on sales ability and experience.

Sales ability is difficult to assess in advance, but perhaps the defining quality for creative services is an ability to recognize the difference between prospects' needs and their wants. Understanding what a prospect really wants, not just what he or she needs or is asking for, makes for happier clients and leads to better, more satisfying, and more profitable work.

Assessing an individual's sales experience is less difficult. Those with the right type of experience typically have worked as creatives themselves. Some might prefer selling the work rather than actually doing it; others might be returning to the field after an absence. No matter what their motivation, they know the creative process and can talk persuasively to clients about what works, what doesn't, and what it costs. Also worth considering are creatively talented printing and paper salespeople who wish to be involved more in the creative side of the business. They bring previous sales experience, understand needs, and have client connections.

Individuals with previous agency account executive experience are another possibility, especially if the firm's business mix includes advertising or PR-type work. However, some candidates—particularly if they've had large agency experience—may have to be cautioned not to focus on client service (easy to do) to the detriment of new business development (difficult to do). The challenge is often in finding an individual with the right sales versus service inclination. Former magazine space reps are also good potential candidates. (Paying by commission will cure the tendency to over-service. See "Arranging Compensation" below.)

GETTING APPLICATIONS. Put the word on the street that your firm is looking. Talk about your needs among peers at creative club meetings and similar events. Ask every printing salesperson you deal with if he or she knows of any good reps, or anyone with sales and creative talent who is looking to get into a slightly different line. Ask the same of paper salespeople and any media reps you work with. Put a job opportunity notice on your Web site and social media pages. Place ads on organizational Web sites (e.g., AIGA) and online employment sites (e.g., Monster).

SCREENING APPLICANTS. By definition, good salespeople have a different set of skills and objectives from most of the creative staff. So don't hold it against them. They should be more polished, more aggressive, and have a certain nonchalance about rejection. When necessary, they should also become a client's in-house advocate. And most important, they should be more interested in the salability of the work than in its craftsmanship. In today's buyer's market, where clients have so many choices, good sales talent is the ideal complement to good creative talent. Each enhances the other by making sure that all interests—quality and needs, shop's and client's—are constantly addressed.

One of the classic screening tests for sales applicants is to hand over a pen and ask the applicant to try to convince you to purchase it. If the applicant has the right instincts, she or he will first attempt to find out what kind of writing you do, then describe the pen's features in that context rather than just detailing its size, grip, ink flow, color, and so on. Although this particular test might not be appropriate, the concept of first finding out the prospect's needs (and wants) is especially important in a service business. Look for it in applicants, and devise your own way to test for it.

INVOLVING THE STAFF. Although hiring decisions are always the responsibility of principals, it is a good idea to have key staff members involved in the interviews for top applicants. They should participate in deciding who will be presenting their work. Including them in the selection process helps build morale and impresses on them the important role of sales.

REQUIRING A NON-COMPETE AGREEMENT. This should be a condition of employment: a signed agreement restricting after-employment solicitation or acceptance of work from a firm's clients or from a potential client contacted when in its employ. Although this issue is subject to varying state enforcement restrictions, requiring a new salesperson to sign a non-compete document sends a clear message that you consider your clients to be an important business asset and will fight to retain them when necessary. The agreement should also state that database and CRM (Customer Relationship Management) records, including all personal entries to them, are the firm's property and cannot be copied or taken if the individual leaves. (For a sample non-compete agreement, see Appendix III.)

ARRANGING COMPENSATION

There is no clearer indication of the importance a firm puts on the sales function than the extent to which its salespersons are compensated. Principals who are dissatisfied with performance often combine unrealistic expectations with unrealistic compensation. Guidelines follow.

COMMISSION. Paying salespersons on a commission basis is arguably the best arrangement for project-based firms because it provides a strong performance incentive and minimizes a firm's cash flow exposure. In addition, it removes the artificial earnings ceiling that jeopardizes the entrepreneurial spirit every good salesperson must possess to be effective. (A potential downside of commission arrangement is the possibility of an aggressive salesperson bringing in too much of the wrong type of work. This is a situation to address through a principal's management.)

On new client work, the standard industry commission is 15 percent of a project's fee income and 15 percent of any markup income (e.g., 15 percent of 20 percent). On follow-on work or that from existing clients ("house accounts"), a slightly lower commission (10 or 12 percent) often provides an incentive to seek out new ones. However, reducing the commission can also penalize a salesperson who has invested unpaid months trying to land a large client, only to find her or his reward is cut on the second project. As a result, many firms standardize on 15 percent across the board, believing that reducing the commission can be unfair and may cost more in incentive than it promotes in new business. On accounts that accompany a new salesperson, 20 to 25 percent of fee income is typical for the first project, with 15 percent thereafter unless the firm's follow-on commission is lower.

Most salespeople working on commission expect to have a draw arrangement—that is, they can draw a regular "salary" from the firm's payroll account that is periodically replenished by their commissions. The size of the draw is negotiable like any salary. But there are two factors to consider: (1) the draw should be high enough so that you can attract good people willing to work on commission without taking a huge risk in doing so, and (2) it shouldn't be so high that there is no incentive to make more by bringing in business. Many firms feel that 10 to 15 percent below what would be an individual's market-rate salary is about right.

The only payroll differences between a commissioned salesperson and other employees involve keeping track of how much is paid out, depositing commissions into the payroll account, and calculating the difference. Any surplus between commission and draw gets paid out in the same manner you would pay a bonus. Any deficit is carried forward. Commissions are paid, either directly or into a draw account, only after the client pays. For tax purposes, commissioned salespeople are considered employees. Most firms also provide salespeople the same benefits given to salaried personnel, which might also be required.

If a new salesperson does not cover his or her draw by the end of six months, and if there is no real expectation of doing so soon, you should consider termination. This individual will have lost the difference between normal salary and draw. Theoretically you will have lost all you paid out in draw; but this is no more than what you would have paid out in salary anyway, and there is also the possibility that some business will come in after the individual leaves. (If so, you still owe a commission on those sales.) Otherwise, you should expect to balance draw accounts every six months.

As an example of compensation potential, one commissioned salesperson working in a firm with five creative individuals producing $500,000 in fee billings (a low $100,000 per creative employee) would make $75,000 annually.

SALARY PLUS COMMISSION. This arrangement is appropriate where there is a mix of sales and account service responsibilities. It is also appropriate as a temporary step before ultimately moving a salesperson to commission compensation.

The difficulty with a salary plus commission arrangement comes in setting the appropriate ratio. The most common practice is to set the salary component at the firm's lowest professional starting salary and the commission at 8 to 10 percent of a job's fee income. You can adjust the mix later when there is experience on the actual amount of sales versus account service time. Although adjustment may be necessary to reach a fair compensation package, it may look arbitrary to the salesperson, particularly if it results in less take-home pay. As a guideline for determining what is appropriate, the total compensation possible (not necessarily what is paid) should be comparable to the salaries paid to senior creative staff.

Using the same conditions of compensation potential as under "Commission" above, a salesperson with a $40,000 annual base salary and an 8 percent commission would earn $80,000 annually on fee billings of $500,000. If the commission were 10 percent, earnings would be $90,000.

STRAIGHT SALARY. This arrangement is only appropriate for firms with true account service needs—process-based firms, such advertising and PR agencies, and some interactive firms. Project-based firms using account executives (AEs) usually either have too much business with too few clients or need to reassign client service to in-house project, production, or traffic managers.

Pay scales for account executives vary widely, depending on responsibilities and the importance of the accounts handled. When there is a mix of non-billable and billable account work, one benchmark is 10 percent of the media commissions that their accounts generate, along with 33 percent of the total of their billed time. (The difference in the compensation rates reflects the fact that more expenses have to be covered by commission income than by billed income.)

For instance, let's say the AE was responsible for accounts with media billings of $1,400,000, which produced commission income of $210,000. Fair compensation for this activity (10 percent of income) would be $21,000. In addition, 1,250 hours of the AE's time was billed out annually at $125 per hour for $156,250 of income. Fair compensation for this activity (33 percent of income) would be $51,563. Using this formula, fair compensation, the total for both activities, is a salary of $72,563. Note, however, that this salary would be low for AEs with great potential or in tight labor markets; it would be high for hangers-on or in markets where labor is plentiful.

REALISTIC EXPECTATIONS

Unlike new creative hires, who typically fit into an established workflow pattern with other employees, new sales hires are generally on their own, even when there are other salespeople in the organization. Being a salesperson means working solo much of the time, and much of it outside the firm. It also means that a principal's expectations based on experience with creative employees often have to be adjusted.

GETTING UP TO SPEED. Selling creative services is a process of developing relationships, particularly for the most sought-after clients. Sometimes a cold call results in an immediate sale. The client and the salesperson hit it off, and a project just happens to be waiting. But more often it takes time. The bigger the clients and the more lucrative their projects, the more important relationships become and the longer it takes for sales activity to pay off. Unless a new salesperson brings along a roster of established clients, it will usually be several months before even the most energetic efforts return more than they cost.

Be prepared to give new sales help six months to prove they have what it takes. During this time, there should be progress in making good contacts and an increasing number of sales. By the end of the sixth month, though, these salespeople should either be earning their salary or commission draw, or be on the verge of doing so. If not, it is probably time to cut your losses and start looking for someone new.

RESPONSIBILITIES. The major responsibilities of sales help are to prospect, introduce the firm, solicit work, and ensure that clients are satisfied. Once they start earning their keep, however, salespeople's responsibilities should also include helping to set marketing goals, devising selling strategies, determining pricing, recommending promotional activities, and even advising on the hiring of specific types of talent.

This inclusion of overall marketing responsibilities has mutual benefits. For principals, it provides additional, often more objective opinions on how to help grow the business, and it allows the further delegation of responsibilities. For salespeople, the more authority they gain in other aspects of marketing, the more enthusiastic and effective they become in selling. Perhaps the major benefit, though, is that it makes them more sensitive to the need to search for new clients and projects—and to search for more profitable ones.

OBJECTIVITY. Fulfilling a customer's needs with the right, not necessarily the absolute best, product is the formula that spells long-term success for every business, including creative services. No one understands this any better than someone who has to meet with clients every day and listen to their needs. This not only makes a salesperson the clients' in-house advocate, but it also brings into the shop a level of objectivity that is usually missing otherwise. In their effort to do the best possible work, creatives—including a firm's principals—are often blinded to what the client really wants. A good salesperson keeps them focused on meeting the client's objective.

8

THEIR BUDGETING, YOUR PRICING

Budgeting and pricing are obviously related, and they both play a large role in marketing. The lower a prospect's budgets and the higher a firm's pricing, the harder it should be to make a sale. Except that things are never quite that simple. For one thing, budgets are seldom as inflexible as you might be led to believe. Then, too, a low price won't necessarily win the day. Desirable prospects look at the total package a firm can offer—experience, creativity, service, and price—not just price alone. Also, prices that are too low can lack credibility. They call into question what might be overpromised or missing. Not all projects lost on pricing have been priced too high; some are lost because they've been priced too low.

This chapter explains the budget/price relationship as it applies to project-based companies, such as design firms. (In process-based firms, such as agencies, budgets and pricing are seldom as closely tied.) The effects of budgets and pricing in the context of closing a sale are discussed in Chapter 12.

THE BUDGET PARADOX

Regardless of a firm's labor rate, the fee that it will charge also depends on the effort that it will expend—which can be lots, a little, or someplace in between. And the available budget will influence whether more or less effort is required. So knowing how much money has been allocated is more than a little helpful. Is this a project worth pursuing, or is it better to go after something else? Is an "adequate," "good," or "best" effort most suitable?

However, prospects are understandably reluctant to indicate how much money they are willing to spend. Not always knowing what is reasonable, they might not want to show their hand. And should you come right out and ask, prospects might get the impression that no matter what the budget is, you'll find a way to spend it!

BUDGET INDICATORS. Although there is a tactful way to ask (see below), sometimes other indications can preclude the need. *What other firms have they used?*—chances are their budget will be adequate if they've worked before with firms at your level or higher. *How often do they purchase creative services?*—frequent purchasers are usually aware of going market rates. *How big are they?*—there's a strong correlation between professional management and budget sophistication. *What's their reaction to your portfolio?*—being able to appreciate what goes into good work also correlates with realistic budgets. *How concerned they are about price?*—excessive concern will almost certainly indicate a budget problem.

THE RIGHT WAY TO FIND OUT A PROJECT'S BUDGET. It is not by asking directly. Rather, it involves determining where within a range of "adequate," "good," or "best" approaches a prospect's perceptions fall.

With an unsolicited inquiry. If you've never heard of the prospect, ask about the project he or she has in mind and give a typical price range (see below). If the prospect doesn't seem concerned, schedule an appointment. If the prospect does, demur.

With a new prospect. After showing a selection of your work, ask which items were most similar to what the prospect has in mind. Then, after he or she has indicated which are closest in size, style, and complexity to the project, you should say something like this:

"Of course, we develop every project around the specific objectives and budget of our clients. But projects similar to this normally run in the range of ($X to $Y)." [Give a range of 100 percent.] "The lower figure reflects a simple, no-frills approach; the higher one reflects projects for which there is complex development and the client desires maximum impact. Most projects fall in the middle. Where within this range would you think is appropriate? With a figure to start with, and after I get all the details, I can then work up a proposal that will meet your needs and fit your budget."

With a familiar client. The approach is similar to the above, but it acknowledges your firm's past relationship with the client:

"Given our experience working together, I know you're aware that we can handle this project in several different ways. From what you've indicated you have in mind, they would range from a simple, no-frills approach of around ($X) up to around ($Y) for complex development and maximum impact. Can you give me an idea of where within this range you think would be appropriate? With a figure to start with, and after I get all the details, I can then work up a proposal that will both meet your needs and fit your budget."

AN INEXACT SCIENCE. A common misconception is that clients' budgets are the result of extensive management consideration—in other words, that managers set the budget for any given project or program only after making a lengthy review of priorities and finances. It is, therefore, a true reflection of what they want and can afford. Actually, this isn't even close to reality. In fact, most organizations set budgets arbitrarily and more by happenstance than by managerial science. This is especially true in areas where the prospect has little expertise or where the return from the amount budgeted (ROI, or return on investment) cannot be easily measured—the very definition of most creative projects and programs. The smaller the organization, the more this holds true.

In many organizations, a typical budget-setting exercise consists of guesstimating what someone thinks something should cost. Or it may consist of extrapolating cost figures from a similar, past project. Or it may be what feels affordable, despite whether the figure is realistic or not.

Whatever the budget, it is seldom carved in stone. The more specific the item, the more this is so. For example, a corporate marketing department may have to keep within its total budget for promotion, but it can overspend lavishly on some projects as long as it cuts back on others. In other cases, a budget may simply be a guideline, much the same as an individual might use a budget to keep expenses in line with income. Prospects' budgets usually indicate a financial goal; they do not necessarily indicate what the prospects will pay. Most prospects who are impressed by a solid presentation and good samples will willingly pay 10 to 15 percent more than budgeted. (Exceeding this amount by even more is possible but would probably require additional approvals.)

The point to remember is that there is nothing sacrosanct about a prospect's budget. It might be realistic, or it might not.

BEFORE VERSUS AFTER BUDGETS

The above comments relate to a budget before you accept a project. There is, though, another type of budget—the one that you have already agreed on. The budget assigned to a project after work begins is a different animal. Beforehand, it is a goal or aim-point, something subject to negotiation; afterward, it will likely be treated as a commitment, even though you and the (now) client might have agreed that your price (the client's revised budget figure) is subject to change if conditions change.

After accepting a proposal from an outsider (i.e., your firm), the client enters the stated price into her or his company's database of committed funds, and a purchase order (PO) is assigned. It then becomes the new budget for the item, and the client's accounts-payable software "assumes" that the item will be delivered at or below that price. That is, the computer will probably start treating the price as though it were firm. This means that invoices exceeding the funds that have been allocated could be delayed or refused. Avoiding this problem usually requires amending the project's PO when the invoices will total more than 10 percent of its stated amount. (Up to 10 percent overage is usually allowed.) So no matter what the reason, as soon as it is apparent that your estimate (the client's new budget) was too low, ask the client to issue a revised PO for the new amount. Doing so, in turn, will trigger an increase in the project's budget and allow the client's accounts-payable software to pay you on time.

HOW BUDGETS ARE ARRIVED AT

Understanding how companies set their budgets can help you to speak knowledgeably, whether you are pitching a new prospect or helping a small client to prosper. Familiarity with the process is particularly important for firms positioning themselves as "marketing-oriented design," "branding consultants," or "purveyors of strategic communications." It can be necessary for credibility in conducting budget discussions.

Most companies use some combination of three methods when funding their marketing communications programs: (1) calculating a percentage of sales, typically as an expense guideline, (2) identifying the specific items and programs needed to address their marketing objectives, and (3) determining what is necessary to maintain parity with competitors.

THE PERCENTAGE METHOD. The simplest budgeting method involves taking a percentage of overall sales, or those of a given product, and plowing it back into generating more of the same. This method has the major advantage of being more or less predictable; it is most commonly used when markets are stable and products change little. It is also used where there's little else to go on, as would be the case with a new business startup or a product that defines a whole new business category. (In these cases, a percentage of expected sales would be used.)

The problem with using this method exclusively is that it does not take into account several factors. Most significant, it is backward- versus forward-looking: it addresses tomorrow's needs on the basis of yesterday's sales. Also, it is only loosely predictive of effectiveness because sales are seldom directly traceable to a level of promotional spending. Then, too, newer brands usually need to spend more to get to the same level of impact or awareness as more mature ones do. Because the amount that different industries need to spend on various marketing functions will differ, an average percentage for all wouldn't be meaningful. For instance, some industries spend most of their marketing budget on "pushing" activities (sales), others on "pulling" activities (advertising).

There are average advertising percentages by industry as defined by SIC, or Standard Industrial Classification. Although it is unclear how much other types of marketing communications are included, it is good to know about them and to be able to refer a client to these sources if you're asked. An Internet search for "advertising-to-sales ratio by industry" will turn up several sources. One is the report published each spring by *Advertising Age* magazine. The percentages reported range from around 15 percent for liquor to 0.1 percent for aircraft manufacturers.

While few clients will want to match their percentage to their industry's average, many will want to make sure that they are in the ballpark. Awareness of an industry's advertising spending norms can also be useful in helping to set a budget for support materials. (See "Budget Allocation" below.)

THE NEEDS METHOD. This is sometimes called the strategy-based or objectives approach. Rather than being an arbitrary figure, the budget is the sum cost of a number of items and programs, each of which has been selected to meet one or more marketing objectives. The needs method is the primary method that most companies use, and it typically involves several rounds of submissions and revisions. This process ostensibly produces a consensus on the most cost-effective way to meet marketing objectives. There are two variations.

Top down. This is the more common variation. An expense target, not yet a budget, is given to the head of a department (e.g., the marcom manager) based on the company's projected annual expenses and income. She or he then considers, selects, prioritizes, and costs out items and programs, coming as close to the target as possible. If, as is often the case, the needs identified exceed the target, increased funding is then requested. Whether it will be granted depends on the strength of the case made.

Bottom up. Often called zero-sum budgeting, it is the ideal, but not common. It involves starting from scratch without a target or reference to previous activity. With the company's marketing goals in mind, a wish list to meet them is drawn up by the marketing staff, prioritized, and priced out. The list and its price tag is then reviewed, and a decision is made by senior marketing executives regarding how far down the list various items can be funded.

Startup companies also employ this method of budgeting, particularly those with venture funding that want to start off on the right foot. And the method is occasionally useful for established companies that want to review (audit) and possibly revamp their existing programs. In both instances, creative firms are occasionally asked to provide their expertise, not only on what is most effective but also on what is realistic funding.

THE COMPETITOR METHOD. Sometimes called parity budgeting, this method considers what competitors are doing. Their activity is, of course, always a consideration. Yet some companies, particularly in commodity markets, go one step beyond and attempt to match competitor activities one-for-one, often setting off promotional wars. For most companies, though, monitoring competitor activity is just a way of confirming that they are keeping pace and not spending more than necessary.

The obvious problem in looking at competitor spending is that it's tough to find out. It is only close to possible when there are substantial media purchases. Another problem is that parity is seldom a desirable marketing goal. The objective is usually to increase market share, not to stand pat.

BUDGET ALLOCATION. One other aspect of budgeting is of particular interest to firms that are not heavily involved with media: how much of a company's budget is typically allocated to non-media production and placement—that is, to print and online sales and support materials (collateral)? As should be expected, there is no universal percentage. But some guidelines can be useful in talking with clients about the balance of their budgets.

In general, the more high-ticket, considered-purchase items a client markets, the higher the portion of the client's budget that should be spent on support materials, the lower the portion on media. In practice, this means that the percentage of a budget devoted to support materials is highest among marketers of heavy industrial products, lowest among marketers of consumer commodities. Marketers of business-to-business items, not-for-profits, and service organizations fall in between.

This relationship of advertising to support spending makes it possible to set a very rough support material budget mathematically for some clients. That's because spending on support materials for industrial products (heavy equipment, machine tools, etc.) is typically up to two times advertising spending. Spending on support materials for business-to-business goods (computers, copiers, etc.) is about one-third less than advertising spending. For considered-purchase consumer goods (autos, domestic appliances, health insurance, etc.), support spending is typically two-thirds less than advertising spending. And for commodity consumer goods (household expendables), support material spending is miniscule compared to media spending.

A client can check how the support section of his or her budget compares to the advertising section by using the above guidelines. Consider the following examples. A heavy equipment manufacturer spending $100,000 annually on advertising (media and production) should probably be spending around $200,000 on support materials. A client selling business products that spends $100,000 annually on ads should probably spend around $65,000 on support materials. A client selling considered consumer products with a $100,000 ad budget should probably have a $35,000 budget for support materials. And a client selling commodity consumer goods will likely spend little or nothing on support materials.

This calculation can be done as a percentage of a company's sales as well. Let's say, for example, that the company is a manufacturer of consumer hand tools with $25 million in sales; this is an industry where 1.5 percent is the advertising-to-sales ratio. Therefore, an industry-average budget would be around $375,000, of which roughly two-thirds—or $250,000—probably would be for advertising and $125,000 for support materials.

THE PSYCHOLOGY OF PRICING

Although there is no question about the importance of pricing in services marketing, it can be easily overemphasized. Numerous surveys of buyers of professional services have shown that cost is seldom among the top reasons given for choosing suppliers. Usually, more important are considerations of quality, service, experience, dependability, flexibility, convenience, and the like. This makes pricing psychology—your knowledge of the subject and how you approach it—often more important than price itself.

SERVICES ARE DIFFERENT FROM PRODUCTS. Products are tangible, finite, and usually able to be exactly duplicated, so it is possible to specify them in terms that are conducive to price negotiation. For instance: "We'll agree to (X) units, incorporating (Y) features, at (Z) price." In contrast, services are intangible, cannot be directly duplicated, and don't even "exist" when purchased. So it is next to impossible to specify them in the same terms as products. Purchasing services requires making advance judgments based on a number of qualitative factors. Buying primarily on price simply makes no sense.

SERVICES AREN'T DIRECTLY COMPARABLE. It's easy to compare the attributes of most products to those of competitors. This makes evaluation pretty straightforward. For instance, features and other things being equal, *Product* A, costing $100, is a better deal than Product B, costing $110. Now consider *Services* A and B at the same prices. Here, attributes are not easily compared, so Service B might well offer more. It might have style, quality, and scheduling that make it a far better value (cost ÷ performance) for the purchaser. Without going beyond a superficial look at price, the true value of a service can never be determined. When there is little quantitative (comparable) information to go on, sorting suppliers by price can too easily eliminate the best choices and reward the cheapest ones.

SERVICES DON'T HAVE SCALE ECONOMIES. The greater the quantity of a manufactured product, the less expensive each item becomes. Higher volume allows manufacturers to lower prices without compromising quality or profitability. Not so with services. Every project is different, so there are few opportunities to gain efficiency by standardizing production. It takes about as much time to do any particular task the hundredth time as the first. And most of a service supplier's costs are in labor, typically around 70 percent (45 percent payroll, 20 percent benefits, 5 percent administrative) in a creative firm. So there is little or no economic benefit for the supplier to lower its prices to get more work.

PROPOSAL AND ESTIMATE DETAIL IS CRUCIAL. Consider this: in many situations, you will be asking prospects to spend money on projects that can only be loosely defined and that will depend on the interpretation and innovation of a supplier (you) with whom the prospect sometimes has only a limited acquaintance. In short, the prospect will need to buy into a promise. Given this, in order to go forward the prospect needs the confidence that can best be provided by a detailed proposal or estimate showing careful attention to and explanation of pricing. How much detail will be necessary? That will depend on the project's size and the prospect's mindset, but any hint of haphazardness concerning pricing will almost certainly bring it to the top of considerations. The extra time taken in estimating and preparing a proposal greatly decreases the prospect's concerns and increases the odds of acceptance. (For more on this subject, see Chapter 13.)

"IT'S AN INVESTMENT, NOT AN EXPENSE." Keep this in mind when discussing pricing, and subtly remind prospects of it: creative services return more to the organization than they cost it. (Marketing is usually considered an "opportunity center," not a "cost center.") This point doesn't mean that prospects should be less concerned about the dollars involved, but it should affect the context in which they view spending. When evaluating pricing, try to get prospects to think in terms of where they will get the most *value* (i.e., the greatest payback) for what they spend. (Again, value is cost ÷ performance.) You need to make the case that the value leader is you.

"YOU GET WHAT YOU PAY FOR." Most prospects believe this rule of thumb, so when you back it up with a detailed proposal, you should be able to treat pricing matter-of-factly: "This is what it will take to meet the goals you have established." Assuming ample information and time to prepare an estimate, any hesitation or lack of sureness will call into question whether your firm has a good grasp of the situation and the right way of addressing it. Hesitation or lack of sureness might also create an impression that you purposely inflated the price (i.e., marked it up so you can later mark it down.) Apologizing for a price is even worse; apologizing is what you do when you make a mistake. Answer questions on how you arrived at your prices, walking prospects through proposals, explaining how long various things actually take, and stressing your firm's quality control procedures.

HAVE THE STRENGTH OF YOUR CONVICTIONS. It is in every prospect's interests to negotiate the best price possible. If you aren't prepared to defend yours, it will be treated as a sure sign that you either purposely inflated or haphazardly calculated your price. Not only will you probably end up reducing your price and losing money, but you will also likely lose respect. No prospect respects a wimp, least of all a hard-bargaining prospect. Also keep in mind that hard bargaining is sometimes a management tactic to test the strength of a supplier's processes and convictions. Another common price-reduction strategy is to refer to supposedly lower competitive prices. The only way to pass these tests is to not arbitrarily lower a price under pressure. Pushing back might be all that's necessary to maintain it. At the same time, if advisable, be prepared to lower your price by knowing your costs of doing business and having a figure you can't go below and still be profitable.

ACKNOWLEDGE THE NEED FOR PROFITABILITY. Just as prospects often use the excuse of supposedly tight budgets to try to negotiate lower prices, you shouldn't hesitate to cite profitability as reason to resist going below a certain figure. Speaking to your own need to make a profit not only demonstrates business acumen but also reminds *good* prospective clients that a supplier's absence of profitability is not in their best interests. It will show up sooner or later in a lack of enthusiasm for collaborating and in the quality of the products being purchased. Similarly, no organization wants to invest in getting a supplier up to speed on its needs only to later see the supplier go bankrupt. And for most large corporations, helping smaller firms in their community to prosper is a part of good corporate citizenship. So don't be reluctant to play the profitability card. If you do end up lowering prices later, be sure that the prospect understands that it is an exception: "Even though meeting your budget will remove most of the profit for us, the opportunity to (provide such-and-such service) makes this a project we would like to work with you on."

PRESENTING AND CLOSING

Central to the marketing of creative services is the role of presentations in securing new business. This section discusses the factors that contribute to making successful presentations that generate new business. These factors are described in four chapters, more or less in the order that need occurs. Chapter 9, about preparation, addresses building self-confidence, arranging presentation time and space, and dealing with unpredictable events. Chapter 10 covers the crucial difference that differentiation makes when competing against others and suggests ways to incorporate it in presentations. Chapter 11 explains the two different types of new business pitches—portfolio and process—and when each is most suitable. Chapter 12 discusses presentation closings, or asking for the order; presenters often ignore this need because of their personal reluctance, or else they simply overlook it. (For more on presenting proposals and concepts, see Chapter 14.)

9

PRESENTATION PREPARATION

Regardless of a presentation's particulars, they all have one thing in common: the need for the individual(s) conducting them to be confident, at ease, and in control. Yet few of us have any presentation training, and even fewer have intuitive stand-up skills. So some discussion of what makes one a successful presenter is in order. The following can serve as a primer for those who are less experienced or as a refresher for seasoned pros.

OVERCOMING PRESENTATION JITTERS

This subject comes first because it could happen to any of us, novice or experienced, depending on who our audience is and how much is at stake. So if your knees tremble a bit at the thought of doing a new business pitch to a roomful of client heavies or giving a speech before a large audience, you're hardly alone—especially among fellow creatives, who are a bit more introverted than the population at large. Nonetheless, being able to speak articulately before a group is an important business skill and a crucial one if you are responsible for selling your firm's capabilities and concepts.

Overcoming uneasiness or nervousness is the critical first step in making well-received presentations. The best ideas and greatest concepts can fall flat when audiences are distracted by a speaker's visible nervousness. Even mediocre ideas can impress an audience when a confident speaker presents them. Whatever the occasion—off-the-cuff stand-up or formal speech—*you* are the first thing an audience reacts to. The material is secondary. Only after the audience is comfortable with you will they begin to listen to what you have to say. To paraphrase an old saw, the medium (you) is a very large part of the message.

DEVELOPING SELF-CONFIDENCE. Nearly all speakers, including the most practiced, rarely step in front of a large audience without feeling some level of uneasiness. But what makes them seem to be relaxed is that they have developed the self-confidence that enables them to confront and overcome their fears. It works for small presentations, too. Not only will strengthening your self-confidence help to banish the jitters, but it will spill over into other aspects of business as well—everything from having greater courage in pushing the creative envelope, to working more effectively with co-workers and clients. It takes only desire and practice.

MODIFYING DESTRUCTIVE MANNERISMS. Many mannerisms insidiously sabotage confidence-building efforts. The following ones can be particularly damaging. *False modesty*—never be reluctant to take credit for what you've accomplished; you've earned it. *Apologies*—don't make them where it's unnecessary, such as when discussing pricing or scheduling. *Wishy-washy phrases*—statements such as "I guess so" create an aura of being unsure of yourself or lackadaisical. *Mousiness*—failure to look others in the eye and limp-wristed handshakes undercut your authority.

REVIEWING YOUR STRENGTHS. No matter what your background may be, remember that you are a unique blend of talent, accomplishments, and experience. No one else, anywhere, has all your qualities. It will help build your self-confidence to set aside some time and review what these are, remembering the praise you've received, the awards you've won, the challenges you've overcome, the insights you've developed.

Many of us blame ourselves when things go wrong, but we never think to praise ourselves when things go right. So over time we develop a negative mental state from more thoughts that tear down our confidence than ones that build it up. You can reverse this imbalance by patting yourself on the back when handling a situation well and being less critical when things happen to go less than perfectly. The more specific you make the self-praise, the more powerful it will be. Reinforce it by occasionally looking in the mirror and praising yourself out loud. This might sound a little hokey, but it will be more effective than you think. Seeing and hearing yourself describe your triumphs fixes them in your mind.

ADVANCE PREPARATIONS

Think of all the bad presentations you've sat through where the presenter either wasn't well organized or generally fumbled and bumbled. Nothing has a greater negative effect on an audience than someone who has not taken the time to be prepared. Although how far in advance to get ready depends on circumstances, for stand-up presentations where there's adequate notice (e.g., a new business pitch), it's a good idea to set a goal of at least several days beforehand. By having decided on content well in advance, you'll have a cushion in case something unexpected comes up or there's a need to make last-minute modifications.

Formal presentations (e.g., speeches) require longer preparation to provide adequate time for rehearsals and rewrites. When making a commitment to address a large audience sometime in the future, schedule a begin-preparation date several weeks in advance, and stick to it. A bad presentation caused by rushed preparation will almost surely have the opposite effect of your intended purpose.

GOING OVER YOUR STRENGTHS AGAIN. This time, think of your unique talents and experiences in the context of your audience's specific interests—for example, your experience in solving problems for similar clients with similar needs. Then, stop and repeat out loud something like the following: "We are the best choice for their rebranding because we have the experience, knowledge, and talent that (competitive firm) can't match." Repeat this mantra as many times as necessary between now and your presentation.

KEEPING THINGS SIMPLE. The more complex a presentation, the more impersonal it becomes. Yet establishing personal rapport—the "likeability factor"—is a crucial element in winning confidence. Although visual aids are often necessary when addressing large groups, they tend to dehumanize a small-group presentation and can become crutches that hinder the development of stand-up skills. Avoid them wherever possible.

Use a laptop only when necessary to show Web site development or to demonstrate interactivity and programming skills. Use PowerPoint presentations, projection visuals, pitch books, and flip charts sparingly, if at all. Also, whenever possible, give your audience a hands-on, real-time experience. Navigate them through an interactive Web site, show an ad campaign in the magazines it ran in, hand over an annual report, and walk through the effective ways the creative product enhances the strategy. (See also "Scripting," below.)

RESEARCHING A PROSPECT. Few things impress prospects more or have a greater impact than knowledge about their organization and industry. Not only will this make it easier to orient a presentation around what is most likely to appeal to them, but it will convey an interest in their business that goes beyond just making a sale. The extent to which prospect- and industry-specific information is incorporated is a strong differentiating factor in competitive presentations. Prospects will often overlook flawed presentations from firms that are knowledgeable; they'll dismiss polished ones from those that aren't.

Not much background is needed, and it is not difficult to get. As little as an hour spent on the Internet checking the Web sites of the prospect and competitors may be all that's necessary for smaller clients. For larger, more significant ones, you can purchase company profiles (e.g., from Dun and Bradstreet), and industry and corporate analyses are often available from brokerage houses (e.g., Merrill Lynch).

DETERMINING HOW MUCH TIME YOU HAVE. Knowledge about the prospect also has other advantages: it makes it easier to select suitable samples and to structure a presentation that's more relevant. Those customized to a prospect's specific interests are shorter, more focused, and better received. Moreover, promising short-and-specific makes it easier to get an appointment. How short is short? Half an hour is all it should take for most portfolio presentations; an hour or so is usually enough for most process presentations. (For the differences between portfolio and process presentations, see Chapter 11.) Speeches should seldom exceed twenty-five minutes unless you are a riveting speaker with a fascinating subject.

SCRIPTING. Ideally, a stand-up should be off-the-cuff—your ultimate goal. But it is better to rely on notes than to take a chance on forgetting key points. A dozen or so small (3 x 5") hand-held cue cards—with a simple reminder phrase or two on each—are an unobtrusive crutch that will keep a presentation on track. (Be sure to number their sequence in case the cards get out of order.) Visual aids with bullet points can also provide cues. But unless visuals are *truly* needed to enhance a presentation, avoid them. Visual presentations, especially to small groups, divert the audience's attention away from the presenter and can easily lead to boringly robotic presentations (the so-called "presentation death by PowerPoint").

Visuals are more important for a talk or speech in front of a sizeable audience, and scripting is necessary unless you are a very talented speaker. Again, the more time devoted to organizing, writing, and rewriting, the more familiar the script will become and the easier it will be to stand relaxed in front of an audience when delivering.

DOING A RUN-THROUGH. Since every audience is different and every presentation should be customized, at least one run-through is necessary.

There's too much at stake otherwise, even for practiced presenters. Pay particular attention to the presentation's first five minutes. It sets the stage, serves to orient and position the rest of the session, is seldom interrupted by questions, and creates the strongest impression.

For major presentations and speeches, three run-throughs are often suggested. The first is an opportunity to go over the material in your mind, referring to your notes or reading your script. Practice your ad-libs and pacing, adjust your timing, and polish your delivery. Keep in mind that silent run-throughs can take from a quarter (speech) to a half (stand-up) less time than the actual delivery. Once you are comfortable, do a spoken rehearsal. Select a private space where you will be unheard and undisturbed, such as a conference room. To the extent possible, replicate the speaking environment—roughly the same presentation space when doing a stand-up, or a simulated podium when preparing a speech. Try to imagine the audience and anticipate their questions. Be particularly attentive to how visuals and concepts will be shown and described. Adjust your pacing and the overall length of the presentation. Finally, do a dress rehearsal before a friendly audience, such as staff or a significant other. Solicit comments for improvement.

PREPARING TO FIELD QUESTIONS. It won't be possible to prepare for every question or comment that might come up. But it's possible to be prepared for the most common ones, especially when there's knowledge of a prospect's background and interests. For instance: "What kind of experience do you have in our business? How long do things normally take? Who will be working on our account? How would you handle (a given situation)?"

Quick and facile responses will keep things moving along and reinforce your self-confidence. Conversely, the less you're prepared, the greater the likelihood that you'll respond inadequately or your composure and timing will be thrown off—or worse, the audience will be turned off. Pricing questions in particular are almost guaranteed to come up when you're making new business pitches.

SCHEDULING. Whenever there's flexibility, try to schedule a major presentation or speech mid-morning, early in the week. This gives you the weekend before for making final changes and time for setting up beforehand. The audience will also be fresh and alert, and you'll have less time for fretting. Resist any temptation to make last-minute changes. Lock things up a few days before, and then relax. Last-minute changes can raise your anxiety level and upset what's otherwise well tuned; anyway, they seldom make a noticeable difference to the audience.

A couple days before the presentation, call to confirm the day, time, and who will be attending. This reinforces the event's importance and increases attendance. For large groups, ask to have access to the meeting room a half hour in advance to set up.

THE DAY OF THE PRESENTATION

Be yourself. Be as casual, offhand, and relaxed as possible. Be friendly to the audience, and they'll be friendly to you. Good presentations, whether stand-ups or speeches, are like pleasant conversations—between you and friends. Being too serious, trying to impress, will just add stress and create the opposite effect. Attempting to fight speaking anxiety right before a presentation just makes it worse. Rather, accept it as a natural condition that, when harnessed and directed, will actually make your presentation better. A little adrenaline is a good thing.

APPEAR PROSPEROUS. Everyone prefers to listen to and do business with someone who is successful. And opinions about success are reinforced or belied by what the audience experiences visually. No matter what your sartorial preferences might be, the better dressed you are and the neater you appear, the greater your chances of winning an audience's trust. This is particularly true when presenting to large organizations with large projects and budgets. The best bet is to dress in a manner similar to, but one step above, that of your audience. The audience will take you more seriously, and knowing that you appear prosperous will give you the "stage presence"—the confidence and authority—you need.

CHECK OUT THE PRESENTATION ROOM. Make any changes that will add to your comfort level, such as moving a podium, resetting a microphone, and making sure visual aids and props are to your right if you're a right-handed person. Rearrange seating to provide better sight lines, and readjust lighting. Put a glass of water where it will be easily accessible. For large presentations and speeches, make sure visual aids are in place and operating smoothly. (Malfunctions are a nuclear threat to speaker anxiety.) Once you are comfortable with the room, do a silent, dry run or two of at least the beginning of your presentation. Imagine the audience sitting in the seats in front of you.

OCCUPY THE ROOM'S "POWER POSITION." If possible, take the head of a conference room table when you're addressing groups of up to three people. For groups of four or more, deliver your presentation standing up. Standing focuses the viewers' attention and creates a psychological impression of control on your part. (Audience is looking up; you are looking down.) For groups of more than half a dozen, ask the audience to hold their comments and questions until the end. This will enable you to proceed without distracting interruptions, and it will likely answer many of your listeners' questions before they can be asked.

MEET AND GREET. Conversing with early arrivers helps personalize and make the audience less intimidating. It's easier to speak to a group of acquaintances than a group of strangers.

START STRONG. This isn't the time to be laid back. The more enthusiastic you are, the more receptive the audience will be and the faster your anxieties will disappear. The first couple of minutes or so of the presentation is the most crucial part—in gaining your audience's confidence and dispelling your own fears.

LOOK THEM IN THE EYE When making a speech and first taking the stage, pause for about fifteen seconds and look over the audience. Don't be in a rush to begin. Make eye contact with one friendly-looking individual. Then switch to another. Fifteen seconds will seem like an eternity to you but only a moment to the audience. This initial delay will ease jitters by allowing you to collect your thoughts. It will also make you appear relaxed and connected with the audience.

AD-LIB A CASUAL, PERSONAL OPENING COMMENT. For example: "It's great to see so many fresh faces so early in the morning." Segue into a short preview next: "What I'm going to be talking to you about this morning is (topic) and (why it's important or how you've solved a problem)." Now pause again. Then begin. There's no need for a joke or an audience warmer. Just begin strong and confident. Continue to make eye contact throughout the presentation, selecting individuals randomly. Keep the audience friendly by being democratic—by not focusing on the more important attendees. Unwarranted attention to some could turn off the rest.

SPEAK SLOWLY, AND PAUSE AT KEY INTERVALS. Speaking rapidly is a nervous giveaway. It can also accelerate over the length of a presentation. (If you have this tendency and are making a speech, put a reminder to slow down in your notes or on every third page of your script.) Don't speak so slowly, though, that you lose enthusiasm. Here, too, written reminders help. After saying something important, leave a gap. Let your words hang for a few seconds. A "pregnant pause" signals to an audience that something is important, slows things down, and lets you catch your breath. Also, pause every so often to take a sip of water.

ENGAGE THE AUDIENCE. Where the format allows, such as in a stand-up pitch, stop occasionally to ask, "Is this clear? Does this raise any questions?" Whether to take questions during a formal presentation or to leave them to the end is a personal call. Although leaving them to the end avoids disrupting your message, stopping for questions during the presentation does allow you to regain composure that might otherwise slip away. Do what makes you most comfortable.

DON'T APOLOGIZE. Any acknowledgment of your uneasiness or lack of public speaking experience will only call attention to something that is almost surely of greater concern to you than to your audience. Likewise, mistakes will almost always be more apparent and significant to you than to them. Except in extreme cases, don't acknowledge mistakes or omissions of information. Most go unnoticed. Only you know what you were supposed to say; the audience knows only what they've heard.

COMMAND YOUR SPACE. Be active. Move around when doing a stand-up (but avoid pacing). When making a speech, don't hide behind the podium or grasp it for dear life. Occasionally pause, commit a couple lines to memory, and deliver them away from the podium. Always answer questions while standing apart, with nothing between you and the audience. Doing so forces an audience to be attentive and is also effective in reducing stress.

THINK OF AN ABSURDITY. Whenever you feel tension creeping up, banish it with a mind exercise, a bit of private, secret humor. For example, imagine that everyone in the audience is suddenly naked or that the audience is composed entirely of Homer and Marge Simpson look-alikes.

AVOID DISTRACTING MANNERISMS. A fidgeting speaker makes an audience uneasy, and any visible uneasiness on their part will make you even more so. Don't play with change in your pocket or fiddle with a paper clip. Keep your arms above your waist, and use gestures sparingly. (Tip: touching your thumb with the forefinger on each hand will help make your hand motions feel more natural.)

DEALING WITH THE UNPREDICTABLE

No matter how well you might have prepared for a presentation, there are often situations—and individuals—that surprise you. Although you can't prepare for these instances specifically, you should be aware of the following possibilities and be ready to confidently respond.

YOU GET UNEXPECTED QUESTIONS. Don't get caught flat-footed. Beforehand, try to think of every potential question the audience might ask. Even if they end up asking none, preparation will increase your confidence level and contribute to a better presentation. And should you get hit with unexpected questions, being able to provide quick responses will be crucial to maintaining your cool, especially if the questions come midway in your presentation.

YOU'RE ASKED A QUESTION YOU CAN'T ANSWER. Admit that you're stumped. You aren't perfect, and the audience doesn't expect you to be. Offer to find out and get back to the individual later.

ONE INDIVIDUAL AGGRESSIVELY CHALLENGES YOUR CONTENT. Don't get defensive. Have strength in your convictions, hold your ground, and explain the rationale of your approach. Most likely the challenger is an individual trying to make points with the boss or impress the audience. A presenter who stands up for what he or she believes in wins the audience's esteem; one who buckles under pressure doesn't.

YOU LOSE YOUR TRAIN OF THOUGHT. Don't let it rattle you. Smile or chuckle and say, "Excuse me, let me go back to (topic) and start over again." Everyone in the room has experienced something similar. They'll be sympathetic.

MEMBERS OF THE AUDIENCE GET UP AND LEAVE. Ignore them. It's not about you or your presentation. They simply have something urgent to attend to, like finding a restroom.

SOMEONE IN THE AUDIENCE IS UNINTERESTED, MAYBE EVEN ASLEEP. There's always someone. Perhaps he's hung over, or she was out partying until the wee hours. Pay them no heed. Unless everyone is fidgeting, it's not about you.

AUDIENCE MEMBERS START TALKING AMONG THEMSELVES. When this happens during large presentations, you can ignore it; during small presentations, nip it in the bud before it gets out of hand. Don't let the audience hijack your presentation. You need to stay in control to maintain self-confidence. Look directly at the individuals, and ask whether there is something they would like you to explain in more detail.

10

DIFFERENTIATION AND NEW BUSINESS PITCHES

New business pitches are, at once, both the most crucial and the most difficult of presentations. They are the most crucial because unless they produce orders there will be no business, no future presentations. They are the most difficult because unlike proposal and concept presentations (see Chapter 14), the prospect is unknown, so there's little of the ease that comes from presenting to familiar faces. The spotlight is as much on the presenter as on the work, there is typically less than an hour of face time in which to be persuasive, and there's seldom a second chance to get things right.

THE DIFFERENTIATION IMPERATIVE

In any new business pitch, the first consideration should be what you have to offer the prospect. The second consideration should be how to put it into a narrative that speaks to the prospect's needs and interests. And the third consideration—too often missing—should be finding ways to stand apart from your competition. In a market where there are numerous talented (and sometimes less expensive) competitors, firms that can't differentiate their services give prospects few reasons to choose them and many reasons to question their fees and procedures.

However talented, respected, and experienced your firm might be, never make the mistake of believing that it is not important to explain in detail what makes it unique. Many presentations are compared to competitors'. The winner in head-to-head comparisons will be the one that best differentiated itself. The extent of differentiation can be based on actual fact, such as greater experience, or on what can be reasonably assumed, such as depth of talent. Moderately exaggerating what makes yours more attractive is okay as long as you do it in moderation and do not mislead. Don't be so concerned about the accuracy of what you claim: that competitors with fewer reservations make stronger pitches and land better clients. And don't be concerned about exclusivity, either. It doesn't matter. Value lies in talking about your firm's differences and (one hopes) becoming the firm with which one or more attributes become identified.

WHAT MAKES GOOD DIFFERENTIATORS?

The answer is anything that sets your firm apart in a positive, value-producing way. What follows are the most common differentiators and how they should, and in some cases should not, be used.

THE FOUR ESSENTIALS. *Sincerity*—chances are you'll never convince a prospect of your firm's distinctiveness if you aren't convinced yourself. Statements about how your firm is different must be honest beliefs, not just ploys to land new business. *Distinctiveness*—uniqueness might not be possible, but unusual is. The more unusual your firm appears to be, the more memorable and the greater the chance to be remembered after the presentation. *No gimmicks*—differentness should benefit the prospect, not signal attention-getting or showmanship on your part. *Preemptiveness*—although not essential, the best differentiators are ones that can't be easily imitated or also claimed by competitors.

PRICING DIFFERENTIATORS. They are listed first here because pricing is often the first thing that comes to mind, especially when business is slow. Below are the four most common.

Lower fees. As a generalization, differentiating by price is a bad strategy. There are several reasons: it is self-defeating because there will always be someone whose pricing is lower; prospects tend to associate low prices with low quality; low prices attract demanding, bargain-shopping prospects; and low prices often mark a firm as "hungry," which just encourages negotiating for even lower prices.

An exception is for single-person and small firms, particularly when competing against larger ones. The reasoning is straightforward and valid: you can offer lower prices for comparable quality because your overhead is lower—no large payroll, less expensive digs, and so on. To ensure that this rationale is credible, however, keep the following guideline in mind: pricing should probably not be less than 75 percent of what a larger firm with a similar level of talent or service would charge. (See also "Size" below.)

Added value. It is easy to promise but difficult to prove. One approach is to incorporate value propositions—statements of benefit/cost relationships—

into the creative development of selected projects. A presentation discussing how a firm employs them sets it apart by emphasizing the depth of its strategic thinking. The same applies to detailed creative briefs. Many firms use them in some form during project development. But few think to also show examples to prospects as a demonstration of the rigorous process a firm goes through to ensure that its creative product is strategically focused. (For samples of a value proposition worksheet, a creative briefing questionnaire, and a creative review checklist, see Appendix III.)

Specialization. Just focusing on a specific market is by itself a differentiator. But there's a downside that must be addressed: the common belief that specialists' prices are higher. Confront it by including in your presentation words to the effect that experience and special procedures enable you to operate more efficiently. In turn, this reduces your expenses. These savings are passed along.

Eliminating markups. This might be worth considering on small items if they are not large contributors to your firm's bottom line. Markups often lead to questions and concerns. Eliminating them gives a firm a promotional talking point. More important, it differentiates the firm from nearly every competitor, sometimes at a very small cost.

Potentially more costly is having clients pay for printing directly. Foregoing the markup added for handling the billing can be an even stronger differentiator, especially for those with large print orders. (It is already the norm for many large clients and creative firms.) While this could mean the loss of significant income for many firms, it's possible to offset such an outcome by billing for printer selection time and press checks, or, as some firms do, by simply adding a 10 percent production supervision fee to all invoices. Whichever approach you follow, it will take your firm out of the risky role of financial middleman, it will encourage your firm to concentrate on its core strength of creative problem-solving, and it will eliminate the distractions of buying and selling what has become a commodity.

QUALITY DIFFERENTIATORS. Because they align with our own self-images and how we want to be known, these are the ones most of us are most comfortable employing.

Creativity. This is, of course, the ultimate differentiator because it is unique to every individual and firm. Yet unique doesn't always mean more effective. And effectiveness—not innovation, aesthetics, style, or craftsmanship—is what prospects are really looking for. So any emphasis on the uniqueness of a firm's talent and creative muscle as a differentiator has to be on how it provides better returns on clients' investments. In other words, creativity has to be put in the context of a means, not a result.

Marketing orientation. This is the second most commonly cited quality differentiator, and one that can be problematic as well. That's because many firms making the claim are really focused on creativity, not on marketing. They lack experience or interest beyond its most superficial aspects. There's nothing inherently wrong with this. But if it defines you, don't risk your credibility by promoting marketing skills unless you are presenting to inexperienced prospects. To coin a phrase, don't talk the talk unless you're truly comfortable walking the walk.

Award-winning. This might seem counterintuitive, but awards should be soft-pedaled except when pitching prospects who are highly creativity oriented. Otherwise, it takes the focus off what the potential clients are most interested in (how you can address their needs) and puts it on what appears to be what you're more interested in (aesthetics and recognition). The right context in which to bring up any industry recognition is in an "oh, by the way" comment after describing the material. This approach is more powerful because it provides third-party certification of what you've just discussed. Further, downplaying awards fosters the impression that winning them is more or less routine for your firm.

Testimonials. Although testimonials are often overlooked, they can be very powerful differentiators when used sparingly. Here's how: several months after completing a signature project, interview your client contact on what results were achieved. Later, when showing this project to a new prospect, weave those comments into your narrative. For instance: "Two months after we finished this site, I happened to also talk with (John Jones), their IT manager, who told me that he was surprised to find that in addition to (one result), which we expected, they also experienced (second result)." Be careful not to overplay this card, though. Save it for the one or two items—especially those done for prestigious clients—that could burnish your credentials. (Caution: while it is fine to use testimonials in this context, never use them publicly without getting written permission.)

Questioning. Good presentations are as much, maybe more, about finding out the prospect's needs as they are about demonstrating your capabilities. The more questions asked about the prospect's organization, product, market, and objectives, the more impressed she or he will be. And the more it will differentiate your firm from competitors, most of whom are content to talk about what makes them unusual rather than questioning prospects on what makes *them* unusual. The extent and sophistication of a firm's inquiries are often what sets competitive pitches apart. (To see how to employ this strategy, see "A Differentiation Example" below.)

Interviewing prospective clients. An impression that your firm is selective in choosing clients, even when this occasionally means turning down work, can be a powerful differentiator. Your rationale is that a productive relationship often takes a partnering (team) approach to problem-solving. This approach requires a firm to be as comfortable with a client as the client is with the firm.

Pushing back. Some prospects interview suppliers by putting presenters on the defensive. The idea is to see how well the presenters stand up to criticism and to test the credibility of their claims. Those who don't perform well under pressure get low grades. They either don't get the business or have to make compromises to get it. Conversely, those who meet confrontational prospects head on, who push back when it's called for, differentiate themselves from their more timid competitors and often end up getting the business.

SERVICE DIFFERENTIATORS. These aspects of a supplier's business can also be powerful because, as most prospects realize when evaluating suppliers, even world-class creativity and quality will come up short unless there's service backing them up.

"How we work" information. This is perhaps the easiest service differentiator to provide, and yet it's one that's often missing. It is equally suitable for individuals who work alone and for firms with dozens of employees. That's because even experienced clients are often unsure what to expect when they consider hiring a new creative firm: How does the firm charge? What is its development process? How long do things take? What is the process for making changes? Although it's possible to address these questions and many more in a project proposal, many prospects need a general idea before getting to that point. This is why having a "how we work" sheet or small brochure for handout at the close of a presentation can be so impressive. It is surprising how seldom this type of client-friendly information is provided, opening an opportunity for firms that are smart enough to do so. It is a prime example of the truism that the hallmark of winning presentations is anticipating and answering questions before they are even asked. (For a sample "How We Work Together" form, see Appendix III.)

Mission statements. While mission statements are not as informative as basic working procedures, they provide prospects with insight into a firm's business philosophy. This can be an important plus to some prospective clients. There's usually no need to discuss a firm's mission statement. Simply having one and adding it to handouts at the end of the presentation is enough. It's a small differentiator, but one that is typically overlooked. (For a sample mission statement, see Appendix III.)

Size. Whatever size your firm happens to be, it can act as an effective presentation differentiator when going head-to-head against a smaller or larger competitor. Depending on the prospect and the project, relative smallness or largeness could be the deciding factor. The smaller the firm, the more important it becomes to emphasize that less really can provide more—lower prices for comparable quality, faster turnaround, and truly personal service. The larger the firm, the more important it is to emphasize the benefits that clients will get from bigness—varied "been there, done that" experiences, more resources and backups, and greater depth in talent.

CLICHÉ AVOIDANCE. In addition to the differentiators described above, there are two others (actually, positioning positions) that are somewhat predictable—a focus on branding and/or a focus on strategy. Both often provide fair descriptions of how a firm operates and are usually handled well. But they are also prone to overuse and exaggeration, which for many sophisticated clients can be more negative than positive.

Branding. Branding has become something of a catchword among marketing communications practitioners, whether on the client side or the creative firm side. It seems to be the ideal, overarching concept that fits all situations. It's what every client wants its products to embody; it's what every creative firm says it's capable of providing. But a small company's branding needs—a couple brochures and a Web page or two—are far removed from those of a large one, which might involve everything from a new corporate identity to makeovers of the company's retail stores. Stressing branding too strongly, especially when pitching large organizations, can open up a credibility gap among those prospects who might easily know more about it than you do. Except when making presentations to small companies, be careful not to imply that you know more about this complex marketing subject than is actually the case. (For more on branding, see Appendix II.)

Strategic focus. During the last several years, it's become an article of faith that business success for creative firms of all sizes depends on their "strategic focus"—that is, how well they can develop and execute communications strategies. Many firms feel that emphasizing strategy moves projects farther up a client's food chain. Coming up with a client strategy first and a creative strategy second is still the right approach for advertising and PR campaigns. The same holds true for significant design, editorial, and interactive work. The more that's at stake and the greater the challenge, the more important developing a strategy becomes. This notwithstanding, the reality is that many types of projects, such as collateral, don't need to be strategy-driven. They just need to be done well, on time, and on budget. Acting as though more is at stake when it really isn't can damage a firm's credibility by making it appear naive or, worse, prone to overselling.

A DIFFERENTIATION EXAMPLE

Most of the differentiators identified above can be easily woven into a presentation. As an illustration, the following sample dialogue builds on the questioning differentiator, abetted by the forms previously mentioned and available in Appendix III. We pick up the dialogue right after the presenter has ended showing the firm's portfolio:

"Frankly, there are lots of other firms out there that do what I do, and many are excellent. But one of the things that I believe sets my work truly apart is what I call 'creative management.' It combines talent and strategy in a unique way.

"It involves two steps that every new project goes through. First, I hold a thorough creative briefing with you. One purpose is to get all the product information—features, benefits, and so on—that I will need to do a good job. But even more important is that I help you define the strategic objectives for the piece in a way that is achievable. The form I use for this is my Creative Briefing Questionnaire. (Show.)

"Following our meeting, I go back to my office and, using the briefing as my marching orders, I develop a creative concept through several trial-and-error refinements. Before I return to show you what I've come up with, though, it first goes through my own quality control checklist. This is Creative Review form I use. (Show.)

"As you can see, I check to make sure not only that the piece meets the objectives you have defined, but also that it meets a number of my own criteria. Some, such as ensuring that your logo is used correctly, is just detail checking. But others, such as checking with vendors to confirm it can be produced on time and budget, are crucial for scheduling.

"I am not familiar with competitors doing anything similar."

THE INVISIBLE KILLERS

Not everything that can differentiate a firm in a new business pitch is positive. Nor are omissions the only things that can work against it. Some differentiators are negative, and they often go unnoticed by the presenter, although seldom by the prospect. If there are too many negatives, the firm just never gets the business or another call.

NOT ADDRESSING THE PROSPECT'S INTERESTS. The most common mistake in making new business pitches occurs when the presenter concentrates on what she or he is most enamored with, not what the prospect would be most interested in. An example involves spending time showing irrelevant "award-winning" and craft-intensive samples instead of demonstrating how the firm interacts with clients in defining objectives, preparing creative briefs, and gathering necessary input.

Sometimes this happens because it is simply easier to talk about what is best known. It can also arise from pride-of-creation or from not knowing a prospect's real interests due to lack of preparation. Whatever the cause, the effect is to confuse the presenter's interests with the prospect's, despite the fact that they're substantially different. Prospects are primarily interested in results and only secondarily in the creativity that is produced to achieve them. A presenter's (your) interests are probably opposite. When making a new business pitch, you must take care to concentrate on their interests, not yours.

SPEAKING YOUR LANGUAGE, NOT THEIRS. Similarly, it is easy to fall into the shop-talk trap: too much about aesthetic issues. It can create an impression that craftsmanship is of more importance than selling a prospect's products or communicating its messages. Whether in showing samples or describing processes, creativity and innovation are obvious; they don't need much explanation. Restrict any commentary to what your prospects are most comfortable with: how a novel approach or creative technique was critical in meeting a previous client's business objectives. Anything more will appear gratuitous.

NOT PRESENTING WELL. The person who conducts a firm's new business pitches can have a huge effect on differentiating it. The importance of having a pleasant and skilled individual in this position cannot be overemphasized. She or he becomes its public face. And because creative services essentially imply a business of relationships, connection on a personal level is crucial. More than half a presentation's impact is in the presenting person's hands, for better or worse. This is a tall order for anyone, and it's one reason why larger firms employ sales professionals. Fortunately, however, becoming articulate and comfortable is largely a function of practice. (For more on sales skills, see Chapter 7. For the relative importance of presenting well, see Appendix I.)

COMMENTING ON THEIR MATERIALS. Commenting on a prospect's materials is always risky, even when improvement is clearly needed. There's no accounting for taste, and you never know who might have been involved in developing the materials. So it's advisable to resist any temptation to differentiate by suggesting how things could be done better. If a prospect volunteers displeasure with his or her materials or current relationships, merely respond that you're sure he or she will be much happier with what you'll be able to accomplish. If asked to critique, say something like this: "Well, it isn't the approach we would take, and it also isn't our style. But I don't know the objectives, budget, or other conditions, so I really can't give an informed opinion."

NOT TREATING EVERYONE AS EQUALS. While there's usually a pecking order evident in group meetings—for example, a boss and his or her underlings—it should never influence which person you direct the presentation to or your response to an individual's comments and questions. Don't differentiate here. You can never be sure where the power in an organization lies. For instance, the nerd who interrupts with annoying comments just might be the boss's trusted advisor. Also, underlings always resent outsiders who pander to their boss, even when they're guilty of doing it themselves. So when making a presentation (although not necessarily later on), take care to address, listen to, and treat everyone in the audience as though they were all of equal importance, because they just might be.

GIVING IDEAS AWAY. Don't succumb to the mistake of discussing specific approaches to a prospect's challenges as a way of proving your firm's abilities and differentiating it from competitors. Whether requested or volunteered, it is just another variation of spec work with the same risks. Moreover, because any idea would be spur-of-the-moment, it can easily backfire as proof of ability. If a prospect asks how you would approach a specific challenge, the safest response is to talk about how you responded to something similar for a previous client. If pressed for ideas on a project at hand, respond this way: "As much as I would like to, it really isn't possible to come up with anything I'd feel comfortable with on such short notice. A solution to this problem will take some thought and will involve trying a few things out."

11

YOUR PORTFOLIO
OR YOUR PROCESS?

Which would be more convincing to a prospect, your portfolio or your process? It all depends. A firm's portfolio helps prospects evaluate its style, see examples of who else it has worked with, and helps them decide what they are really looking for. A firm's process—that is, how it thinks and works—explains the ways in which it brings innovative and strategic problem-solving to client challenges. Actually, no presentation should be all one way or the other. A good portfolio presentation also addresses the firm's procedures. And a good process presentation includes portfolio samples. But there is a difference in emphasis. Knowing which is appropriate and when can easily be the deciding factor between winning and coming in second or third when competing for a new project or account.

MAKING A GREAT PORTFOLIO PRESENTATION

For most project-oriented work and prospects, a new business pitch revolves around a firm's portfolio. After making an introduction about the firm, and before asking for the order, the presentation is about showing and discussing work done for prior clients—a show and tell. The implication is: "If we can do work this good for others, we can do something at least as good for you." While the process of working together should also be a key component, the samples are the convincers. Prospects often have little or no direct experience with the firm or individual presenting, and they want to see hard evidence of competence. Portfolio samples provide proof of talent and instant credibility. Whether it's the work of an individual or a group of employees, and irrespective of their specialties, portfolio samples are our equivalent of the in-home vacuum cleaner demonstration or the test-drive of a new car.

This is the case even when most prospects have likely already checked out a firm's work on its Web site. Think of that activity as the qualifying round before the real thing. The form a presentation portfolio takes, what's in it, and how it's shown can still make or break any new business pitch.

HOW THE MEDIUM AFFECTS THE MESSAGE. A few years ago, when a creative spoke of a portfolio he or she usually meant just that—a black carrying case with samples of work, usually mounted within protective sleeves. While these traditional portfolios still have their place with students and illustrators, for everyone else "portfolio" should be thought of as a generic term for whatever best shows off their work. Today there are several ways to show portfolios. The one thing they have in common is that each affects the selling process in a different manner.

Web sites. They've forever changed the way many prospects view portfolios for the first time—alone and left to form their own impressions. Prospects often expect to check out a firm's work before committing to a face-to-face meeting. For distant ones, it may be the only way to show capability. Although few clients will be persuaded solely by examples on a site (possibly excluding Web and three-dimensional work), Web sites become, nonetheless, a crucial first step in the process.

When showing print and three-dimensional work, the mini-portfolio treatment usually works best—a section of the Web site, organized by both industry type and medium, with up to a couple dozen examples. Each industry or medium page shows several small examples, each of which can be enlarged. Some print items should use flip-page examples; others should use three-dimensional ones, rotating perspectives. A very brief description of the client, the objective, and the results should also be included. However, this may not be necessary for larger firms that can show multiple examples from prestigious clients, as the implied testimonial is often enough.

When showing Web or digital work, use two examples (screens) of each project to indicate treatment, as well as a link to the finished URL whenever possible. Broadcast samples can be presented in entirety.

Portfolio cases. A frequent mistake, especially among the less experienced, is thinking of the case and its contents as synonymous. Actually, in many situations the best portfolio showing requires no case at all; it simply involves carrying samples in a good-quality briefcase and handing them to the prospect as you explain them. Sitting across the table and talking about the work while the prospect handles it puts you in control of timing and sample selection; it also enables you to address the prospect's interests by custom-tailoring as you go along.

Mounted samples are usually appropriate only when the piece is delicate—original artwork, ad tearsheets, and the like—or when it's important to protect prints of oversized or three-dimensional work. Handing an actual sample to a prospect to examine is far more interactive and effective than merely turning portfolio pages or projecting a visual. It provides an important sense of involvement. In addition, for printed pieces it provides the opportunity to feel the stock, check the printing, and peruse the copy. Most important, it gives you a better opportunity to describe the piece on your terms, not to wait for the prospect's reaction. Samples that are inaccessible in cases with bound pages work against all this by encouraging routine, formulaic presentations—the antithesis of what a firm should project.

THE PRESENTATION IS AS IMPORTANT AS THE WORK. Depending on the prospect, usually half or less of the impact made during most new business pitches is from the creativity of the samples. More than half comes from a combination of their appropriateness to the prospect's interests, how well they are organized and described, and the overall impression of the firm's competence, service, and talent. In short, the impact comes from the presenter's presentation skills. If you happen to have great samples, the presentation can build on them. If you are relatively inexperienced and have only a few good ones, you can still use the presentation to establish yourself in a prospect's eyes as an up-and-coming talent. Regardless of your situation or experience, your demeanor and presentation skills can make a portfolio better. (See also Appendix I.)

Be able to do it in half an hour. Thirty minutes is about the right amount of time for most portfolio presentations—long enough to say what is important; short enough to conserve the prospect's valuable time, and yours. When making an appointment, promise that it won't take a minute longer. And practice to make sure you can live up to the promise. Conversely, try to avoid accepting an appointment of less than half an hour. ("I will really need a full thirty minutes—no longer—to explain why I did what I did, my pricing, working procedures, and so on.")

Think of the presentation in three sections. The first third of the presentation, comprising small talk and getting to know the prospect, should take about five minutes. The second third, actually presenting the work, should take twenty minutes or so. The last third, closing the presentation and answering questions, should occupy the remaining five minutes.

Begin by developing personal chemistry. The bigger a potential job or account, the more likely it will go to whomever the prospect feels most comfortable with. Even if you can show world-class work, your chances are slim if the prospect doesn't like *you*. So take the first five minutes or so of your allotted half hour to get to know the prospect. Break the ice by asking about her or his business and looking for areas of common interest. Then segue into explaining a little about your firm's background, stressing those areas where its experience and skills are particularly relevant to the prospect's situation.

Focus on problem-solving, not on creativity. We all know this, of course, but we also need reminding. Whether expressed or not, most prospects are looking for results. Creativity shows; you don't have to talk about it. What you do have to talk about is how your talent and experience produce results. Keep in mind that most good prospects consider business sophistication and flexibility to be of paramount importance. After all, raw creativity is readily available and cheap. What is much harder to find is consistent, dependable performance.

The best way to show each sample in your portfolio is to use a formula: why the client chose you (versus someone else); the problem you faced; the specific objective of the piece; any investigation or research involved; why you took a particular approach (particularly if it supports the research); timing and budget (when suitable); and the results obtained. Not only does this approach string things out and make each piece more significant, but taking the same approach each time constantly reinforces professionalism and a problem-given/solution-provided narrative. It makes prospects feel more comfortable, and it also creates a psychological impression of value. In this sense, it is a preemptive strike to minimize any potential pricing concerns the prospect may be harboring.

Pay attention to your body language. You want to convey a relaxed, informal, non-threatening sense of confidence during the presentation. Confidence (or lack of it) is unmistakably communicated through the firmness of your handshake, your degree of friendliness, looking the client directly in the eye, and easily handling pricing inquiries. In short, be professional while also maintaining a sense of amicability.

ORGANIZING THE MATERIALS. Now let's consider how to best organize a portfolio presentation and how to make the most of what you have to show.

No more than a dozen samples. This should be all you need to show style, demonstrate versatility, and draw out the prospect's interests. It also gives you time to tell a short, interesting story about each sample. Showing more tends to confuse the prospect and leads to a boring presentation.

Organize the samples by category. Put those most important to the prospect first, the least important last. For instance, the order might be brochures, then packaging, then Web work. Think of each category as a different chapter in a book. Don't mix different types of samples, except when it may help to show all the work for a single client or industry together.

How much variety? The first three to five samples shown should represent the type of work the prospect will be most interested in seeing—assignments similar to the type you hope to get, or work your firm has done for similar organizations. Devote the balance to different types of work to show your firm's ability to meet diverse challenges.

Don't necessarily focus on your best work. Is this heresy? Not at all. A great portfolio shows the prospective client what he or she wants to see, not what you want to show. Most prospects are more interested in work you've done for similar organizations, or in meeting challenges similar to theirs, than they are in knockout creativity. (Possible exception: agency creative directors looking at freelance talent.) Appropriate good is usually much better than inappropriate best.

Have a dozen or so other, varied samples available if needed. This enables you to modify the presentation as you go along or to show more of a particular style or type or work that the prospect indicates is of particular interest.

What if you don't have appropriate samples? No matter how experienced your firm is, prospective clients will occasionally ask to see samples of a type of work you've never handled before. ("We'd like to see samples of brochures you've done in our field—developing real estate investment trusts in Central America.") The only way to handle such situations is honestly: "Although I don't have any specific samples of this type of work to show you, I think you'll see from the variety of challenges handled in the past that we could do a great job. And, of course, because we don't have any preconceived notions, we'll bring a fresh, new approach to the work." If you are just starting out or wish to break into a new area, use spec samples to show your capability. Replace them with actual work as soon as you can. One mediocre printed sample is worth two great spec samples.

What if the work isn't all yours, or the client messed it up? Turn a negative into a positive. "This is a job I teamed on when I worked on the Framitz account at Bozo Agency. I handled final copy implementation." (Truth: you were the copy editor.) This approach allows you to slightly enhance your role, while also indicating that you are a flexible, team player. Alternatively: "On this assignment, we were asked to work within the guidelines of a corporate style manual. So the approach wasn't what we would have preferred. Frankly, I think that the Circus Gothic typeface is rather garish, but that's what was necessary, and we were pleased to be able to produce something that the client was happy with."

HANDLING QUESTIONS. Questions concerning working arrangements, schedules, availability, and so forth are specific to the presentation and can be addressed as they come up. Defer questions regarding pricing until the end unless the prospect presses you. ("I'll be going over our pricing at the end of my presentation.") Since pricing is potentially the only negative thing in a good presentation (no one likes to spend money), talking about it is better after the prospect has had an opportunity to see the quality that it can purchase. If there is no question about pricing, there is no reason to bring it up. Assuming a prospect has been qualified (see Chapter 6), one who doesn't ask can probably afford you.

When asked, you can cover pricing questions at the end of the presentation by referring to one of the samples in the portfolio that the prospect seemed particularly interested in. "To give you an example of our pricing, the design and preparation of a typical 8- to 12-page brochure like this normally runs from ($X) to ($Y) depending on complexity. (Give a range of 100 percent.) Of course, we always give a specific estimate as soon as a job is clearly defined."

Unless your firm is being considered for a retainer or ongoing account work, it is usually best not to volunteer hourly rates because some prospects might think they sound high. But don't hesitate if asked. For example: "Our labor rate is ($X) per hour, which is low for firms of our quality. Of course, we always give a specific estimate as soon as a job is clearly defined. And we stick to that figure unless the scope of the job changes."

MAKING A GREAT PROCESS PRESENTATION

A process presentation is oriented around the way a firm thinks and works. As would be expected, it is the type of new business presentation best suited to process-based firms involved with ongoing account work, such as agencies. But it is also the right approach for project-based organizations, such as design firms, when prospects' needs are strategy-heavy, multi-faceted, and long-term. Generally, in such situations a prospect will be most interested in a firm's investigational, creative, and implementation processes, and less interested in examples of its previous work. In other words, the higher the level and more unusual the challenge, the more important a firm's problem-solving and challenge-addressing processes become.

Aside from agency account pitches, projects for which an emphasis on process is usually more effective include branding and identity, packaging, new product introductions, industrial design, interactive site development, public relations representation, and communications consulting. Assignments in these areas are often unusual enough that samples of previous work are not nearly as relevant as how a firm goes about addressing the challenges it's been given. Showing samples can also be somewhat irrelevant where high-level work is involved because the reputations of those invited to compete are often well known and respected. The firms' competence, their ability to produce an outstanding creative product, is a given. What's not known—the purpose of the presentation—is how they will rise to a challenge, the depth of their strategic thinking, the resources they can marshal, their relevant experiences, and how well their personnel will team with a prospect's.

All this makes a process presentation more demanding. Whereas presenting a portfolio is routine "show and tell," describing processes requires specific "explain and persuade." With less to show, a presenter has fewer crutches. The need to describe intangibles puts greater emphasis on verbal skills. And each pitch has to be highly customized. Nonetheless, a good process presentation is well within the capability of any reasonably articulate individual.

HOW MUCH TIME? The length of a process presentation meeting should, of course, depend on the prospective client and the opportunity. This said, one hour is usually sufficient for all but the most involved projects. It provides time enough to get to know the prospect and to introduce your firm's experience, processes, and capabilities. Short meetings are respectful of the prospect's time, an important consideration when several individuals are involved. They are also easier to schedule, which can otherwise be a problem. And they force presenters to be organized.

THE TEAM. Although not an option for single-person firms or firms without appropriate personnel, the best process presentations are team efforts. The norm is a team of three: a principal, whoever will be responsible for the business (sales person or account executive), and the person responsible for the product (creative director).

When large organizations are pitching small clients and opportunities, principals need not be involved. At least a senior officer should be, though. Presentation psychology dictates that every prospective client feel important enough to warrant the attention of senior management. On the other end of the scale, a team of more than three might be appropriate for large clients and significant opportunities. Having additional staff describe the firm's capabilities in specialized areas, such as programming, copy development, and media planning, is often helpful. When doing so, however, be sensitive to presentation overkill: as a rule, presenters shouldn't outnumber the audience.

DEFINING THE PROCESS. There's no universal approach or nomenclature; different firms define the way they work—their processes—in different ways. Four distinct processes are most common. The first is *definition*: establishing the client's needs and objectives. The second is *investigation* or exploration: the research that will ensure the correct approach. The third is *development*: the creative process, including review and modifications. The fourth is *implementation*: quality control and any production. No matter how a firm defines its processes, they should be the same as they are presented in its project proposals.

HOW MUCH SHOW AND TELL? For some clients and opportunities, especially larger ones, a single case history example can make a firm's processes more understandable by turning the abstract into the specific. This approach carries some risk, however. The project chosen must not only demonstrate an ideal process but also be interesting and prospect-relevant. It should be a supporting player that illustrates and reinforces, not an end unto itself. For some prospects, especially smaller ones, a mix of process presentation (showing few or no samples) and portfolio presentation (providing little description of procedures) might be most appropriate.

ZERO-BASED. It's important to weave this theme through every process presentation. It means that your firm approaches each project without preconceived notions. The fact that your firm's work starts from scratch and proceeds through a series of increasingly demanding steps ("working it through") enhances its value and helps deter clients from asking for a solution too quickly.

TALKING THE TALK. The words used in a presentation are just as important as the meaning they convey. Never try to snow an audience, but also don't diminish your firm by making its skills sound ordinary. To illustrate, first consider the following statement, taken from the description of a firm's investigational process: "One of our strengths is the research we conduct into whether our clients' branding should be brought up-to-date in light of today's global economy. We look especially for existing elements we can strengthen to make the brand more contemporary while also increasing customer visibility." The statement is straightforward and sufficient, but not very motivating.

Now here's how the same process could sound: "One of our strengths is the research we conduct in brand viability and exploitation, specifically relating to core franchises and global line extensions. Our investigational process often indicates that the best way to accomplish this is through adapting existing elements to trade off equities, telegraph value more effectively, and lead to stronger facings. We look for instantly recognizable, sustainable elements that can become the nucleus for forming a strong emotional connection with customers wherever in the world they happen to be located."

WHO PRESENTS? Ideally, each member of the team should present in turn. The principal acts as the host and begins by giving a short (five or so minutes) overview of the firm, a definition of its processes (see "Defining the process" above), and how its background, capabilities, and experience are a good match to the prospect and its needs. This sets the stage, creates what could be the strongest impression of the firm, and serves to position the rest of the presentation as certification of the points summarized.

Next, the presentation is turned over to whoever will be the prospect's primary contact—a sales person or account executive. She or he details the firm's definition and investigational processes. This individual stresses the importance of developing solid objectives and strategies, along with the firm's partnering approach and the role of feedback. She or he weaves in whatever is already known about the prospect's needs and style.

An explanation of the firm's development and implementation processes follows, described by the creative director. She or he provides a step-by-step account: from concept generation, to approval, to quality control at production. The emphasis is on how thoroughness ensures both impact and effectiveness within each client's strategies and objectives. Any other developmental needs, such as high-level programming, are also covered.

The sales person or account executive concludes the presentation by summarizing what differentiates the firm from its competitors and pointing out why these factors are particularly appropriate for this client at this time.

Finally, the principal ensures the audience of her or his personal involvement, passes out the presentation book (see below), and asks when it would be appropriate to check back (or schedule a meeting to begin work). (See also Chapter 12.)

THE PRESENTATION BOOK. Provided to each attendee, this is an essential element of every process presentation. A customized (usually spiral-bound) booklet, it summarizes the firm's history and its experiences specifically as related to the prospect's industry and needs. The book illustrates selected examples from the presentation and includes biographies of each employee who will be working on the proposed project.

BECOMING A CREATIVE "PARTNER"

No matter what presentation approach a firm chooses, woven through it should be an emphasis that the firm is offering the opportunity to partner in a mutually beneficial business relationship. In this arrangement, the prospect will provide marketing objectives and direction; you will provide the innovation and creativity needed to meet them. It is a classic business arrangement in which the prospect will contribute what he or she knows best, and you will contribute what you know best. Both parties benefit.

The notion of a partnering approach in pitching for new business is preferable promotionally, operationally, and philosophically to the traditional client/vendor approach. First, it puts you mentally on an equal footing with the prospect—you have something the company needs, and it has something you need. So why not do business together? For the prospect, it implies a positive, working-together relationship that most good ones truly desire. The bigger the project, the more that hangs on it, the more important this can be. And from your standpoint, partnering can mean pretty much what you want it to mean, depending on the prospect and the project. It can cover working closely together for months on a complex branding strategy, or simply sitting down with a prospect to understand her or his needs for a small brochure. In short, if partnering—working closely with clients—poses a problem, you're probably in the wrong business.

12

PRESENTATION CLOSINGS

The last part of a new business pitch is its close: bringing decision-making issues to the fore, reducing procrastination and delay, and—one hopes— bringing home the business. It is often the most trying part because it should include asking for the order, or at least asking for an indication of the prospect's future plans. This is not something most of us like to do. It seems a little intrusive, if not downright pushy. Yet it is not as difficult or as tactless as it might seem. When done correctly, it reflects positively on the professionalism of the presenter and her or his organization, not to mention greatly increasing the odds of getting the business.

ASKING FOR THE ORDER

Let's say you've just made a great presentation. You covered your capabilities well, were relaxed and articulate, answered questions knowledgeably, and related everything to the prospect's needs. The prospect was interested and engaged, seemed impressed. Even if this wasn't exactly how it went, the end of a presentation is still the moment of truth. You want to get the business, close the sale. Or if yours is one of several firms under consideration, you want to make sure you leave on the inside track. So what's the best way to close a presentation?

As any actor will attest, exiting the stage is one of the more telling aspects of any performance. With a sales presentation, how it is wrapped up can mean the difference between winning and losing. Yet, after cold-calling, closing is the most difficult part of making a new business pitch for most individuals, especially creatives. Indeed, many presentations simply wind down; there is never a real closing.

A DIFFERENT STYLE. The first lesson in learning how to close a presentation, and a sale, is to clear up any misunderstandings. Its importance notwithstanding, the closing of a creative firm's new business pitch should be different from what's suitable in other sales situations. Most significant, and whether for a single project or an account, the presentation is about professional services that involve as much consultation and interaction as the end product. Think of it as the first step in a relationship-building process.

In this type environment, style and subtlety matter—a lot. In addition, prospects typically have an involved decision-making process, especially when awarding accounts and large projects. Therefore, the closing techniques widely touted by sales gurus seldom work. These include trying to ferret out customers' concerns, getting them to say yes through leading questions (the "yes ladder"), and otherwise using a variety of rhetorical devices. If fact, they can easily backfire because they oversimplify prospect decision-making and emphasize techniques over substance. An important factor in any presentation involves knowing how much selling is enough and how much will be too much.

MOVING TOWARD ACCEPTANCE. While common sales closing techniques aren't suitable when pitching for creative projects and accounts, some others are. They'll only work, however, when the rest of a presentation has been handled well.

Presenting. A good closing never rescues a bad presentation. Prospects first have to like what they see and accept the value of what you're offering. All a good closing will ever do is accelerate what's inevitable or provide the tipping point of acceptance. The more convincing a firm's presentation of its capabilities, the more effective its closing efforts. An informative, polished presentation sets up the prospect to be receptive, and it provides a presenter with the self-confidence needed to be a little more assertive.

Segueing. While it helps to think of a presentation as having a beginning, middle, and end, it should appear seamless. The warm-up should slide into introducing the firm's capabilities, which should move effortlessly into seeking a commitment. The closing of the presentation should not be telegraphed by a break or a change in tone or emphasis.

Wrapping. Every presentation should conclude with a couple-minute summary (the firm's "elevator pitch") immediately before the close. Its purpose is not only to make the benefits of working together more concise and memorable, but also to relate them to whatever client objectives ("hot buttons") were previously known or have become apparent during the presentation.

CLOSING CONSIDERATIONS. Three factors influence the effectiveness of closing efforts. Every presenter needs to keep them in mind.

The procrastination factor. Most people, prospects included, find it easier to put off committing themselves, or even to say no, when asked. As every salesperson knows intuitively, customers often need help in finding ways to say yes—to justify making a commitment—even when that's their ultimate desire and in their best interests. So a presenter should never automatically accept a delayed decision, a "we'll call you when we're ready," or even a "no thanks." Instead, he or she should look for ways to help the client come to a positive decision. Essentially, this is what closing is all about.

The desirability factor. If the above comment sounds a little manipulative, it is not. Truth is, most prospects, like most of us, like to be pursued. Few things are more complimentary and convincing than being enthusiastic about the possibility of working together and asking for the order to get started. This is especially true when the presentation is being made at the prospect's request.

The reluctance factor. This can often be the biggest closing hurdle of all. Many presenters are too polite or too shy to come right out and ask for the business. Or they're afraid that doing so will make them appear desperate. Presenters who are excessively polite or shy should not be making new business presentations. Being mildly aggressive is a plus in the business world, not a negative. As for appearing desperate, it won't happen if you handle the closing well. Pursuing new business to grow an organization is an admired trait, particularly to prospects who are involved in marketing. (Isn't it, after all, what marketing is all about?) Moreover, and quite significant, if you don't ask for the order after making a presentation, there's a strong possibility that a competitor will.

THE ROLE BUDGETS PLAY

Chapter 8 covered prospect budgeting and how it interacts with your pricing. In addition, prospect budgets can play an important role when closing a presentation.

"WE ARE VERY INTERESTED, BUT OUR BUDGET IS LIMITED." If there's one statement you're likely to run into when concluding a new business pitch, this is it. Some prospects will throw out a low figure, saying it is all they can afford, and then wait for a take-it-or-leave-it reaction. Others won't let on what their budget is until you've taken the time to prepare a detailed proposal.

Either way, you're at a disadvantage. The first instance indicates that there's little or no room for price negotiation. The second instance implies that whatever price your proposal comes in at, it is well beyond the prospect's budget and must be greatly reduced. Does that mean the discussion is over? It shouldn't be. Not, that is, once you understand how client budgets are determined (see Chapter 8) and know how to respond.

LEVELING THE PLAYING FIELD. There is, of course, nothing wrong with a client trying to get the lowest price possible when purchasing. You would do the same thing. But you need to realize that when clients bring up "the budget," it is often nothing more than a tactic to get the best deal possible. Having an established budget to refer to makes it easy for your contact person to claim that she or he has little or no price flexibility. It is out of that person's hands. In addition, referring to a budget figure puts you at a psychological disadvantage because some supposedly knowledgeable higher authority has decreed that only so much money would be suitable—in other words, that any greater spending would be out of synch with market norms.

THE BUDGET EXPERT. It is you, not them—for a reason no more complicated than this: project pricing is something you do all the time and they do almost never. So don't be misled or intimidated. A price honestly figured by an experienced firm that knows its labor costs, expenses, and how long things actually take will always be closer to the going market rate than what appears in a client's budget. (See also "Price Negotiations" in Chapter 13.)

WRAPPING UP

Wrapping up smoothly creates a lasting impression and increases the chances of a positive outcome. Be particularly careful not to overstay your welcome. Never exceed the time you've been allocated unless there's been an expression of continuing interest.

THE TRANSITION. Start wrapping up with comments similar to this: "Well, I see my time is almost up. Let me conclude by saying that this morning I've only been able to touch on some of the things that make our firm worthy of your consideration. I hope you've sensed from what I've shown and described how positive I feel about our ability to work (partner) productively with you. Also, how much we would like the opportunity. And I hope I've demonstrated that (insert a very brief summary about your firm's capabilities)." Include any specific points or hot buttons that might have been uncovered during the presentation.

If you are ending a pitch with no specific project in mind, say something like this: "Finally, is there anything coming along that I might be able to help you with?" If you get a positive response, say: "When would be a good time to give you a call about it?" If not: "I'd like to check in every so often to see if anything is coming up. Whom should I contact? Can you give me her or his e-mail address?" (The e-mail address is for general promotions. Inquiries should be made by telephone.)

If you are ending a pitch for a specific project, say: "Are you prepared to make a decision today?" If so, block out a rough schedule on the spot. If the answer is no: "Can I assume that we are still a contender? When do you think you will be able to make a decision?" Say that you will make a note of it, and be sure to give the prospect a call later that week. Indicating that you'll follow up, not wait for them to call you, demonstrates confidence. It also shows the importance you put on being selected to work with them.

THE COST QUESTION. If pricing came up during the presentation, use the same response as in Chapter 8: "You asked earlier about pricing. Well, as a rough guide, the preparation for a typical (project) such as the (name of project) I discussed earlier normally runs from ($X) to ($Y), depending on complexity. (Give a 100 percent range.) We always provide a detailed estimate as soon as the project is clearly defined, and we stick to our estimates unless the scope changes."

Using an example from the presentation just concluded puts price in the context of a quality deliverable. Giving a 100 percent range is high enough to eliminate tire kickers, low enough to encourage serious prospects. It is usually better not to volunteer hourly rates unless you're being considered for a retainer or ongoing account work. Such rates can appear high to some prospects. But also don't hesitate if asked. For instance: "Our labor rate is ($X) per hour, which, as you are probably aware, is low for firms of our quality."

THE GUESSTIMATE. Avoid it. However casually given and qualified "ballpark" prices are, they usually end up as what prospects come to expect. Insist on full project details and the opportunity to go away and prepare a careful estimate. Further, don't be tempted to offer a great deal on a first project with the expectation of getting higher prices on future ones. A first-time experience usually sets the standard for what clients will expect the next time, assuming that there will even be a next time.

THE LEAVE-BEHIND. Every presentation needs one. What's appropriate depends on the type of presentation, as covered in Chapter 11. For most portfolio presentations, it is advisable to provide all attendees with a folder containing your business card, your firm's brochure, and a "How We Work Together" summary. (For an example, see Appendix III.) For most process presentations, a bound, customized booklet or binder providing a summary of the firm's procedures, case histories and samples of previous work, and biographies of team members should be provided to each attendee.

CLOSING MOTIVATORS

When faced with a prospect's reluctance to move ahead, consider responding with one or more of the following approaches.

THE OPPORTUNITY CLOSE. "I recognize your need to wait and talk this over (with . . .). But I also don't want you to (be pressured later) (fall behind the competition) (miss a time window). So let me suggest that you make a tentative commitment today. You can always cancel it later if necessary. Will this be okay?"

THE QUALITY CLOSE. "As I hope you saw in my presentation, we always use the very best (printers, photographers, programmers, etc.) in the work we do for our clients. The downside of this is that the only way to ensure their availability is to book them well in advance. I'd like to make sure we can lock in the very best for your (project) (account). Is it possible to come to a decision today so I can start making some calls?"

THE SAVINGS CLOSE. "One of the things (I noticed earlier) (you mentioned) is that budget is of a particular concern to you. What we have found in the past is that the farther out we can schedule our workflow, the lower our prices can be. I could put you into our schedule now, even though it will be several weeks before you're ready to get started. At that time I can prepare a detailed proposal for you. Would you like to take advantage of this opportunity?"

THE LOWER PRICE CLOSE. "I hear what you're saying about our proposal's price tag, and I know we can do better now that I have a much better understanding of your needs. Let me go back and rework our numbers. In the meantime, can I assume we can work things out so I can reserve a spot for you in our schedule? You can always cancel if the numbers I come back with aren't acceptable."

THE PORTFOLIO CLOSE. "You'll remember from my presentation that we don't have (as much experience as we'd like) (a previous client) in your industry. This is something we really need in order to flesh out our portfolio. If you could make a commitment to us today, I can ensure you'll get (our top-level talent) (priority scheduling) (prices that are at least 20 percent lower than what we normally charge). Is this attractive to you?"

Note that nowhere in these scenarios is there mention of competition. Although whether to ask about it in another context is a matter of taste and judgment (some do, some don't), competition has little relevance to sales closing. Attempts to sell against another firm in this context will be counterproductive.

WHEN IT DOESN'T GO YOUR WAY

Being selected for a project or an account involves a combination of capability, chemistry, price, timing, and luck. Since it is unlikely they will all fall into place every time, a firm with a high level of presentation success is probably under-pricing or not going after the more desirable and challenging clients. (For a discussion of how much presentation success is typical, see Chapter 13.)

In addition, two or three tries are often needed before some prospects are comfortable selecting a firm, and three to five contacts can be required before some will switch business from one supplier to another. So even when a presentation isn't successful, it often brings a firm one step closer to ultimately scoring with the prospect.

When informed that your firm didn't get selected for the project or account, it's appropriate to ask why. Recognize, however, that this can be potentially embarrassing to the prospect; so if your intent is to increase your chances for success on future projects, how you ask is important. Here's a suggestion: "Of course, I'm very disappointed to hear that. I think you realize how much we looked forward to working with you. Could you share with me where our (presentation) (proposal) came up short? It would help us improve what our firm offers, as well as our chances of perhaps working with you in the future (on another project) (if things don't work out)."

Regardless of the prospect's response, say the following: "Thanks for your candor. Although things didn't work out as I wished, I enjoyed learning about (company) and your needs. Can I check back from time to time to see whether there's something else we could help you with? Could you give me your e-mail address so I can send you occasional updates on what we are doing?"

FOLLOWING UP

A week or so after making a presentation, write a short "thanks for the cour-tesy" note to the prospect contact. Resist the temptation to do it immedi-ately. Wait until the presentation starts to fade from the prospect's memory. That way, the thank-you will serve as one more contact.

Maintain regular contact through periodic mailings and e-mailings thereafter. Don't close the door on a latent opportunity through inattention. The payoff for some presentations occurs months, even years, later.

SECTION FOUR

FOLLOWING UP

Although it often goes unrecognized as such, marketing doesn't end when a prospect has agreed to receive a proposal or even become a client. The chapters in this section describe the post-presentation marketing process. Chapter 13 covers what type of paperwork is most appropriate in presenting project details, how it should be formatted and presented, and how much success can be expected. Chapter 14 addresses the step after winning the business: the all-important process of getting your ideas and concepts accepted. Chapter 15 deals with after-marketing, including how to strengthen relationships, recognize possible dissatisfaction, and keep your clients coming back for more.

13

PRE-PROJECT PAPERWORK

When a prospect requests an estimate or proposal, the focus first has to be on the numbers—their budget, your pricing—as discussed in Chapter 8. But the way prices and terms are presented can also have a large impact, both initially in whether or not you'll get the business, and later in avoiding potential misunderstandings. Which format—contract, estimate, letter of agreement, or proposal—is most appropriate in which situations? What should be covered? How much detail is necessary to protect yourself? How much detail do prospects expect? How important is personal (versus a mailed, e-mailed, or faxed) delivery? These are the subjects of this chapter.

"GOD IS IN THE DETAILS"

In an ideal world, business would be done on a handshake. Each party would be secure not only in the trustworthiness of the other, but in the accuracy of his or her memory as well. Indeed, for some long-standing client relationships a handshake is the only form of agreement necessary. And for a few fast-turnaround jobs there isn't always time to prepare a written agreement. In both cases, less paperwork will save you time and lower your costs. But it always comes at a risk. Unless you are a gambler or are secure in the knowledge that the chances of later disagreements are very low, never begin a job or take on client representation without a clear, signed agreement on schedule, terms, and pricing.

For more than 90 percent of projects, some form of up-front written agreement is an important requisite. Most prospects require documentation that stipulates what will be done, when, and for what price. They need it to budget funds, evaluate suppliers, and allocate expenses. For suppliers (that's you), written agreements help reduce misunderstandings, by far the major cause of later problems. They help ensure appropriate remuneration by forcing consideration of all aspects of a project. They provide the records by which to track and improve your future performance. And they provide some protection should you get into a shoot-out with a client later.

Firms that represent clients in placing ads or other transactions—that is, act as their agent (as in agency)—should have an agreement (letter of agency) outlining the extent and limitation of their responsibilities. Although not absolutely necessary (agreements can be oral), it is desirable to avoid later conflicts and misunderstandings. It is immaterial whether the creative supplier is a traditional advertising, public relations, or design firm, or an individual freelancer. A sample agent agreement is shown in Appendix III. The balance of this chapter addresses documentation for project-based work.

HOW MUCH EFFORT? Despite the importance of pre-project paperwork, every hour spent on it is potentially non-billable overhead. Only when it results in actually getting the project is there an opportunity to recoup the cost, and even in these cases it is sometimes difficult. This results in a paradox: the less time you spend on prospect-impressing paperwork, the more you reduce your chances of getting a project. In contrast, the more time you spend, the less money you make. So there is a strong incentive not only to choose your opportunities carefully but also to be as efficient as possible.

MATCHING EFFORT TO POTENTIAL. *Creative Business* newsletter surveys indicate that the average dollar value of crunching the numbers and preparing presentation paperwork (but not including the time and costs of making the presentation) should probably not exceed 2 percent of a job's estimated billing.

As an example, the cost of estimating and preparing a proposal for a job estimated to bill out at $15,000 would be $300 or lower, or a couple hours of time. This assumes normal information and procedures, as well as the use of templates and copy that can be easily customized.

KEEPING OBJECTIVES IN MIND. There are three primary goals for pre-project paperwork. One is to answer questions a prospect may have about how you would handle the work—your procedures, pricing, and scheduling. The second is to promote yourself—your style, experience, and capabilities. And the third goal, should you get the project, is to define your creative, production, and billing processes in a way that provides some protection against client disagreements later on.

The latter is important because no matter how good the prospect or how detailed your discussions, it is difficult to verbally cover the critical aspects of working together. In addition, putting things in writing can help refresh lapsed memories and avoid simple misunderstandings. Although written agreements are important for these reasons, there is seldom as much actual legal protection in them as most of us would like. The reason is that our "product"—creative executions—is unique, hard to define, and subjectively evaluated. This provides so many potential loopholes that a client desiring to find one usually can, especially if the client has legal staff on retainer. Also, enforcing an agreement through the court system often takes more time and money than many small creative firms can muster. If an unscrupulous client wants to violate the terms of an agreement, even a tightly worded one, he or she can probably find a way. Even if you do fight it out in the courts and ultimately triumph, the victory may cost more than it's worth.

So while most agreements should be in writing, they can't be counted on for anything other than rudimentary legal protection. Written agreements are legally powerful only in very clear violations involving substantial sums of money. Otherwise, what they mostly provide are details that reduce misunderstandings, as well as a point of reference from which to appeal to a client's conscience. ("Our agreement, which you signed off on, clearly states [terms].")

The reason for mentioning the limitations of written agreements while simultaneously encouraging them is to discourage spending an excessive amount of time on their preparation. Certainly, the paperwork must cover the basics. But to attempt to cover every possible contingency is impossible. Moreover, trying too hard eats up a lot of valuable, non-billable time. And the result obtained is only marginally more protective.

STANDARD LEGAL CONTRACTS

All agreements are equally binding; the only differences are in specificity. One way to provide specificity without spending inordinate preparation time is to adopt the wording and appearance of a standard legal contract. Such a contract ("Standard Form of Agreement for Graphic Design Services") is available from the American Institute of Graphic Arts (www.AIGA.org), and similar ones are in the book *Pricing & Ethical Guidelines* published by the Graphic Artists Guild (www.GAG.org).

Yet the format and language of standard contracts are rigid, legalistic, and off-putting to most clients. They counteract the very spirit of working together to mutually solve problems that's so important when soliciting a project. Even in cases where the prospect is not put off by legalistic language—the wherefores and wherebys—such contracts can delay projects and run up legal bills. (An all-too-typical response: "This looks okay to me, but I'd better have our lawyer look it over to make sure. If there are any questions, she'll get back to your lawyer.") Also, contractual forms don't adapt easily to the many types of work most of us do or to the changes often required during a job's progress. And finally, they don't provide that much more legal protection, anyway.

For these reasons there are only two situations calling for formal, legalistic contracts: (1) long-term, large-dollar design or interactive projects, such as ongoing branding or site maintenance; (2) illustration projects with a new or difficult client when there is no personal contact. In these cases, standard contracts are often appropriate.

WHAT'S APPROPRIATE AND WHEN

The most effective and most common pre-project paperwork is an estimate, letter of agreement, or detailed proposal that's been tailored to the unique circumstances of the job and the specific needs of the prospect. Previously prepared templates and boilerplate copy that have been customized entail little more work than a standard contract. More important, the result is always more attractive, persuasive, and effective.

These documents should include just enough to make the prospect comfortable with your professionalism; they should explain your pricing and schedule events. Obviously, the bigger the project and the more that can go wrong, the more information, detail, and pages that will be necessary. The challenge is always to provide as much as, but never more than, necessary. (For examples of simple estimates, letters of agreement, and print and Web site proposals, see Appendix III.)

SIMPLE ESTIMATES. For small jobs under about $3,000, a single-page estimate letter should be sufficient. They take little time to prepare and will provide all the paperwork most prospects need to initiate a purchase order, which is the official authorization to start work. In cases where the prospect doesn't issue purchase orders, a line should be added for the prospect to sign to signify approval.

LETTERS OF AGREEMENT. For jobs between $3,000 and $12,000, a little more detail is normally appropriate. Usually a two- to three-page letter of agreement will suffice. Although it may also initiate a purchase order because of the level of job detail involved, it should be approved by the prospect as well.

When directed to a new prospect, it is best to enclose the letter in a presentation folder that also contains a brief biographical sketch or capability brochure, an up-to-date client list, a business card, and any samples of similar work that may help the prospect assess your capabilities.

DETAILED PROPOSALS. Most substantial jobs ($12,000 and up) require a proposal of several pages. Except in cases of very large, multi-job or multi-month projects, it is usually advisable not to exceed a dozen or so pages. The best proposals not only provide a description of what will happen and how much it will cost, but also reassure the prospect that you have a clear understanding of the problems or opportunities they are facing and that you are competent to deal with them.

The key to writing a good proposal is to segment the project into a few phases (steps) of more or less similar activity. Doing so makes the proposal easy for prospects to read and understand, and it provides the detail most of them want. How many phases and how much detail is a judgment call, but three to five is usually sufficient. For example, Phase I might be orientation and information-gathering; Phase II, concept development and copy/design approvals; Phase III, art direction and photography; Phase IV, creative production; Phase V, print supervision and delivery.

Although some firms include a breakdown of estimated costs with the description of each phase, it is more common to put the costs of each phase, along with their total, in a separate section. When prepared this way, the proposal essentially has two sections: one on job detail, the other on job costs. To allow for progress payment invoicing, the costs for several phrases are often lumped together. In addition, it is usually helpful to indicate other job costs separately (expenses, etc.). This provides the prospect with a total cost picture without exaggerating the amount that actually goes to the creative firm.

When a proposal grows to be more than twenty pages, as might be the case with very large or long-term projects, it should be broken down into three or more distinct sections. In such cases, Section One typically describes and schedules activity in several phases as indicated above, including separate phases for each individual component. Section Two normally contains cost breakdowns. And Section Three usually provides material to help the prospect be totally comfortable with your ability to handle all aspects of the project. Examples of what to include in Section Three are as follows: a brief description of the creative firm and its history; relevant project or industry experience; a list of past clients; biographical sketches of team members who will work on the project; relevant awards; and client references.

RESPONDING TO RFQS

Whether in the form of an estimate, a letter of agreement, or a proposal, new project paperwork involves a price bid, often against one or two other competitors. But some projects require a different and more formal type of price bidding: responding to a formal Request For Quote (RFQ), sometimes referred to as a Request For Proposal (RFP). RFQs (and sometimes "bid conferences") are the method often used by governmental and not-for-profit organizations to procure goods and services, and they are typically sent to many suppliers. The response required is usually lengthy and must follow a structured format; personal presentations are seldom appropriate. Before deciding whether to respond, keep the following in mind.

WHAT'S THE EFFORT VERSUS REWARD RATIO? Ask yourself whether this will be good use of your limited marketing time. Minimal paperwork plus few bidders plus big project equal "probably." Much paperwork plus many bidders plus small project equal "probably not." Also, is the bid for a lengthy contract or a single job? The effort involved in preparation can be significant because many of the responses required are of questionable applicability for a creative firm or project and must be finessed or guessed. (In these situations, it might be possible to save time by first asking your prospect contact if it would be acceptable to enter "NA" [not applicable] to some questions.)

DO YOU HAVE A PREFERRED BUSINESS? Many organizations, particularly government agencies and those receiving government money, are required to give preference to disadvantaged firms. These firms include those owned by racial and ethnic minorities, women, disabled individuals, and veterans. Firms located in certain economically depressed areas also qualify.

DO YOU HAVE A SPECIALTY? Firms with specialties have three advantages. First, having a specialty gets them on a bid list when they might otherwise be overlooked. Second, experience and special techniques often permit lower prices without compromising quality. And third, the prospect may be more inclined to select a specialist—assuming, that is, that RFQ competitors aren't equally well qualified.

ARE YOU INTERESTED IN GOVERNMENT WORK? Although government work is not always as lucrative and creatively challenging as other work, it can be steady and profitable. If you want to pursue it, you will have to deal with RFQs. For U.S. firms, information on becoming a bidder on federal contracts is available at the General Service Administration's Web site, www.gsa.gov. Similar information is available at most state and local Web sites.

IS PRICE THE MAJOR CRITERION? If it is, you will probably either lose out or lose money. However, some organizations do allow their decision makers to exercise some discretion. Don't hesitate to ask. If discretion comes into play, the winning bid does not have to be the lowest as long as the reason it is chosen can be justified by a promise of better-quality service and results. Indeed, some organizations have rules requiring that the second-lowest bid be selected or that the lowest bid not be selected if it is more than a certain percentage under the next lowest. A few organizations even use a weighted formula when making a selection—so many points for experience, so many for price, and so on.

THE DECK MAY BE STACKED. Unfortunately, discretion in awarding projects can work the other way, too. It can also justify the selection of favorite suppliers. Occasionally, the entire RFQ process is a sham, an exercise conducted by an individual solely to meet his or her organization's purchasing rules even though the decision has already been made. The favored supplier might be tipped off, but more commonly its selection will be made on "discretionary factors."

THE RFQ CAN BE A NEGOTIATING TACTIC. Among commercial prospects in particular, sending out an RFQ can be a way of pressuring current suppliers. By seeking multiple bids, companies force current suppliers to match lower prices or risk the possibility of being cut out of future opportunities. Since the current suppliers most often comply, the odds of business changing hands in these situations are low.

WHERE IN AN ORGANIZATION DID AN RFQ COME FROM? Those coming from marketing departments will be evaluated more subjectively and qualitatively than those originating in purchasing departments.

RFQ SUMMARY: LOTS OF DROSS, OCCASIONAL GOLD. The format of an RFQ puts emphasis on quantitative criteria, such as price, scheduling, and production, and not on qualitative criteria, such as innovation and impact. This points to the need to be selective in responding.

PERSONAL PRESENTATION

Today's technologies make it easy to tailor every estimate, letter of agreement, and proposal through style templates, boilerplate copy, and quality color illustrations. (The latitude in RFQs is normally more limited.) There is, however, a downside to the possibilities created by today's technologies: it is the ease of sending by e-mail, phone, fax, courier, or express mail. As timesaving and tempting as this might be, particularly when getting the project might seem like a long shot, you should resist it. Any job worth the time it takes to prepare a letter of agreement or a proposal is worth investing the time it takes for personal delivery and presentation. Sending simple estimates by postal service, fax, phone, or e-mail may be all that a small job's profitability allows, but it, too, is never as good as personal delivery and presentation. And rarely, if ever, should you provide pricing or job detail over the telephone.

THE MEETING. Set it up to allow sufficient time to go over the important points, usually a half hour to an hour. If the prospect says that a meeting isn't necessary ("just send it"), try to convince him or her that it is. You can respond in the following manner: "On projects like this, it usually ensures satisfaction and saves money if I'm there to answer questions and make modifications when you read through my proposal. It will only take a half hour."

THE PRESENTATION. Start by reiterating the prospect's goals and objectives so she or he is comfortable that what you propose will address the appropriate needs. Then pass out the proposal and walk the audience through it, emphasizing the assumptions on which it is based (e.g., availability of information at a certain date), the schedule, what will be expected of the client and when, what the client can expect of you and when, and how you arrived at your pricing. Remember, not everything that will make a prospect comfortable can, or should, be written down. Moreover, you cannot assume that the prospect will read and understand everything. For these reasons alone, the more important the job is, the more important a personal presentation is. (For general presentation tips, see Chapters 9, 10, and 11.)

NEGOTIATING CHANGES. However carefully prepared it might be, many of the assumptions, schedules, prices, and terms in pre-project paperwork will require change before a prospect's acceptance. This makes it important to consider beforehand what changes you will be willing to accept and where you will draw the line. Hasty, on-the-spot decisions almost always work to your disadvantage.

Also, don't be reluctant to negotiate when doing so is appropriate. Some negotiation is a good thing. It often results in fine-tuning a project for the better. Also, many prospects will assume that there is "air" in a schedule or pricing to allow for negotiation. So either play along with up to 10 percent flexibility or make it clear that what you are proposing is "bare bones."

NON-PRICE NEGOTIATIONS. Have three alternatives in mind for most areas that are subject to discussion or change. For instance, in terms of creative treatments, the alternatives would be what you consider crucial, what's important but not crucial, and what you would like to include but isn't crucial. In other areas, consider what's easy to accommodate, what would be difficult but possible, and what could be disastrous. For instance, know when a scheduling delay will begin to cause a problem, when the delay will become serious, and when it will kill a delivery date.

PRICE NEGOTIATIONS. First, know what your costs of doing business are and what is required to make a reasonable profit. Next, know how much you are willing to give up to work with this prospect or on this type of business. Then, set a figure you won't go below. Finally, be prepared to back up your pricing by going over proposals line by line if necessary. Explain the effort involved in each task, why reducing it could have an adverse effect on quality or impact, and how cutting back in one area could have consequences in others.

Making adjustments. When your pricing falls within 15 percent of what the prospect feels is affordable, you should be able to meet it by adjusting the amount of creative (versus production) time involved. In other words, you should be able to move the project up or down on your personal "adequate, good, or best" efforts scale. Within this range, it's usually better to compromise on the way you would approach a project than to lose it over a price/budget mismatch.

Should the spread be larger, you should negotiate until the price approaches the figure you won't go below. At that point, say that you can't go any lower because the project would cease to be profitable. If pressed about cutting your profit margin, say that it is already in the single digits, well below industry averages (and likely the prospect's). Offer as an alternative modifying the prospect's project specifications—and thus the work involved. If you do make a concession and accept the prospect's price, be sure to indicate that it is an exception to your normal pricing for promotional or other reasons.

Addressing lower-quality competitors. When pressure to lower a price is the result of less experienced or talented competition, the most effective response is that it is an apples to oranges comparison. Your higher price incorporates superior experience, service, and talent that will provide a return on investment (ROI) more than making up for the (small) cost difference. In short, your price might be slightly higher, but your product's value will be considerably higher. If you convey this message confidently, it should seldom be necessary to match the price of a less experienced competitor.

When faced with a lower-price competitor whose credentials are similar to yours, the best response is to express surprise. Say that your prices are almost always lower than those of others firms in your quality and experience league. Perhaps the competitor isn't as busy as you are right now or wasn't as careful in estimating. Without denigrating the competitor, cast doubt on how he or she could have possibly come up with a lower price while still offering your high level of quality and service. If necessary, you can then adjust your price as a one-time exception.

SUCCESS RATIOS

What percentage of jobs that a firm bids on does it end up getting? For any given firm, several conditions will affect these figures. Firms that do business with many repeat prospects have a much higher success ratio than those working with many new prospects. Some firms only go after projects with a high probability of success; others go after nearly everything. Creative reputation is also a factor, although it seldom ensures competitive success because it usually comes with a price tag that is off-putting to some prospects. (Of course, this is a cause for optimism among talented, less established creatives everywhere.)

Principals of small firms doing their own selling to new prospects typically get about one job out of every two (50 percent) on which they provide pricing detail. Professional sales representatives in established creative firms don't fare as well, typically getting about one out of every three jobs (33 percent). This is due to the fact that reps cast a wider net and make many more presentations. Although their success ratio is lower, the extra volume of work they bring in more than compensates.

FOLLOWING UP

Losers in a multi-bid situation are not always informed of who won and why. If this is you, don't hesitate to inquire. The prospect may not want to divulge specific information, but asking sends a message about the importance of his or her business and about improving your future bids. Say you are interested because it will help your firm be more competitive. Specifically, try to find out if your bid was "in the ballpark" and what factors might have worked for and against it. If the decision hinged on pricing, say something like this: "That's something we're going to have to work on. I know our prices are (slightly) higher, but I also believe we are (much) easier to work with. So we actually may end up costing less when all things are considered. I hope you'll give us another opportunity to prove that sometime in the future."

14

SELLING IDEAS AND CONCEPTS

While there are countless ways in which client satisfaction can be affected, not least is the initial unveiling of what's being produced for the client—the concept presentation. Unlike most other products that clients purchase, there are few standards by which to judge concepts. This can make a persuasive presentation all that stands between easy acceptance and the beginning of numerous costly revisions or even outright rejection. Here, failure to make a compelling presentation costs more than just a lost opportunity; it costs real money.

PRELIMINARY CONSIDERATIONS

All the elements that make a good new business pitch—preparation, control, confidence, enthusiasm, and the like—are necessary for a good concept presentation. But certain other factors are especially important when first showing ideas and concepts.

LIMITING ATTENDANCE. Concept presentations can be well attended—sometimes too well. Everyone who provided input is potentially interested, and your client contact might also be looking for group feedback. But here's the potential problem: group discussions can degenerate into ones of personal likes and dislikes, and concepts can end up being compromised to death. So it's advisable to request that attendance be limited to decision makers. Moreover, it often helps to show the work to the client contact first, because his or her satisfaction and support could help neutralize in-house criticisms later.

For small- to mid-size projects, the ideal presentation would be to the contact person and possibly his or her assistant and boss; for larger projects, up to six attendees, but seldom more. If a larger group must be involved, ask for two meetings: a small one for the major decision makers, a later one for everyone else. Explain that this will ensure that the concept benefits from the input of the most crucial individuals before it gets shown to others. This arrangement should put the decision makers solidly in your corner when making the second presentation. There will be fewer comments because they will have already reviewed the concept, if not totally approved it.

LIMITING APPROVAL ROUTINGS. Also, when several client individuals are involved, ask your contact to do two (or three or more) separate routings: a small, very restricted list "for approval"; one or more larger lists "for information only."

PRIORITIZING ELEMENTS. Decide which elements of the concept are essential to its effectiveness and which ones aren't. Be prepared to defend the former vigorously, but don't go to the mat over the latter. Clients respect those who fight for what they believe is truly crucial, yet they are not concerned about modifying something that mostly involves individual taste or style. In addition, there's a psychological advantage in allowing some client-suggested modification to be made.

ENSURING THAT THE BUDGET AND SCHEDULE CAN BE MET. A client has the right to expect that whatever you show will meet their budget and production schedule. In situations where there might be benefits from exceeding them, you should prepare two concepts. Present the on-track and less costly one first, explaining its limitations. Then present the preferred one, explaining how it will overcome these limitations for a small addition in time or cost. Be prepared, though, to live with the client's choice. In situations where a client has previously provided only rough budget or scheduling guidelines, you should be prepared to provide detailed costs and time lines following the presentation.

BEGINNING EVERY PRESENTATION

As with new business pitches, there are two separate approaches to concept presentations. One, which we'll call descriptive presentations, focuses on showing final concepts but little or none of the developmental work leading up to them. This approach is useful for collateral, design, and interactive projects (see below). The other, which we'll call refinement presentations, shows much of the developmental work as well as the final concepts. This approach is useful for branding, packaging, and large ad campaigns (see below). Before discussing each approach, the following sections will address issues that are common to both types.

SETTING UP. For group meetings, allow ample time to check out the room and set up, especially if presentation aids will be involved. For small groups, try to arrange seating so that you are at the head of the room or table—in the power position. Have supporting individuals sit on each side. Ideally, the client's major decision maker should sit opposite you. Informal one-on-one meetings excepted, always stand when presenting. It focuses your audience's attention, makes concepts easier to see, and has the psychological advantage of making you appear to be in control. (For more, see Chapter 9.)

MEET AND GREET. Except for situations involving large audiences, try to find out in advance who will be attending. Introduce yourself to any who are unfamiliar to you. Ask for business cards. When presenting to unfamiliar faces, make a note of who is sitting where and keep it in front of you. Address individuals by name when responding to their questions or comments.

GETTING STARTED. Ask your client contact to kick off the meeting by formally introducing yourself, your firm, the challenge you have been asked to address, and (when appropriate) why your firm was selected. This involvement is good for his or her career and also provides an important imprimatur for the work.

REVIEWING THE REQUIREMENTS. Open the presentation with a review of the requirements. For example: "Last month we were asked by (name) to help the company develop a new approach to the (project topic). This challenge is similar to several projects we have handled in the past for other clients such as (name)." Starting off this way helps to (re)establish your bona fides. After all, many clients who are awaiting the unveiling of creative work worry that it will be inappropriate. Their concern is that however innovative and powerful your work might be, it will be directed at the wrong target. The less familiar the firm making the presentation, the greater this concern can be.

To set minds at ease, as a next step it's advisable to go over all the parameters the work was designed to meet—objectives, specifications, and schedule. This demonstrates a clear understanding of what is required and reassures your listeners that that what you are about to show was developed accordingly. Equally important, it helps identify any potential misunderstandings before showing the work. If any arise, this review of the requirements provides an opportunity for you to modify any of your planned comments. And it also stretches out the presentation and makes it more significant.

STRESSING THE OBJECTIVES. Whatever they might be, the objectives are the nucleus around which you should build the presentation. Always describe the various aspects of a concept in the context of how they help meet one or more of the client's objectives. Innovation and creativity are usually obvious, and you don't have to say much about what's obvious. What sells a concept is how well you can promise that it will meet the client's objectives. Whenever possible, add any comments from your own experience that will reinforce an objective and enhance the concept. For example: "My experience is that an additional benefit of your objective of easier navigation on your Web site is that it will also cut down on your need for support staff. As you'll see in a couple of minutes, my approach is going to help you achieve this as well."

Stressing how a concept meets a client's objectives is the only effective antidote to subjective criticisms because it forces critics to be constructive in their comments. It is much harder for an individual to criticize a concept that clearly meets the goals that were established for it.

CLUSTERING COMMENTS AND QUESTIONS. Unless you have a presentation of more than ten minutes, ask your audience to hold their comments and questions until the end. This will enable you to proceed without distracting interruptions, and it will likely answer many listeners' questions before they can be asked.

USING A REVIEW OR A CHECKLIST. These documents can be effective aids in reinforcing not only that you have taken the client's objectives seriously, but also that the concept you're showing has passed your own tough internal standards. For example: "The form I'm passing out shows the information we provided our creative team, which is a summary of what you told us you wanted to achieve in our input meetings. It also indicates that what I will be showing you in a couple of minutes not only meets the objectives you defined, but also satisfies our own rigorous in-house review as well." Seeing their own objectives spelled out, and knowing that a concept has passed an in-house review before presentation, helps further reassure most clients. It will also further differentiate multi-person firms from most competitors. And it will provide a smooth segue into presenting the concepts themselves. (For a sample Creative Review Checklist, see Appendix III.)

ADDRESSING EVERYONE. Present to the entire room. Don't favor certain individuals, even when there is a clear pecking order and some attendees are obviously of lesser importance. Individuals who feel slighted could be troublesome later in asking questions or voicing concerns.

ACKNOWLEDGING INDIVIDUALS. If possible, mention where within the client's organization an idea or certain information originated. For example: "One of the reasons we took this particular approach to the problem is that (Malcolm Geek of the IT Lab), among others, stressed how important it was to (topic of project)." Be particularly sensitive to protecting and enhancing the reputation of your client contact, even if doing so means taking responsibility for something that wasn't your fault. As an example, here's what you might say if you had based your work on what turned out to be faulty input: "Unfortunately, I totally misinterpreted the direction (Marsha Marcom) provided in our meeting." Whatever such a mea culpa would cost in ego and revision time will be more than made for up later by the grateful employee.

THE DNA OF PERSUASION

There are four major elements that contribute to or detract from all presentations whose purpose is to persuade or sell an audience.

SHARED VALUES. Stressing shared values involves relating to a client's self-interest. Talk about what you have in common and how your concept is a great way to achieve it. For example: "I know you're looking for maximum impact on your Web site, and you know I'd love to stretch my creative wings and win a few awards. So what would you say if I were to take (idea) and (idea)?"

ENTHUSIASM. When others sense conviction, they take ideas more seriously whether they initially agree with them or not. For example: "We thought of this really fantastic and innovative way to (idea). You won't believe how simple and effective it is. I don't know why we didn't think of it sooner."

SUCCESS. Base your presentation on something that has worked successfully for others. The closer your idea is to one that's already been implemented and proven successful, the more validity it will have. For example: "Remember the wonderful campaign that (company) did a few years ago? Well, we've come up with something that's different creatively but will generate the same kind of emotional response from your customers."

VANITY. This is an approach to use in situations where the decision maker is ruled by emotional responses. For example: "I (know) (suspect) you don't personally care for this treatment, and it's not my favorite either. But you have to consider that you are a lot more sophisticated than most of the audience we are addressing. We all need to be careful not to let our own personal tastes get in the way of a sound business judgment."

MAKING A DESCRIPTIVE PRESENTATION

The descriptive presentation is the most familiar type of concept presentation, best adapted to regular collateral, single ad, editorial, design, and interactive projects. (The other type, refinement presentations, explained below, would be overkill unless a project is complex enough to warrant it.)

HOW MANY CONCEPTS TO OFFER? It is common practice in design to offer a choice among three different concepts. Many institutions teach this approach, and some clients request it. The rationale is that clients should have a choice because taste is difficult to predict. Also, there is often more than one approach—style, layout, type, color, and so on—that will meet the client's objectives. Presenting several concepts and letting clients choose increases the odds of acceptance.

Unfortunately, offering several choices also puts the spotlight on artistic treatment and takes it off the strategic thinking that should lie behind good concepts. It can exemplify yesterday's thinking: that the purpose of design is simply to beautify or explain, whereas in reality it is to develop what will work most effectively in meeting a client's objectives. The creative firm, not the client, is most knowledgeable in this regard and should, therefore, take the lead and recommend what it feels will work best.

Asking the client to choose among approaches could easily convey a sense of detachment, implying that the creator has no preference and little concern about effectiveness. It could be viewed as a responsibility cop-out, diminish a client's respect, and make any approach more difficult to justify. While creatives might view preparing several concepts as a way to provide alternatives, some clients will interpret it as a lack of experience or a clear point of view. In addition, alternatives can confuse some clients. Worse, they can lead to "cherry picking"—clients select elements from each and ask that you combine them in a new concept.

A preferable alternative is to initially present and try to "sell" one concept: the creative solution that you feel best addresses the client's objectives. For instance, if a client asks you to come back with several approaches when assigning a project, say that you always develop several and they are included in your pricing, but you'd prefer to start by showing the one you believe best addresses the client's need. If the first is not adequate, you'll be happy to show a couple of alternatives. Taking this tack demonstrates that you're knowledgeable and opinionated about what will work best. (See also "Showing Alternatives" below.)

HOW WELL DEVELOPED? How fully to develop a concept is a judgment call, depending on budget, time, and client sophistication. Keep in mind, however, that the more conceptual it appears, the more difficult it will be for even knowledgeable clients to appreciate. What might seem perfectly clear to you might pass over their heads. The closer to "real" a concept appears, the faster the appreciation, the fewer the changes, and the greater the profit. Extra preparation time and effort usually pay off in easier approval. So always prepare the most comprehensive treatment feasible. Today's color printers make preparing lifelike concepts easily affordable.

For design, the ideal concept is complete, full size, full color, and as realistically rendered as possible. A dummy book on the actual stock with several lifelike spreads is always better than sketches, page proofs, or thumbnails. For ads, a printed rendition placed in the context of a magazine in which it will appear is better than one mounted on art board. For Web sites, a laptop viewing is better than screen sketches. For writing projects, the presentation ideal is a full outline, polished heads and subheads, at least one page of copy to show style, and a pagination dummy where appropriate. For illustration projects, the talent sophistication of the art director or art buyer, as well as the degree of free rein given, determine how rough or polished to make a first sketch. Always err on the side of providing more detail than expected.

Whenever there's a choice in a presentation, select what best shows or describes the client's product, not what presented the greatest creative challenge. Don't make the mistake of obsessing over creative nuances instead of how you will showcase the client's product. Choose to show what most interests the client, not yourself.

"SELLING" THE CONCEPT. To reinforce a point from earlier in this chapter, a presentation should always begin by reviewing the client's objectives, and when presenting the concept everything should be described in the context of furthering these objectives. Unless the audience comprises individuals with obvious creative (craft) interest, never try to justify concepts in primarily aesthetic terms. Justify everything in business terms. For example: "One of the objectives we just went over was the need to get maximum impact as economically as possible. For this reason, in approaching this project we decided to use (strategy)." Alternatively: "In keeping with your desire for fast, easy readability, I chose to (strategy)." Or: "To help increase the navigational ease that you felt was crucial now that your site has expanded, we have changed (strategy)." Or: "One of the things you'll notice here is that by using (approach) we've created a feeling of (example), which was one of your major objectives."

This method of presentation—tying creative development directly to the client's own objectives—makes the process more understandable and increases the value of the result. It becomes less artistic and esoteric, more businesslike. More crucial, it makes critical comments easier to handle. Any criticism will be personal and subjective, which is much less likely to hold up after discussion. (See "Responding to Reactions" below.)

Also, be thorough when explaining the concept. For a storyboard or illustration, flesh out the story and describe what's going on. For an ad, read through the headlines and body copy. For a brochure, walk the client through the pages by reading headlines and describing visuals. For a Web site, show all the links and explain how they will be developed and interact. Don't minimize the concept by failing to provide a narrative.

SHOWING ALTERNATIVES. As covered above (see "How Many Concepts to Offer?"), it is usually better to start by showing and trying to sell the concept you believe best meets the client's objectives. You can show the alternatives afterward. These can be more conceptual, less polished. Don't change your preference when describing them, and indicate why they are not your first choice. But also be perfectly clear that anything you show has met your firm's high standards and that individual preference is, after all, subjective. Moreover, the decision is the client's to make, not yours.

If none of these concepts are acceptable, get more detail on what the client has in mind. Then go back to work. Make one more presentation, showing at most two new approaches. If these aren't acceptable, chances are strong that nothing will be. It will probably be better to resign the business.

MAKING A REFINEMENT PRESENTATION

This type of presentation is useful when clients are interested in all the developmental work that has gone into a concept. Although a refinement presentation can occasionally be appropriate for smaller projects, it is most common in branding, packaging, advertising campaigns, and similarly involved assignments. Showing the germ of an idea and how it grows and is refined through several stages demonstrates the extensive thought and effort that are necessary in multi-faceted work. It reassures clients that your firm has thoroughly explored the many factors that can affect the work's success. It also reassures clients that you have considered all their needs and concerns. Additionally, it complements the procedures typically used by large firms in pitching their capabilities and later in carrying out the investigational phase of projects they work on. Not least, it reduces the probability of critical questioning later on.

CONSIDERATIONS. Within reason, the more steps (iterations) you show, the more impressive the presentation will be. Tie as many refinements as possible to meeting specific client objectives. To add impact, make sure the first things you show are rough sketches; those in the middle should be increasingly refined (work in progress), and the last should be very polished (as close to the real item as possible). Display everything in a linear fashion, first to last, so the audience is aware of the progression of creative thought. A conference room corkboard is ideal for printed work or storyboards. Line up three-dimensional items on a conference room table.

AN EXAMPLE. Following is a condensed narrative of a typical refinement presentation. It picks up right after reviewing the client's objectives. (See "Beginning Every Presentation" above.)

"First I want to show you where we started." (Bring out and display the initial idea.) "As you can see, it encompasses many of the objectives that we just discussed. Specifically, it is very strong in conveying (objective), (objective), and (objective). However, we felt it was still lacking somewhat in (example) and (example), so we next modified it by (approach), which addresses these issues." (Display next to the initial idea.)

"In doing this, it became apparent that your objective of (objective) would be even better met if we also added (example). So we did, as you can see here." (Display next to the preceding two.)

"This is very close to what we think works, but it still seemed to lack the shelf presence we felt was necessary. So we decided to take the further step of (strategy), which, as you see, eliminates this concern." (Display next to the preceding three.)

"We liked this concept very much, except for one thing—it doesn't lend itself as well as we would like to future line extensions. So we made one further refinement through (strategy)." (Pause for effect. Then display the final concept next to the preceding four.)

"This, then, is our recommendation. It is (description)." (Describe in detail the concept's creative distinctiveness and impact.) "I think you can also see from the process I've just gone over that this approach meets all your primary and secondary objectives." (Review objectives again briefly.) "Now, can I answer any questions you might have? Is there anything you would like me to cover in more detail?"

THE BENEFITS. A successful process presentation ensures not only that every client objective has been covered or strengthened by one or more refinements, but also that every aesthetic element has been justified in these terms.

RESPONDING TO REACTIONS

Whether you have made a descriptive or a refinement presentation, it is advisable not to ask what the audience thinks of a concept or whether they like it. To do so is to open the door to the possibility of an unnecessary critique. Clients like everything unless they indicate otherwise.

LISTEN TO EVERYONE, PAY ATTENTION TO A FEW. No matter how irrelevant you may feel a comment to be, listen attentively and respond. But don't attempt to accommodate every minor comment and suggestion. Say something like this: "I appreciate your input, and you make a good point. Frankly, however, I think it is probably a little late to accommodate much more than (example) at this point, but let me take another look."

CHALLENGE NEGATIVE OR UNINFORMED COMMENTS. If you don't do this, you'll lose the prospective client's respect while damaging your own self-esteem. First, restate the comment in your own words. Then, in a friendly and non-threatening way, question the wisdom behind it. "Let me play the devil's advocate here for a minute. If I were to use the approach you suggest, wouldn't that position the product very close to that of your major competitor? Is this really wise?"

WHEN SOMEONE EXPRESSES GENERAL DISAPPROVAL, ASK FOR PRECISE REASONS. Then, if you don't agree, explain why, noting that you will of course ultimately follow the client's wishes. Not standing up for your work, especially when criticisms are uninformed or irrational, is a sure-fire way to encourage additional ones.

BE PREPARED FOR COMMON RESPONSES. Although the variety of client responses is limitless, many are familiar. Following are suggestions on how to acknowledge several common responses.

"I (we) would like to get a few other opinions." Whether the "other opinions" will be from subordinates, friends, or even a spouse, a concept will probably end up in trouble if you are not there to explain it. Respond with something like this:

"Our experience is that this is seldom a good idea. Unless the others have been equally involved, they won't have the benefit you have in knowing the objectives we are trying to meet, or our development limitations. Then, too, everyone you ask will probably feel obliged to have an opinion, and uninformed opinions usually just muddy the water."

"I don't like . . ." Get the individual to explain exactly why. If the reason is objective and rational ("The product is not shown correctly."), then you should agree and make the fix. If the criticism is subjective or irrational ("I've always hated . . . "), respond this way:

"Personally, I'm not necessarily in love with (issue) either. But the concept does meet your objectives, and it is unlikely that most of your target audience shares your aversion. I believe it would be unwise to change something that otherwise works so well for what is, in actuality, a purely personal reaction."

"We like it, but we think it would be improved if you changed . . ." Agree to any minor changes. But resist any that would seriously impact the work's effectiveness. Here's how to respond to the latter:

"I'm afraid that . . . is one of this concept's essential (elements) (building blocks). It (relates to) (reinforces) . . . and provides a crucial (sense of) (bridge to) . . . . To make the change you are suggesting would require also modifying . . . and . . . , which would (weaken) (effectively emasculate) the concept. Of course, we'll do whatever you wish, but I don't think this is a good idea. Trust me on this one."

"Why didn't you . . . ?" There are an infinite number of ways to approach creative challenges, yet time and budgets are always finite. So attempting to justify what you did or didn't try is pointless. Defuse this reaction this way:

"It's interesting that you mentioned this, because we did try something similar. We felt, however, that adopting this approach would be a bit too . . . Also, we felt that . . . does a much better job of meeting your objective of . . . so we didn't take that approach any farther."

"We think it should be much simpler." This reaction, more often to copy than to design, may be valid. But it often comes with a statement about how viewers (client customers) are too busy to read or too mainstream to appreciate a sophisticated design. So the client wants every-

thing reduced to simple graphics and bullet copy. Your best response:

"One of the things I have learned over my (many) years in this business is that it is better not to underestimate the taste or sophistication of customers. Well-written, interesting copy will be read and remembered. And good, arresting design will not only attract attention and increase interest and readability, but will also provide the additional benefit of making a positive statement about a company's sophistication. We can do whatever you desire, but all my experience tells me that what you see here is pegged at the exactly the right level."

WHAT KIND OF SUCCESS?

Presentation perfection—concept acceptance with no changes—is unusual, especially with complex projects. There are too many variables, ranging from individual tastes to valid differences regarding strategic direction. So a realistic goal is not to expect perfection; it is to keep changes—refinements—manageable and within the project's budget.

15

AFTER-MARKETING

In the first chapter of this book, we discussed why marketing needs to be continuous despite how busy a firm might be. Without a regular effort, there's the possibility of experiencing feast-or-famine ups and downs, becoming too dependent on a few clients, missing out on new challenges, and having to deal with inefficient workflow—to mention but a few of the downsides. Subsequent chapters have covered implementing the many aspects of marketing that lead to increased business. Now, in this final chapter, we look more deeply at a subject raised under "Contact Mining" in Chapter 6—after-marketing, or the activities that will keep good clients coming back for more. This aspect of marketing deserves more than a little consideration for two good reasons: (1) previous clients don't require getting-up-to-speed, and (2) they come with little or no marketing expense. As a result, they can be up to 20 percent more profitable than new clients.

STRENGTHENING RELATIONSHIPS

A successful services business requires building good client relationships, whether they're for a few days or a lifetime. Clients want to work with whoever makes them feel most comfortable. This statement is not intended to underplay the role of such objective factors as talent, experience, and price; it simply emphasizes the importance of the "likeability quotient." In fact, it takes a powerful combination of objective factors to overcome it. Truth is, clients make selections at least as often on personal, subjective factors.

This reality is particularly telling when it comes to follow-on business. As large a role as the likeability quotient plays in initial selection, it becomes even more significant later on. Unlike companies that sell products, where customer interaction, while important, is relatively limited, in service businesses interaction is longer, more intensive, and more personal. Getting continued business takes paying close attention to the interactions and relationships that develop. There must be a constant awareness of ways to improve service, nurture and retain current clients, and entice former ones back. All this constitutes the human side of CRM (Customer Relationship Management), previously introduced in Chapter 6.

TEN REASONS WHY CLIENTS LEAVE AND WHAT YOU CAN DO ABOUT IT

While it is impossible to provide remedies for personality conflicts (see "They Don't Like You" below), many of the reasons new clients become short-term rather than long-term ones are predictable. Following are ten of the most common reasons for client defection, more or less in order of frequency.

BEING TAKEN FOR GRANTED. The excitement of a new challenge, the freshness of working together, giving 110 percent of what's expected—all will understandably diminish with client longevity. This effect may well be offset by understanding clients' needs better, adding more efficiency, and cultivating closer relationships. But be cognizant of the risk, and when you feel the work is becoming routine, look for ways to rejuvenate the business before the client stops calling. This often happens with little or no warning or explanation. For the reasons why, look first in the mirror. After all, most clients don't stop doing business; they just stop doing business with you.

DOING DESIGN / ADVERTISING / ETC. But, you say, isn't this what clients pay you to do? Often, yes. But at least as often the *real* assignment is to help the client implement a strategy, communicate a message, create an impression, or strengthen a brand. It is the result, not the process, that counts. Thinking of your firm narrowly—for instance, exclusively as a design studio or an interactive agency—risks ensnaring yourself in the same trap that has done in countless companies of all types over centuries. They failed because they focused on their processes, not on what their customers were paying for. The more broadly and inclusively a creative firm thinks, the more likely it is to come up with innovative, value-added solutions. Good clients realize this and can be quick to dismiss firms that don't.

CUTTING CORNERS. Every client wants work done as inexpensively as possible. Few, however, would admit to wanting it done cheaply. Each wants the highest possible quality and service for whatever it's willing to pay. Smart firms modify their creative and production procedures as needed to try to meet a client's budget. But they never go so far as to compromise their own standards. Not-so-smart firms cut whatever corners are necessary to get business. They fail to realize that the aftertaste of a bad experience will stay with clients long after the pleasure of low price has disappeared. A firm that sells price at the expense of quality and service will eventually lose out to one that doesn't.

DEVELOPING A "CAN'T DO" ATTITUDE. Most clients are not knowledgeable about the creative process or what's likely to be effective. So they occasionally ask for something that you can't easily accomplish or that might not be suitable. Yet most will respond positively to a rational, businesslike alternative, especially if you couple it with an economic rationale. What no one ever wants to sense, however, is that his or her request is inappropriate, unsophisticated, or too difficult to consider. No matter how unusual a request might be, successful firms approach it with a "let's see" attitude. Conversely, firms with a "can't do" attitude approach unusual requests only from the narrow perspective of their own experiences and desires. Although this reaction is rarely intentional, they're dismissive of other ideas and approaches. And in doing so they're likely to offend.

TRYING TO RESTRICT USE. Creative products—intellectual property—are legally distinct from those that most clients deal with every day. So it is little wonder that misunderstandings often occur over ownership of copyrights and production files, as well as subsequent restrictions on their use. Where copyright ownership by the originator has clear precedents (e.g., in photography and illustration), you can avoid the possibility of later misunderstandings by discussing use restrictions up front and by making sure ownership is defined in proposals and contracts.

Where precedents on copyright ownership are less clear-cut (e.g., in design and advertising), all paid activity on the client's behalf should be accepted as work-for-hire. Anything otherwise will surely lead to an unhappy client, not to mention the possibility of an expensive legal challenge. Charge adequately for services provided, and let it go at that. As for turning over production files, which are usually held to be the legal property of the creative firm, be selective and don't deny them to a good client with a legitimate need. Doing so will threaten most relationships.

OVER-PROMISING. When trying to land a desirable client or project, especially a hotly contested one, it's easy to promise more than you can absolutely guarantee. Likewise, when trying to placate a current client with an urgent request. Although such promises are usually well motivated and seldom are an attempt to mislead, any need to later renege will have the same effect: destroying client confidence.

The ability to count on a supplier to deliver what's promised when promised constitutes the foundation of a solid, long-term relationship. Wise firms know that it is better to confront reality up-front than to risk client displeasure later on. Under-promising and over-delivering is the way to keep clients; the opposite is a sure way to lose them.

HAVING PAROCHIAL INTERESTS. Clients don't expect outsiders to be as interested in their industries, organizations, and products as they are. But they do expect somewhat more than just passing interest or only enough to get the job done.

Increasingly, they look for firms that have broad, not just parochial (e.g., creative), interests. They want those that can act as strategic partners, ones that have a broad enough understanding of their business and needs to "think outside the box." This is impossible when a firm's knowledge of a client and its products and environment is limited to the task immediately at hand. Firms with the best bet to hold on to clients are ones that display a broad interest in their clients' businesses. Firms most likely to lose clients are those that limit their interest to a current project, despite how well they handle it.

COMPROMISING SERVICE. Two words describe the businesses of most readers of this book: "creative" and "service." Yet in most firms there's a strong, if understandable, emphasis on the former. This is no problem unless service gets short-changed, which often happens. Reasons run the gamut from a firm's culture being insufficiently service oriented, to lacking adequate staff, to service time being non-billable or less profitable. Regardless of the reason, many clients put as strong a premium on the process of working with a supplier as on the results produced. Firms that don't provide both outstanding work and outstanding service are delivering only half of what their clients pay for. Savvy clients recognize that in today's competitive market they don't have to accept this outcome, and they start looking for an alternative.

THEY WANT TO TRY SOMETHING / SOMEONE NEW. Most creative firms have a distinctive style. While this uniqueness is beneficial in attracting clients (it is the major differentiator among competitors), it can also be a reason for ultimately losing them. Occasionally clients want a "new look" or a fresh approach. Firms—both single- and multi-person—that don't occasionally offer it can inadvertently shorten their tenure.

The most successful firms are those that are the least predictable in their creative approaches and styles. Single-person firms should guard against the "sameness" problem by occasionally pushing the creative envelope. Multi-person firms can do the same by rotating creatives assigned to the account. Also, multi-person firms should be careful to hire new employees for their creative diversity, not for their similarity.

THEY DON'T LIKE YOU. Don't take it personally, but in this scenario the problem is personality. There's a mismatch. The chemistry isn't good. What to do about it? Accept the inevitable and prepare to move on. You should expect to get along well with most clients most of the time, but not with all clients all of the time. So when you have one you can't work comfortably with, recognize the inevitable and tactfully resign that business. Don't fret or try to save it. You'll be happier, and your firm more profitable, when you concentrate on clients with whom you see eye-to-eye. Forego the others.

WHAT IMPRESSES CLIENTS

What motivates a client to call again and again? Good work, surely. But there are also other factors—some practical, some psychological—that are equally important.

APPEARING TO BE IN DEMAND. Busy businesses are the ones that other businesses seek out. The busier you appear to be, the more in demand you'll likely become. You can't change reality, but you can change the perception of reality. Never talk about inactivity; instead, talk about what you are doing. Discretely drop the names of prestigious clients whenever it's appropriate to do so. Increase your visibility through promotions, pro bono work, or community activities.

BEING EASY TO WORK WITH. Everyone prefers to work with someone who is cheerful and pleasant. Having this reputation helps particularly in getting the larger, longer, more profitable projects. In addition, there's another benefit: the more clients like you personally, the easier it will be for them to accept any strong opinions or unusual creative approaches you offer.

BEING CURIOUS. Taking an interest beyond what's required to do the project—being genuinely curious about a client's business—is a sure way to earn trust and confidence. Clients often assume that you need to know more than is actually necessary. And because they're so involved in their business, they often want to share their interests with you. Equally significant, the more knowledgeable you become, the better the position you'll be in to suggest additional ways you can help them out.

TAKING CHARGE. All clients want to relax, believing their project is in capable hands. So give them this confidence. Leave little to doubt. The more you appear to be in control, the more the client will come trust your judgment and the more easily things will proceed. Conversely, the more nervousness or lack of confidence you display, the more the client will question your judgments, work, and prices.

BEING 100 PERCENT RELIABLE. Show up for appointments on time, even early. Never be late. Deliver what you promise, when you promise. And never let a client see you sweat. There's little that worries clients more than missed deadlines, cover-ups, or lackadaisical attitudes. If you do mess up, be 100 percent honest about it. Most clients want you to succeed and will forgive an honest mistake or two.

BEING ATTENTIVE TO DETAILS. Take nothing for granted. In many cases, clients have only the most superficial knowledge of what you do. They expect you to tell them how you work, the process, the schedule, and when and what will be required of them. They also expect you to keep them informed of all changes and to provide options when appropriate. Cater to their idiosyncrasies. And check all the details as if a mistake could cost you your career.

TAKING A PERSONAL INTEREST. It's human nature: we all prefer those who take an interest in us, and clients are no exception. So don't make the mistake of being so businesslike that you ignore the personal component of a business relationship. Be particularly careful not to neglect individuals at lower echelons in an organization. They not only influence how assignments proceed today, but they may move up to a more influential position tomorrow.

DEFINING CREATIVITY THEIR WAY. When we discuss creativity, we often define it in terms of talent, originality, fashion, trends, and praise by creative peers and opinion leaders. Clients, however, usually think differently. To them, creativity is usually defined as an original way to sell their product or communicate their ideas. When you are with clients, make sure you talk their language.

BEING FLEXIBLE. Good clients expect you to handle a project in the way you believe will best achieve their objectives. But when a client disagrees with your approach, you have to be flexible enough to willingly make changes. After all, every project is nothing more than a collection of subjective procedures and results. Never forget: they pay the bill, so they have the right to have it done their way.

TREATING THEIR MONEY LIKE IT'S YOUR OWN. If you follow this advice, chances are that's where more of the client's money will end up—with you. Big or small, today more clients than ever are budget conscious. Sticking to a budget figure is important. Finding novel ways to reduce it is even more so. The challenge is to convince your clients that you are frugal about their money while at the same time being fussy about the quality you provide.

GETTING FEEDBACK

Service businesses have a concern that those who sell products don't: getting a read on satisfaction. Product businesses quickly see from receipts just how well they've met customer expectations. Sales soar for well-liked products; they sag for less-liked ones. The relationship between a sale and expectations is less direct in service businesses. Except where there's major dissatisfaction, a sale takes place on schedule. What may not happen, though, is a repeat sale or the opportunity to be considered for something bigger or better in the future.

HOW IMPORTANT IS FEEDBACK? Principals who work directly with senior client personnel usually have a good feel for satisfaction. Where there's a close, one-on-one relationship and client personnel also have decision-making authority, there's little direct benefit to soliciting feedback. Any formal process for asking might appear to be overkill. Much more often, however (especially among larger clients), mid-level personnel have project responsibility. Or a firm's staff, not a principal, is mostly involved. In these cases, any inquiry into client satisfaction can be informative and appreciated.

The bigger both organizations are, the more important soliciting feedback becomes. In other words, the farther removed project responsibility is from both client and firm management, the more fruitful it is to ask for feedback. There's little worse than not knowing what's really going on or having clients feel they're being taken for granted.

BENEFITS OF FEEDBACK. Perhaps the most misleading belief about feedback is that client dissatisfaction will be apparent. While this may be true in major instances, it usually isn't otherwise. Or it is, and we're not sensitive enough to pick up on it. In fact, many clients and projects are lost because of dissatisfactions that the clients won't volunteer. Or future working relationships become strained because of unmentioned and often-imagined offenses. It's important to point out that soliciting feedback not only aims to correct problems or ward off threats to future business; usually, a more important goal is to shore up the positive aspects of a relationship.

It says "you're important." It is easy to forget that every client wants to feel important, despite how large his or her firm is and how small yours is. While you can, and should, address this issue in numerous ways on a day-to-day basis, nothing conveys it with quite the same impact as soliciting feedback on the client's satisfaction.

It reinforces "partnering." If "partnering" with clients to further their success is to be anything more than an empty word, it has to be backed up. Talking the talk is not the same as walking the walk. Feedback on what needs to be done better in the future is a crucial element in true partnering.

It encourages referrals. Referrals are an essential source of new business for many firms. Soliciting feedback encourages a client to provide referrals because it helps recall good experiences. Conversely, a willingness to hear (and, by implication, address) dissatisfaction can forestall unhappy clients from discussing it with others.

It inspires loyalty. Soliciting feedback makes clients feel appreciated, and appreciated ones are more likely to stick around. Not only does having loyal clients reduce business acquisition (marketing) costs, but the costs of working with them average 10 to 15 percent less. And lower costs increase profitability.

It differentiates. If not exactly rare, formal soliciting of client feedback is nonetheless unusual. Surveying first-time clients can be very effective in setting a firm apart from others. Occasional surveying of long-time clients reinforces its uniqueness and helps keep established relationships from going stale.

It provides testimonials. Complimentary comments from previous clients, particularly well-known ones, are among the most powerful ways to impress prospects. They are especially effective for individuals and small firms that are competing against larger, better-known organizations. A note of caution, though: any testimonial that you intend to use publicly must have separate approval. Individuals who are effusive in their casual remarks are often hesitant to commit to having the same words appear publicly, or their employer might have a policy against use of the organization's name for promotional purposes.

It improves products and services. While the aforementioned benefits of feedback are mostly external, the most important benefit of all is actually internal. It involves listening to clients about their satisfaction with the quality of a firm's products and services, and then taking those comments to heart and using them to improve its future performance.

WAYS OF GETTING FEEDBACK. How to solicit feedback depends on relationships and what you hope to learn. Inquiries about the general satisfaction of ongoing clients are usually best handled in one-on-one reviews; those regarding occasional clients are usually best handled impersonally through surveys.

One-on-one reviews. It is easy to keep abreast of day-to-day and job-to-job satisfaction for clients who provide a continuous stream of work. But maintaining strong relationships over time usually requires something more. It usually also requires a means of staying sensitive to overall satisfaction. Not to keep tabs on client satisfaction is to risk being blindsided by concerns that might ultimately lead to a client's sudden departure.

The key to maintaining sensitivity to issues that are not readily apparent is to have an annual (or more often, if warranted) review of the firm's performance by the client. The objective is to reinforce the idea that the client is special and that his or her concerns warrant special consideration. Probably the best way of doing this is at an occasional one-on-one lunch: a firm's principal(s) hosts the key client individual(s) in surroundings that are conducive to discussion and befitting the meeting's importance. Doing it on the "boss-to-boss" level helps keep the focus on the big picture, not on details, while the social environment helps keep everything productively informal and cordial.

Informal should not mean unprepared, however. Have a loose agenda in mind: areas of potential improvement, things that might make working together more efficient, capabilities the client may not be aware of, possible opportunities of mutual benefit. As a way of prepping the client and making the meeting more significant, you can outline talking points in a letter sent a week or so in advance. Whatever the agenda, keep it simple enough to discuss easily in a couple of hours. Let the client direct pacing and adjust content. And keep in mind that just having such occasional "summit meetings" is as important as what you hear at them. (Remember: the medium is also the message.)

Web surveys. Surveying software and online surveying are widely available and inexpensive. (Do a search for "survey software.") They enable a firm to compose its own personalized survey and transmittal letter to send to any client whose e-mail address is available. Responses are automatically tabulated. In addition to the ease and professionalism of conducting surveys this way, responses can be anonymous, which encourages participation. Although client anonymity would not be credible when a single-person firm with few clients surveys a new one, it could be credible if sent to all a small firm's clients once a year or sent to a list of numerous client contacts. (For a sample Web survey form, see Appendix III.)

Mail surveys. Although mail surveys are used less often, they can be effective for larger firms for which client anonymity is less of a consideration. In these situations, a survey is mailed once or twice a year to contact individuals at selected client organizations.

Whether sent by e-mail or the post, survey questions should be specific to a firm and its interests. Nonetheless, there are a few general rules that make surveys more impressive and add to their usefulness: they should come from a firm's principal, not an account person; unless sent to several individuals, they should go to the contact person at the client organization, not his or her boss (for empowerment); they shouldn't be longer than two pages; questions should focus on how well your firm's work met the client's expectations and business objectives; questions should be short, direct, and mostly answerable with key or pen stroke (little writing needed); when a firm specializes, questions should be industry-specific; if mailed, a postpaid envelope should be provided; if e-mailed, an anonymous "reply to."

Other survey methods. Surveys can also be conducted by telephone or fax. Telephone surveys are impressive, but they need to be conducted by professional researchers, a fact that makes them expensive and typically suitable only for larger firms with an extensive client list. Fax surveys are unprofessional and offer little in the way of advantages. Surveys of client happiness with a firm's competitors—that is, surveys whose aim is to solicit new business—are different in nature and shouldn't be confused with surveys of a firm's own clients.

WHAT TO EXPECT FROM CLIENT FEEDBACK. Don't expect a lot. But, then, don't let this be the criterion. Again, it is the act, not necessarily the result, that's most important. The very process of asking forces one to think about priorities—what's important to clients and, by extension, the health of a service business.

The response to most surveys is poor. You should feel lucky if one in five is returned. Clients with business-killing gripes don't wait for a survey to voice them. And when there's a history of small problems, many clients feel more comfortable avoiding discussion and simply moving their business to another firm. Because of this, you should take very seriously any critical comments you receive. By and large they come from clients who are, in varying degrees, disappointed but wish to continue working with your firm. They are, in other words, the very clients your firm should cultivate. In addition, there's a strong probability that every problem they identify will have troubled several other clients who have decided to let it pass.

The other side of survey feedback is to downplay most positive responses. They can easily lull a firm into complacency. Also, they are seldom representative of a firm's client universe. Satisfied clients are more apt to respond than dissatisfied ones. And even those that might see a need for improvement often succumb to the tendency to avoid being critical when a firm's efforts are well intentioned.

Feedback from one-on-one review meetings is typically more detailed, but not necessarily more forthcoming. The friendly, informal nature of such meetings can make it difficult for clients to be totally honest. They might be reluctant to mention small issues, feel they can't adequately articulate major gripes, or want to keep their feelings private. Indeed, it is not unheard of for a client to dump a firm shortly after a review meeting when all signals were positive. Office politics, business changes, and personal feelings can upset a relationship in a heartbeat.

Bottom line: treat any feedback seriously, particularly when it is critical. But think of most benefits of feedback solicitation as coming out of the process itself. Consider any actionable specifics to be an unexpected bonus.

SECTION FIVE

APPENDICES

SEVEN EXAMPLES OF MARKETING MISTAKES

The need for better marketing that this text emphasizes can be illustrated and summarized by looking at some of the misguided approaches that firms routinely take. The mini case histories that follow describe real-life situations, what factors need to be considered, and what remedies will produce future improvement.

#1 HAVING NO PLAN

Tom is a freelance writer, coming from the corporate PR world a year ago after being downsized. He has yet to do any formal marketing, and he has no strategy or plan for doing so. His reasoning: there's no need.

THE SITUATION. Before going out on his own, Tom had informed friends, made over a seventeen-year career in the pharmaceutical industry, of his plans. His experience and knowledge led to many promises of future assignments. Although most proved empty, a few came through. In fact, after just one year Tom has about as much work as he can comfortably handle. So he feels no pressure to spend his still limited funds on soliciting business that could possibly overwhelm him anyway. And having supervised employees in his previous career, he has no desire to grow and add staff. He relishes the freelance lifestyle. So what's the problem?

WHAT NEEDS TO BE CONSIDERED. The problem is that Tom is betting on things continuing to go as they have gone so far—in other words, he's relying on his industry friends and good luck. Unfortunately, both are quite fickle. By not planning for future change, he is in denial about the reality of being in business. No serious business should ever adopt a take-every-day-at-a-time approach. Here are a few things that sooner or later will introduce Tom to reality:

Contacts dry up. According to the U.S. Bureau of Labor Statistics, one in five employees (20 percent) changes jobs annually. This makes it unlikely that most of Tom's friends will be in the same positions five years from now. Of course, a friend who moves might continue to give Tom business, and Tom will also be making new contacts as he handles his assignments. Nonetheless, without an effort to actively develop new contacts, chances are that Tom's base—the foundation of his success—will ultimately erode to the point of uselessness. And there's no plan for refreshing it.

Business conditions change. As inevitable as losing his contacts may be, even more so are economic cycles. Tom has been fortunate in being in business during a period when conditions are generally good. Clients are spending. That's not always the case, though. Economic downturns and their effect can never be accurately predicted. But there's one thing that can be predicted: when times become tough and everyone is scrambling for business, a few contacts, even good ones, aren't enough. Tom is also totally vulnerable to the pharmaceutical industry's ups and downs, which may not track with the national economy. If this industry should catch cold, his business will develop life-threatening pneumonia.

Developing new business takes time. Typically, it takes months from the time a person puts together and implements a marketing program until it starts to produce results. The more ambitious the program and the higher the prospect level, the longer it takes. This delay makes it important for Tom to expand his contact base before he has to. If he waits until it's necessary, it will probably be too late.

THE REMEDY. Tom needs to develop a strategy and a plan for expanding his contact base immediately. The main purpose is to build a broader foundation of contacts—enough to ensure that his business will have stability and staying power despite the attrition of friends or an economic downturn. Tom also needs to reduce his dependency on the pharmaceutical industry. He should plan to begin marketing to other healthcare industries. Related clients will provide a cushion and will likely enhance his status with pharmaceutical clients as well.

As for developing too much business through marketing, Tom shouldn't be concerned. Having more opportunities than he can handle will enable him to be more selective in the assignments he accepts. Turning down work seldom results in any long-term loss of opportunities. Instead, the perception of being in high demand usually makes one's services all the more desirable.

The process of planning will also encourage Tom to be more objective in working with his clients. He needs to think more like the CEO of a small business and less like an individual working with friends. Thinking about what is best for his bottom line in the long run is crucial to ongoing success. As an example, the close client/freelancer relationship he enjoys may work to his disadvantage. Such arrangements usually favor clients, who tend to take too much for granted and expect "friends" pricing. Without going beyond his current contact base, Tom might be missing out on securing better clients with bigger budgets. Finally, developing a plan is not that difficult or time-consuming. In Tom's case, it need involve nothing more than a few hours of thinking and then committing a short list of objectives and a schedule of actions to paper. It is the process that's important.

#2 RELYING ON REFERRALS

Viral marketing . . . word-of-mouth . . . referrals. Whatever it's called, it's the preferred mode for most creative firms. And that's okay—as long as it's not the primary or, worse, the only form of marketing. To illustrate why that can be a problem, let's take look at Renvii & Company, a six-person interactive firm enjoying plenty of business.

THE SITUATION. Aside from a Web site and a brochure for those inquiring about its services, Renvii spends nothing on marketing. Yet the phone still rings. One client tells another, who tells another, who tells another. And so on. That's the way it has been for five years now, and that's the plan for the future. Sounds ideal, doesn't it? What's to criticize? There are no dreaded telephone prospecting calls to make and fewer competitive bids to agonize over. With no marketing expenses, including non-billable selling time, profits should be higher, too.

WHAT NEEDS TO BE CONSIDERED. Like so much in life, what seems to be at first, actually isn't. When a firm relies exclusively on referrals for new business, there are more downsides than upsides.

Less efficiency. Referrals are notoriously unpredictable. Yet predictability is the crucial element in efficient productivity. Without knowing how much work of what type to expect, a firm's principal will find that workflow and scheduling are disorganized and in constant flux. Even more important, firms with inconsistent workflow typically have higher labor costs. Because there's no "normal" workflow, there's no way to be staffed efficiently. The result is that employees are often either overcommitted and being paid over-time, or underutilized and being paid for time that's non-billable.

Lower profitability. It is true that Renvii saves on marketing expenses. But it is also true that its operational costs are substantially higher because of lower efficiency. What Renvii and many other firms fail to appreciate is that when it's done well, marketing is not a cost (a profit subtraction); rather, it is an investment (a profit addition). In short, its costs are more than made up for by the increase in business profits. Also, and at least as important although impossible to calculate, is the potential of lost-opportunity profits. These are the bigger jobs and better clients that usually only come through active solicitation.

Fewer opportunities. It is a rare creative firm that is totally satisfied with its current clients and projects. Nor should one be. The essence of creativity is new challenges; the essence of business is new opportunities. Referrals fall short in both counts. Firms that rely on them usually end up doing much the same types of work for much the same types of clients. How so? Because individuals who provide referrals normally do so to others who operate at their own business level or lower. And they usually make such referrals for familiar types of work. Referral business tends to move down the desirability scale over time. Moreover, doing the same types of projects for the same types of clients is creatively uninspiring and will likely pigeonhole a firm to future clients.

Abdicating control. The more aspects of its operations a firm controls, the better it is positioned for success. Whom it works with on what projects is perhaps the most crucial area of control. Referrals take control away from the firm and hand it to over to clients. When a firm relies on referrals, it ceases being proactive—deciding whom it wants to work with under what conditions. Instead, it becomes reactive—putting aside what's best for itself in favor of what's best for outsiders.

THE REMEDY. The above comments do not intend to make a case against referrals. Indeed, referrals should be an essential part of every firm's business mix, even solicited from happy clients when appropriate. A stable creative business needs referrals as a balance and supplement to its marketing activities. Further, active marketing programs actually increase the number and quality of referrals by reminding past clients of a firm's capabilities. Referrals are only a problem when they become a firm's primary source of business, as is the case with Renvii.

What's the right mix of referral versus solicited business? It depends on many factors, including a firm's size, its obligations, how much of its business comes from regular clients, and the regularity and desirability of referrals.

As a benchmark, though, referrals probably shouldn't average more than 50 percent of a firm's new business. Finally, Renvii and other firms that depend on referrals should keep in mind a disturbing statistic: the drying up of a referrals pipeline is among the major reasons why creative businesses fail.

#3 LACKING CONTINUITY

Lucinda has no problem with marketing per se. Indeed, she does what's necessary to drum up business for her three-person design firm. But addressing the need for more work through a sudden flurry of activity is never the best approach. Being smart trumps hustling more.

THE SITUATION. As in all creative firms, the workflow and income of Lucinda's are inconsistent. Sometimes there's a lot in the pipeline; at other times there's little or nothing. Lucinda's viewpoint is that it's foolish to waste time and money on something for which there is no immediate need. So she waits until she starts to see a drying out of the pipeline, and then she gets busy contacting former clients and making cold calls. And it works. Business picks up. As it does, she cuts back on her efforts and expenditures until they're no longer needed. It is a cycle that she has come to think of as natural.

WHAT NEEDS TO BE CONSIDERED. Lucinda is right in one sense. The roller-coaster effect, sometimes referred to as feast-or-famine, is inherent in businesses that offer occasional services. In contrast to product-based or commodity-based businesses, which are relatively stable, demand fluctuates. But this doesn't mean it can't be minimized. A primary function of a creative firm's marketing should be to even out fluctuating demand so that it matches consistent supply. Good marketing efforts will do this. Bad ones will either fail or, worse, exacerbate the problem.

There are also two other factors that a creative firm's marketing should address. One is the fact that the larger and more lucrative projects are, the less often they come along. For instance, a large Web site redo for a client may only surface once every couple of years. In contrast, less lucrative projects, such as small brochures and ads, happen regularly.

The second factor is that few clients actually do a search for the best firm to handle their account or project. Most commonly, they ask firms they are already aware of to submit proposals, or they select one based on familiarity. Essentially, firms that clients are most likely to remember are the ones most likely to get a nod. In other words, out-of-memory equates to out-of-consideration.

THE REMEDY. For the reasons cited above, inconsistent marketing is inefficient marketing. This does not mean that it doesn't work, just that it works less well and at a higher price. So a firm's marketing emphasis should not be just on what works, but also on what works *best*.

What defines efficiency versus inefficiency? Consider this: there are two fundamental ways in which a firm's marketing time and money can be allocated. One way involves doing big things less often; the other involves doing small things more often. The former is called opting for impact; the latter, opting for frequency. Either way—impact or frequency—the effort and expense can be the same. But the results usually aren't. Many firms, Lucinda's included, make the wrong choice: they go for bigger efforts less often. That's because the time they make available for marketing is limited, the need is not always constant, and splashy promotions are more fun to work on and create more buzz.

But the price tag for the lack of continuity can be high. In Lucinda's case, limiting marketing to when she sees a need results in uneven orders and workflow. Her approach enhances, rather than reduces, the very roller-coaster effect she should be trying to minimize. Equally costly is the fact that sporadic marketing is hit or miss. Except for clients who happen to be looking when Lucinda is active, much of her activities go unnoticed. It normally takes many contacts before a client is well aware of a firm and its capabilities. Client memory is also short- lived, and there's high turnover among personnel. So to be "top of the mind" when a client is choosing a supplier not only requires overcoming the initial awareness threshold, but necessitates maintaining it as well. In addition, with only occasional activity there's little of the multiplier effect that comes with consistent activity. In short, by limiting her marketing activity not only does Lucinda spend more, but she also gets less. Frequent contact increases the odds of getting business and lowers the cost of getting it.

What's the lesson here for other firms? The buying patterns of creative services clients are occasional and protracted. In such an environment, smart marketers eschew occasional efforts in favor of regular ones. A marketing-savvy creative firm never allows prospective clients to forget about it.

#4 HAVING UNREALISTIC EXPECTATIONS

How much business, how fast, can a creative firm expect from its marketing activities? When firms aren't realistic, they not only waste money on what's ineffective but also become discouraged about future efforts.

THREE SITUATIONS. To set the stage for some reality benchmarks, the following scenarios relate the experiences of principals from three firms.

No awareness. Harry and Henry started a new ad agency with two clients six months ago. To get the word out, they've sent an announcement mailing, drafted a press release for the media, and started a monthly "e-zine" that goes to those whose e-mail addresses they obtained from past contacts. They've also networked at industry events and blanketed award shows (several of their entries have won). Despite this, they've had no inquiries. When they've made cold calls, prospects have never heard of them. Shouldn't they be better known by now?

Few leads. To revive business at Michelle's three-employee design firm, she bought a mailing list with the names of a hundred local marketing managers. She used it to send a personally addressed letter seeking an appointment, enclosed a reply card, and followed up with phone calls. Of the hundred letters, she netted six appointments. So far, they've produced no new business. Wasn't this a lot of effort for little result?

Telemarketing disconnect. Before starting her marketing communications firm, Jan was in sales. So she's not turned off by cold-calling. But she has been turned off by the results it yields. Cold-calling hasn't paid off in enabling her four-person operation to move up the ladder to better clients and bigger projects. Most of the time she can't get through, and when she does the prospects are uninterested. What's she doing wrong?

WHAT NEEDS TO BE CONSIDERED. The marketing process can be frustrating and easily misunderstood, especially when there is pressure to land new business. A helpful analogy is that it's like growing a garden. How bountiful the crop will be depends on doing proper preparation, planting the right seeds, and maintaining constant care. Luck doesn't hurt, either. And like a garden, some marketing efforts will pay off quickly, then wither away; others will be slow to bloom but will remain long-lasting.

It also helps to remember the way that clients choose a creative firm. For most clients, it is an infrequent—if not rare—event. It's a considered—not impulse—decision, too. This means that the more visible and better known a firm is, the better its chances of scoring business. The relevance here is that in each of the three situations, clients' lack of familiarity with the firm is the common problem. What's different with each situation is how the problem should be addressed.

THE REMEDIES. Following are some realistic expectations, along with suggestions for improvement.

Building awareness. Because of greater client risk, agency accounts (advertising, PR, and interactive) take longer on average to land than project-based accounts, such as design. So six months is not unusual. This said, the clock has barely started ticking for Harry and Henry. So far their awareness-building efforts have been directed mostly at others in the industry—their competitors. To become known among potential clients, they need to immediately refocus on the larger business community. Schmoozing at industry events and winning awards is great, but those are no substitute for addressing potential clients.

Getting leads. An appointment-soliciting mailing is typically the most cost-effective way for firms to get immediate leads. Six appointments from a hundred-piece mailing (6 percent) is also better than average. A well-written personal letter to a qualified list should return around 5 percent when there's both a postpaid reply card and a follow-up telephone call. A typical conversion ratio is about one out of every five appointments. So Michelle shouldn't be discouraged; she might be having bad luck. She should continue the mailings by buying another hundred names. If that is not possible, she should wait several weeks and re-mail to those who didn't respond the first time. Sooner or later, the law of averages will catch up. When it does, the cost-per-new-client will prove to be low.

Getting connected. The effectiveness of telemarketing is heavily influenced by how well known a firm is. Calls from recognized ones get through where others don't. Good sales reps (business development persons) from recognized firms contacting qualified clients score as high or higher than one appointment out of every ten calls. So Jan's problem is probably that her firm is not well enough known. The long-term fix is to develop a promotional strategy that will get her firm better known to those she calls. The short-term fix is to simply stick with it. Telemarketing is a numbers game. If she makes enough calls, she will score some business. Since the costs are low, the major downside is avoiding discouragement.

#5 DISLIKING SELLING

Creative firm principals are apt to consider selling as the least attractive part of marketing—perhaps necessary, but not highly regarded or rewarded. This is a shame, because doing it on the cheap invariably means doing it ineptly, as Charlie's experience illustrates.

THE SITUATION. In ten years, Charlie has grown his firm from just himself to seven full-time employees. During this period, his "selling" has consisted only of "showing the book" to referrals and prospects generated through networking and occasional promotions.

As the firm has grown, though, there's been an increasing need to make workflow consistent. Charlie also has had less and less time for creative direction and management. In short, he's come to recognize the need for a business development (BDP) or sales person. She or he could cold-call and make presentations, leaving Charlie involved with only the last stage of prospect contact, which he enjoys.

Hiring a former employee part-time several years ago was an expensive failure. Recently Charlie hired a former printing saleswoman full-time. The arrangement is that she gets a salary of $400 weekly, plus a 6 percent commission on fee income on the first job from a client and 4 percent on all subsequent ones. After six months, Charlie has paid out $14,400 in salary and $18,350 in commissions earned on $367,000 of sales. The saleswoman's income to date is $32,750, which works out to $65,500 annualized. She has been unhappy with this arrangement and wants to renegotiate. He doesn't. In fact, he has been somewhat disappointed with her performance ($734,000 in sales annualized).

WHAT NEEDS TO BE CONSIDERED. Principals are often dissatisfied with the salespeople they hire because of unreal expectations, ineffective incentives (compensation), or both. Occasionally there is also a personality clash—the extroverted go-getter (hunter) confronting the introverted doer (gatherer). Regardless of the situation, the reality is that for project-based firms to get a dependable influx of new work and clients, they should have one acquirer (a full-time business development person) for every four or five doers (creative employees). An alternative is a principal devoted full-time to sales.

Because everyone's job depends on sales, those with this responsibility should be professionally qualified and have internal stature and compensation similar to those of the firm's most senior creative employees. To earn their keep, in addition to prospecting these salespeople should be directly involved in setting a firm's marketing direction and consulted when new creative talent is hired. They also should be largely responsible for pricing and scheduling their projects. And they should stay in contact with their clients during production, but turn daily responsibility over to a project manager.

It normally takes several months before efforts begin to pay off; new salespersons should have at least six months to prove they have what it takes. During this period, there should be progress in making good contacts and an increasing number of orders. After half a year, though, they should either be earning their keep or be well on the way toward doing so.

THE REMEDY. In project-based firms (e.g., design), it usually works better for both parties if business development persons work on commission. Full commission of 15 percent of fee-based gross income is the norm. A little less desirable is a combination of salary and commission, depending on individual preferences and responsibilities—for instance, some salary when account service is involved. Generally, the higher the percentage of commission income, the more incentive the salesperson will have to perform.

According to this benchmark, Charlie is underpaying. His salesperson's $367,000 in bookings should have earned her about $55,000 in income to date, not $32,000. If he doesn't change his compensation formula, he risks losing a valuable contributor. This could be a big loss, as good salespeople are extraordinarily hard to find. A better arrangement would be to keep her salary the same but change the future commission percentage to 8 percent on new business and 6 percent on repeat business. Doing this should provide the incentive necessary to keep her happy and productive.

#6 PRESENTING POORLY

Landing a new project or client almost always requires a presentation—a new business pitch. Many turn out to be unsuccessful because of a lack of preparation and a misunderstanding of what clients really want.

TWO SITUATIONS. There are two ways to pitch new business. One focuses primarily on a firm's portfolio; the other focuses on its processes.

Wecandoit Inc. is a two-person studio going after a variety of print and interactive work. Their small clients want to see proof of competence. The studio addresses this request through portfolio presentations showing what they have done for other clients.

GetNoticed LLC is an eight-person PR agency. Their clients are most interested in how the agency works. So their presentations emphasize their process of interacting closely with clients.

WHAT NEEDS TO BE CONSIDERED. Whether a presentation emphasizes a firm's portfolio or its process (neither is mutually exclusive), there are three general rules to follow. First, the more a presenter knows about a prospect's business, the more receptive the prospect will be. The prospect will quickly dismiss a polished presentation from someone who doesn't know much about her firm; she'll overlook many flaws from someone who does. Second, it is important to say what the prospect wants to hear, not what the presenter wants to say. "Here's what we did" is dismissive of the prospect's interests. Far more persuasive is "We've helped many clients similar to you achieve their objectives by (describe strategy)." Third, it is essential is to spend as much time discussing prospects' needs as your firm's capabilities. The more prospects participate in a presentation, the more convinced they will be.

PORTFOLIO REMEDIES. Presentation blunders made by Wecandoit's principal, Sarah, are typical and easy to correct.

Trying to be too businesslike. Sarah wants to make sure that prospects take her seriously. So she overcompensates by holding down the amount of small talk and getting right into her presentations. By being too businesslike she makes it harder for prospects to warm up to her and trust her. Only half of a prospect's impression normally comes from a firm's portfolio samples. The rest comes from personally liking and trusting the presenter.

Focusing on the wrong examples. Sarah leads with and concentrates on showing her firm's best work. No problem there, right? Wrong. A firm's best work isn't necessarily what will be most persuasive. Her presentations should be about what prospective clients want to see, not what Sarah wants to show. Appropriate good is almost always better than inappropriate best.

Showing too much. Sarah's passion is design, which comes across well in her presentations. Unfortunately, it also causes her to show many examples, which she describes in too much detail. A half dozen examples should be all that's needed to show style, demonstrate versatility, and draw out a prospect's interests. Unless requested otherwise, a portfolio showing shouldn't take longer than about thirty minutes—long enough to say what is important; short enough to show respect for a prospect's time. Long presentations cause clients to tune out, and they demonstrate a lack of time-sensitivity and discipline.

PROCESS REMEDIES. Now let's look at the mistakes that GetNoticed's principal, Terry, made when describing the process of working with his firm.

Not showcasing the team. As the chief honcho, Terry believes it is his role to explain how the agency works. Yet a solo presentation belies the very premise of a process orientation—interaction and teamwork. A three-person presentation would be more appropriate and effective: Terry to do the introduction and close, an account executive to talk about seamlessly working together, and the firm's creative director to explain the development process.

Relying on aids. As talking points and to highlight how his agency works, Terry uses presentation visuals (e.g., PowerPoint), as do many clients. Presentation visuals are necessary when speaking to large groups. But for smaller ones they more often serve as presentation crutches, destroying the personal rapport that's a crucial element in soliciting business. They should be avoided in most new business pitches.

Scant partnering emphasis. A productive relationship in a process-driven business requires client and creative firm to work closely together as a team—that is, to function as partners. Presenters who are not specific about what their firm expects of its clients (their partners) can lose respect and be eliminated from consideration. And should the firm win the account anyway, not having clearly defined expectations ahead of time will cause numerous problems later on.

#7 AVOIDING CLOSING

The end of a new business pitch is the moment of truth. In Equidad's case, everything goes well and the prospective clients seem impressed. But often there's no commitment. To come right out and ask seems crass. But is it really?

THE SITUATION. Equidad Ltd. is a twelve-person branding firm. Their presentations, handled by one of two business development persons, go well. But their conversions—presentation into project—are only about 30 percent. How can they increase their closing ratio?

WHAT NEEDS TO BE CONSIDERED. New business presentations should have three parts. The first involves breaking the ice or warming up. It involves becoming comfortable, assessing the audience, and developing rapport. This part is important because the likability factor strongly affects the presenter's credibility and the audience's receptivity. The second part—the major part of a presentation—is its substance. It involves finding out the prospective client's needs, showing work done for similar clients, explaining the firm's processes, maybe even going over pricing.

The third part of a presentation is the ending or close. It's usually the most difficult because it is the least familiar and is often associated with aggressive selling. Neither need be the case. Closing can be both natural and professional. When done correctly, it is a seamless part of the presentation that reflects positively on the presenter and his or her firm. Think of it this way: when you don't ask for the order, there's a strong possibility that a competitor won't be as reluctant to do so.

THE REMEDIES. First, a reality check: all a good closing will ever do is accelerate what's inevitable or provide the tipping point of acceptance. It won't rescue a bad presentation. So Equidad's concern might have deeper roots than presentation closing. Surveys reported in *Creative Business* newsletter find that firms average being successful in about 50 percent of multi-bid pitches to new clients. The success rate in competitive pitches to regular clients is about 75 percent (three in four). Firms in very competitive situations often average as low as 25 percent (one in four). Equidad's closing rate is not far from the norm. Nonetheless, they should rethink how they are handling presentation closing.

Recognizing procrastination. Most people, clients included, find it easier to put off or even say no than to commit themselves. So a presenter should never automatically accept a delayed decision, a "we'll call you when we're ready," or even a "no thanks." Instead, he or she should look for ways to help the prospective client come to a positive decision.

Being moderately aggressive. Truth is, most clients like being pursued. Few things are more complimentary than a suitor being enthusiastic about the possibility of working together and asking for the order to get started. This is especially true when making a presentation at the client's request.

Overcoming reluctance. This can often be the biggest closing hurdle of all. Presenters are often too polite to come right out and ask for the business. Or they're afraid that doing so will make them appear desperate. It is not impolite, nor will it appear desperate, particularly to clients who are also involved in marketing.

Wrapping up the presentation. After thanking an audience for their time and attention, every presentation should end something like this: "I hope you sensed from my presentation how positive we feel about our ability to meet your challenge, and how much we would like the opportunity of working with you. Do you have any further questions? Is what I have (said) (shown) enough to allow you to make a decision today?"

UNDERSTANDING THE WORLD OF BRANDING

It would be unusual, to say the least, to be in the communications business today and not encounter the word "branding." It is a word that's much overused, a concept that's often misunderstood. And therein lies a danger. Individuals who aren't careful discussing branding, particularly when dealing with knowledgeable clients, can find their credibility being questioned. Conversely, those who understand its many facets can be much more effective in helping their clients. They can also be much more effective in promoting their own services. So let's clear up some of the misconceptions and ambiguities surrounding branding. (For more on branding in the context of a firm's marketing strategies, see Chapter 2; for branding as a presentation differentiator, see Chapter 10. Also, many branding terms are defined in Appendix IV.)

FIRST, DEFINITIONS

The connotations and everyday use of language, not dictionary definitions, are what count in the real world. Nonetheless, knowing what's correct can provide a good feeling for what's appropriate.

A BRAND. As used in marketing, the noun "brand" defines a distinctive name or symbol (trademark) that identifies and differentiates a certain manufacturer or its products. A brand can denote a single product, an entire line of products, or an organization. When registered (with the Patent and Trademark Office in the United States, and with comparable agencies in other countries), brands also have a legal status. They are intellectual property owned by their registrants, and their use is legally proscribed. Use is authorized only to their owners and only in the ways and for the purposes for which the brands were registered. Even when not registered, a name or symbol used consistently in commerce over an extended period can acquire legal status. Although the type, recognition, impact, and value of brands vary, they all have one thing in common: they define a specific entity. In most cases, this entity has legal protection.

BRANDING. In contrast to the above, the gerund "branding" defines a process. Like most processes, it can be whatever those involved say it is. There are no hard definitions, no legal considerations. Generally, though, as practiced by creative firms, branding falls into two broad categories. In the more traditional category, branding is just a new way to describe what used to be called identity, or corporate ID, work. Think of this as branding with a small b. It can encompass something as simple and straightforward as developing a small logo or mark. Or, at the other end of the scale, as complex as developing a corporate identity program—investigational research, developmental refinement, implementation standards, occasionally even manufacturing. Whatever the case, any firm involved in establishing or modifying an identity is certainly involved in branding.

Yet, while many disparate factors and talents can be involved in this process, and invoices can run well into the six figures, identity work—branding with a small b—is primarily visual. This limitation is what differentiates it from an all-encompassing process—Branding with a capital B. Increasingly, particularly in consumer areas, this type of branding is seen as a process that goes well beyond just providing visual distinctions. It refers to providing a well-coordinated and consistent approach to everything a customer experiences. It is nothing less than a way of doing business. In this context, visual items (logos, trade dress, etc.) play an important role through meaningful and compelling differentiation. But so, too, do many, often intangible attributes as varied as product design, product mix, pricing, sales environment, and customer interactions.

EXAMPLES. The familiar, worldwide Starbucks coffee chain has distinctive stores and a logo and trade dress (identity) that visually differentiate its products from others'. There is more to its branding, however. In addition, there's a distinctive product mix, tiered pricing, retail ambience, and numerous other experiential factors. In their entirety, these make up the uniquely Starbucks "brand experience" that cuts across language and culture barriers. Starbucks' branding is not just about well-designed products and stores. Starbucks also exemplifies a young company that has grown through controlling—branding—the entire customer recognition/interaction process.

Other companies have used branding to reshape, reorient, and remake their organizations. FedEx is a recent example. While creatives might have been more attuned than other people to its redesigned logo and distinctive new color palettes, these were but a small part of a total effort that encompassed everything down to reclassifying services and reshaping customer experiences. FedEx's rebranding was not just about repainting its trucks. FedEx exemplifies a mature organization rebranding itself to keep its lead in a highly competitive marketplace.

These two examples—Starbucks, whose branding was orchestrated primarily in-house, and FedEx, whose branding was orchestrated primarily outside—go well beyond the needs of most clients. Nonetheless, they illustrate that while great brands always have consistency in design and communications, considerably more is involved in the branding process. It is a lesson that's as relevant to small clients as it is to large ones.

OVERKILL? Brands and brand management have been around for a century. But branding, particularly in its all-encompassing mode, is essentially a product of the last couple decades. Much of its current popularity is driven by increasingly competitive marketing environments, especially the one in which large commodity businesses operate. Much is also just plain hype—a new name for familiar services. Few creative firms today don't genuflect to the branding God; many actively promote their expertise in it, and some have made it part of their identities.

In this sense, creative firms are in tune with the times. A Web search will turn up several sites devoted to branding. As of this writing, at least three magazines and one scholarly journal cover the subject exclusively: *Brand Marketing, Brandweek, Personal Branding*, and the *Journal of Brand Management*. Amazon.com carries nearly three hundred books on the topic. And branding is a hot subject at marketing seminars and conferences. Branding has even been employed by governments to improve international perceptions (e.g., "Cool Britannia").

So it is not a bad horse to ride, as long as you ride it carefully and knowledgeably.

REALITY. In its essence, branding is about the marketplace perception of value—for sellers, establishing it; for buyers, assessing it.

For sellers (brand sponsors or owners), there are several value aspects. From the marketing perspective, branding means easier customer recognition and faster sales. From the financial perspective, it means the security of predictable income. From the legal perspective, it means ensuring that an organization's most valuable assets are protected. For buyers (customers), the value of branding is in its shorthand: it offers easy product recognition and quality assurance in marketplaces cluttered with choices.

With this as an overview, we can now consider the ways a creative firm can best brand its own business, and what beyond creative talent clients look for when evaluating a firm's branding credentials.

IMPROVING YOUR OWN BRAND MANAGEMENT

There's no way to say this diplomatically: as a group, creatives, most of whom talk the branding talk and walk the branding walk for clients, are poor managers of their own brands. Branding irony—doing for others what you don't do for yourself—defines the situation.

It is easy to forget that every business with a name—whether a small creative boutique or a multinational employing tens of thousands—is also a brand. Moreover, every brand is defined and constantly redefined—if not proactively by its owners, then by its customers. Of course, what techniques are appropriate and how they are applied differ from business type to business type. Unlike many clients, creative firms are service businesses, not product businesses; there are no retail environments to consider, no mass-media opportunities to exploit. Moreover, creative firms are rarely multinational or cross-cultural. But if branding efforts will never be as far reaching for creative firms, they are no less important.

Think of brand management as two separate areas that complement each other. The first is everything that clients don't directly experience—a firm's internal branding decisions. Primarily, they determine how a firm positions itself in the marketplace. The second is everything that clients do experience— all the strategies a firm uses to implement its positioning (branding) decisions.

A FIRM'S POSITIONING. How a firm should be positioned—in essence, its branding strategy—is one of only two responsibilities that principals should almost never delegate. (The other is financial control.) Positioning involves identifying a market environment and then defining the firm in ways that enhance its standing within that environment.

The process. The first step involves acknowledging long-term market trends. This means placing more emphasis on creative services that are strategically driven, and less on those that are craft driven. However else you may decide to position your firm, don't make the mistake of being on the wrong side of a shifting marketplace. Positioning is about your firm's future, not the past or even what's current.

Next, consider the direction in which you would like to take the firm. The smaller it is, the more this will be a personal decision. Where do you want to be in five years or ten? (For example: What type of clients? What type of work? How much or little specialization by activity or industry?) Now, take an educated guess as to how your firm is, or would be, perceived by desired clients with these opportunities. Finally, take a look at how competitive firms are positioned.

The analysis. The purpose of the positioning process is to encourage realistic thinking about effective ways to reach selected clients. In doing this, be careful not to define your firm as something it clearly isn't just so you can attract a broader business base. Such attempts almost always backfire. However, don't be afraid to push the creative or business envelope a bit either. Positioning is about enhancing perceptions. Reality should be a foundation, but not a limitation. As long as you don't carry the positioning process to excess, you are what you say you are.

BRANDING IMPLEMENTATION. Unlike positioning, branding is not a process. Rather, it is a singular and consistent context, theme, or approach to all external contacts and communication. It is the application of a firm's positioning (brand essence) throughout its marketing strategy, marketing plan, and more. Through the use of a common theme, branding enables a firm to define itself instead of being defined by default through the market. Moreover, when based on sound positioning, branding does this in a way that enhances the firm's market standing and share. There are three major elements to successful brand implementation: consistency, inclusiveness, and regularity. Although these are common to every organization and branding challenge, there are specific factors that creative firms need to consider.

Consistency. This is the holy grail of branding. Without a uniformly consistent message, there is no branding. Consistency does not mean that every promotion or medium should carry exactly the same message. In fact, quite the opposite is true. Branding effectiveness is increased when a variety of techniques and approaches serve to keep messages fresh and interesting. Nonetheless, the central theme, the brand essence, should come across in everything. The same is true with new business presentations and ongoing client relationships. How a firm's brand essence is conveyed should take different forms to best fit the situation. But the underlying theme should never change.

Inclusiveness. Each time you touch the client (figuratively), you communicate something about your brand. To ensure branding success, a firm's positioning statement should underlie and reinforce every form of external contact and communication. It is easy to understand how branding includes stationery, Web sites, promotions, new business presentations, and client relationships. Not quite as easy is understanding that branding also includes a firm's sophistication level, its operations style, its facilities, the way its personnel conduct themselves, the way in which its work is presented, and the extent of its after-project follow-up. All these are but a few of the more obvious impression points.

Regularity. Any firm that follows branding principles is better off than one that doesn't. Market consistency always has a multiplier effect. But building a brand requires going beyond just ensuring consistency in a firm's materials and everyday client contact. It requires regular promotional activity, too. How much activity depends on how well the firm is known and whether its objective is to create market perceptions, to change them, or merely to enhance them. Regardless of the situation, regular activity is required. Both establishing and sustaining brand awareness must involve client contact of some type at least two or three times each year.

KEYS TO ENSURING A BRAND MANAGER'S LOYALTY

Responsibility for a client's branding is typically at a high level—senior executive or brand manager. Pleasing these individuals involves recognizing several specific needs and interests.

BEING FLEXIBLE. Unlike most other types of clients, these individuals typically have few additional responsibilities. Their primary, often sole, task is to increase a brand's performance, which directly affects their careers. While they welcome strategic input and creative innovation, when all is said and done they expect their directions to be closely followed. There's no room here for prima donnas or those who can't work well with pragmatically oriented MBAs.

LEAVING A LITTLE ON THE TABLE. The branding community can be close-knit, and your firm will probably be around for a while. Therefore, not only are referrals important, but you're also likely to cross paths with some individuals several times, often in new contexts or organizations. So don't get greedy when negotiating project prices, especially with well-heeled clients. A small pricing compromise today can be a great investment in getting more business tomorrow.

TREATING THEIR MONEY LIKE IT'S YOUR OWN. Branding often involves extended, high-profile work that's substantially budgeted. This is often the case for large organizations. But spending a lot of money doesn't mean that a brand manager will be any less cost sensitive. In fact, because he or she may have profit center responsibility, there could be even greater cost sensitivity. You'll win loyalty by watching every penny as closely as if it were coming out of a child's piggy bank.

USING THE PRODUCT. Branding or rebranding a product requires a certain amount of investigational research—acquiring knowledge of the product and its marketing environment. But knowledge of a product gained by doing research is different from that gained by actually using the product in the real world. To a brand manager, the product is his or her "baby." Brand managers want your firm to be nearly as familiar with its features as they are. They'll also appreciate objective comments and criticisms. You'll only get to really know a product when you use it day in and day out.

FOLLOWING UP. It's always good business to inquire later about the effectiveness of any project in meeting a client's needs. But it is even more so with branding. Never forget, this is a revenue-crucial interest for most clients. Your continuing interest in implementation and market success can make or break any relationship. The best way to sell the next branding project is to stay in touch with the last one.

APPENDIX III

SAMPLES AND FORMS

Full-size, editable copies of the examples shown in this appendix can be downloaded for your own use from www.creativebusiness.com/marketbook. html.

Press release. Press releases on newsworthy events provide indirect marketing by helping to keep a firm's name known. (Referenced in Chapter 3.)

Sample Standard Press Release Form

(print on letterhead)

For more information, contact: Morris Minor

DATE: June 15, 0000
RELEASE DATE: July 1, 0000

SELDOM-DONE GRAPHICS REDESIGNS STAFF O'LIFE PACKAGING

St. Paul, MN. Seldom-Done Graphics has redesigned the packaging for Plains Baking Company's popular Staff O' Life brand all-natural breads. According to Morris Minor, Principal of Seldom-Done, the new design represents, "An evolution in combining contemporary graphics with more extensive consumer nutrition information."

Plains Baking first introduced the Staff O' Life line of six all-natural breads five years ago. The Company initiated the packaging redesign this year to provide even more of the healthy-eating tips and nutritional information that have become increasingly popular with consumers, as well as a hallmark of Staff O' Life products.

The newly-packaged Staff O' Life breads will be first distributed the week of July 15.

Seldom-Done Graphics provides packaging and other graphic design services to firms throughout the upper midwest from offices in St. Paul.

# # #

ENCL: photograph with caption

Basic business/marketing plan. For small organizations, business and marketing plans are more or less synonymous. (Referenced in Chapter 4.)

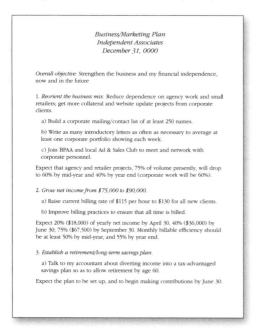

Marketing plan worksheet. Helping small clients to establish marketing plans can burnish a firm's marketing credibility. (Referenced in Chapter 4.)

Typical business/marketing plan. For most creative services organizations, marketing is a major portion of a yearly business plan, as shown by four of this firm's five objectives. (Referenced in Chapter 4.)

Marketing Plan
Dedicated Associates

Prepared: December 15, 0000   Reviewed/Updated:

Summary:

Operations: The addition of Jerry Talentoso as a junior designer in November has eased our occasional overtime crunch by assisting Sally Doue and Joe Begaafd. Keeping Karen Specialist busy next year might pose a problem, depending on what happens with Big Client. Helen Codego should see an increase in web projects in 0000, but should be able to handle it with outside programming help. My dual role as creative director and new business development person is becoming more and more of a problem.

Finances: Income for 0000 is projected to come in at 10% higher than 0000. Expenses are expected to be about the same as 0000, but monthly expenses are now running nearly 15% higher. The addition of Jerry has reduced our overtime burden, but this savings has only covered about half his salary and benefit costs. Maintaining profitability in 0000 looks like it will be a problem.

Market: Client activity appears stable. We have so far worked with five new ones in 0000 as opposed to four new in 0000. But only one new client has provided more than one project. More significantly, the new management team at Big Client has indicated that they intend to do a review of all the corporation's outside suppliers after the first of the year. A cut-back by them could be partially covered by more web projects.

Needs: Increased salary and benefits costs have to be covered through new business, increased billing rates, or better billable efficiency. We need to try harder to keep the business from Big Client, as well as develop a broader client base should they cut-back. Sales activity has to be separated from creative direction so workflow can be smoothed out and new clients developed.

Objective #1: Increase Income

Situation: Our hourly billing rate of $135 per hour has not been raised for four years. During this time inflation has averaged 2% yearly. Our current pricing appears to be about average among comparable competitors, so there appears to be an opportunity to raise prices without undue risk.

Goal: Increase gross income by $40,000 annually.

Plan: 1) Raise billing rate to $150 effective January 1st

Expect: 1) Gross income will be at least $200,000 by June 30th.
             2) Gross income will be at least $500,000 by December 31st.

Assumptions: Business volume will be stable, and billable efficiency will improve during the year.

Objective #2: Improve Billable Efficiency

Situation: Employees are lax in accounting for billable time, often forgetting, assigning it to house accounts, or working after hours and not recording it. This has resulted in unacceptably low billable efficiency of only 49%.

Goal: Achieve 55% billable efficiency by year end.

Plan: 1) Research and purchase management software in January to better track billable time on each project.
             2) Require all employees to track working hours electronically.

Expect: 1) All employees to be fully conversant and operational on the new software by June 30.
             2) Billable efficiency will be at or exceed 55% by September 1st.

Assumption: The volume of work in 0000 will at least equal that of 0000.

Objective #3: Protect Our Big Client Business

Situation: Big Client currently accounts for 22% of income and as much as 30% of profitability. While this concentration would normally be acceptable, their new marketing team could reduce or eliminate this business.

Goal: Keep Big Client's business.

Plan: 1) Hold meetings to introduce their new marketing team to the variety and depth of our capabilities, and how our knowledge of their business allows us to do better work less expensively.
             2) Offer a retainer as a way to reduce their costs while also locking in their business.

Expect: 1) To hold the meetings by February 1st.
             2) To hear their decision on their 0000 suppliers by March 1st.

Assumption: Big Client is open minded about choosing suppliers.

Objective #4: Prepare To Replace Big Client's Business

Situation: If Big Client decides to reduce or eliminate much of the business they provide us, it could lead to drastically reduced volume, and the possibility of staff reduction. Yet developing too much replacement business could exceed our capacity should they decide to keep us.

Goal: Prepare to find replacements for Big Client.

Plan: 1) Update our previously-successful direct mailer.
             2) Do a mailing to our contact list soon after we hear that Big Client will cut our business substantially.
             3) Make follow-up sales calls as necessary.

Expect: 1) To hear Big Client's decision by March 1st.
             2) To replace half of the revenue loss with new work by July 1st, the balance by December 31st.

Assumption: Staff reduction should not be necessary.

Objective #5: Divorce Sales And Creative Direction

Situation: The effect of having Dedicated's sales efforts and creative direction handled by one person results in each function being short-changed. If the firm is to grow, an increased and consistent sales effort will be necessary.

Goal: A full-time, dedicated sales effort.

Plan: 1) Keep personally doing sales and delegate creative direction.
             2) Promote Karen Specialist to creative director.
             3) Assign Jerry Talentoso to assist Karen with Big Client's business if required.
             4) Increase sales calls.

Expect: 1) To discuss this arrangement with Karen in January.
             2) To make the transition by the end of the first quarter (March).
             3) To increase new client sales calls by 25% by July 1st.

Assumption: Karen will want the additional responsibility.

Referral request letter. Referrals don't have to come by happenstance. You can generate them by sending letters to satisfied clients. (Referenced in Chapter 4.)

Client backgrounder. The more you know about a prospect up front, the better your chances of landing the business. Forms like this provide a way to organize client background information. (Referenced in Chapter 6.)

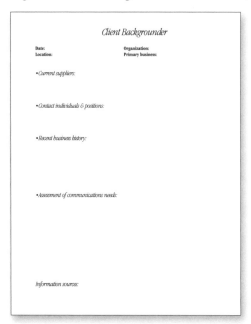

Prospecting letter. Sending a letter such as this, followed up with a tele-phone call, is an inexpensive and time-proven way for a firm to introduce itself to prospective clients. (Referenced in Chapter 6.)

Database record. Maintaining a history of all your firm's prospects and cli-ents is a crucial element in building long-lasting relationships. (Referenced in Chapter 6.)

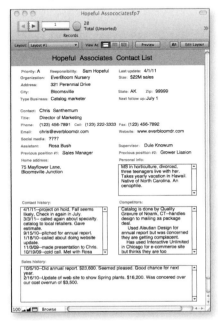

"How We Work Together." Providing pre-project information such as this is reassuring to prospective clients. (Referenced in Chapters 6, 10, and 12.)

Non-compete agreement. Although enforceability can vary, signed agreements provide a powerful deterrent to sales and other employees who might consider leaving a firm and taking its clients with them. (Referenced in Chapter 7.)

Value proposition worksheet. In competitive situations, being able to define and articulate what makes a firm a better value than others can be the difference between winning or losing a prospective client. (Referenced in Chapter 10.)

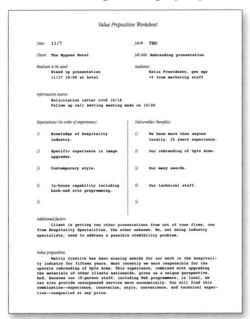

Value Proposition Worksheet

Date: 11/7   Job#: TBD

Client: The Bygone Hotel   Job title: Rebranding presentation

Medium to be used: Audience:
    Stand up presentation   Katie Frontdesko, gen mgr
    11/17 10:00 at hotel   +5 from marketing staff

Information source:
    Solicitation letter rcvd 10/18
    Follow up call setting meeting made on 10/20

Expectations (in order of importance):   Deliverables (benefits):

1) Knowledge of hospitality   1) We know more than anyone
    industry.   locally. 15 years experience.

2) Specific experience in image   2) Our rebranding of UpIn Arms.
    upgrades.

3) Contemporary style.   3) Our many awards.

4) In-house capability including   4) Our technical staff.
    back-end site programming.

5)   5)

Additional factors:
    Client is getting two other presentations from out of town firms, one
from Hospitality Specialities, the other unknown. We, not being industry
specialists, need to address a possible credibility problem.

Value proposition:
    Matrix Creative has been winning awards for our work in the hospitali-
ty industry for fifteen years. Most recently we were responsible for the
upscale rebranding of UpIn Arms. This experience, combined with upgrading
the materials of other clients nationwide, gives us a unique perspective.
And, because our 15-person staff, including Web programmers, is local, we
can also provide unsurpassed service more economically. You will find this
combination—experience, innovation, style, convenience, and technical expertise—unequalled at any price.

Creative brief questionnaire. Using an input form during a creative briefing can help ensure that you will address the client's objectives. (Referenced in Chapter 10.)

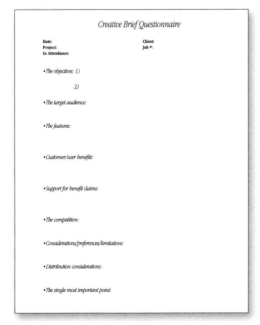

Creative Brief Questionnaire

Date: Client:
Project: Job #:
In Attendance:

• The objectives: 1)

              2)

• The target audience:

• The features:

• Customer/user benefits:

• Support for benefit claims:

• The competition:

• Considerations/preferences/limitations:

• Distribution considerations:

• The single most important point:

Creative review checklist. Used internally, this checklist ensures quality control; used externally, it shows clients that you have addressed their objectives. (Referenced in Chapters 10 and 14.)

Mission statement. In addition to serving internal purposes, a statement of a firm's guiding principles will impress many clients. (Referenced in Chapter 10.)

Agent agreement. Although not necessary to handle a client's advertising or public relations, an agent agreement provides a firm with specific authority to act on the client's behalf. (Referenced in Chapter 13.)

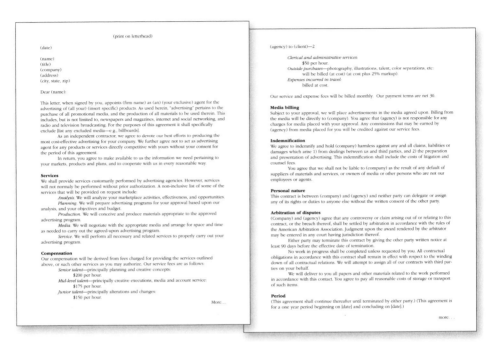

Estimating worksheet. A standard, repeatable approach to estimating makes the process more accurate and makes pricing easier to justify to clients. (Referenced in Chapter 13.)

Estimate letter. A simple description of what your firm will deliver, when, and for what cost should be all that is needed to get approval on projects under $3,000. (Referenced in Chapter 13.)

Letter of agreement. When signed, it is all that is normally needed to begin on projects from around $3,000 to $12,000. (Referenced in Chapter 13.)

(letterhead)

June 1, 0000

Mr. William Prospect
Vice President, Sales
Breakthrough Medical Products
198 Swansea Drive
Dayton, OH 45427

Dear Bill:

This letter will constitute an agreement for Squeamish Graphics to develop a single-page magazine advertisement and a Web page announcing the introduction of the CleanSlice Ligament Cutter. Placement of the ad in appropriate magazines and implementation of the web page on Breakthrough's web site will be handled by Breakthrough.

Schedule: The project will include the following on approximately the dates indicated:

July 1—Fact gathering meeting with your staff and appropriate personnel from the product development group.

July 10—Presentation of our ideas and conceptual approaches for review and input.

July 18—Presentation of final ad and Web page layouts.

July 19/August 1—Photography, artwork preparation, copywriting, electronic file development, and coding.

August 1/8—Approval routing at Breakthrough.

August 8/15—Final modifications and changes by Breakthrough.

August 15—Electronic files sent to Breakthrough's multimedia department for Web implementation.

more . . .

SQUEAMISH TO PROSPECT—2

September 1—Ad films sent to appropriate magazines by Squeamish from a list supplied by Breakthrough.

Fees: The following is an estimate of our fees for this project based on the information you've provided. Please note that if conditions or the schedule changes, the actual price may be higher or lower. We will, however, keep you informed of any change which exceeds 10 percent of the estimate.

Phase I—Research and concept development $1,750
Phase II—Photography, copywriting, and artwork $3,250
Phase III—Art direction, typography, and layouts $2,500
Phase IV—Electronic file and films $1,600

Expenses: Out-of-pocket expenses will be billed at a 25 percent mark up, which covers our handling costs. Such items normally include deliveries, service bureau charges, and long-distance phone calls.

We estimate total expenses for this project will be:$ _250

Estimated project cost: $9,350

Ownership. All original photographic film, including transparencies and negatives, remain the property of the photographer selected. All preparation materials, including original artwork and electronic files and printing films, remain the property of Squeamish Graphics. All ideas and concepts not used remain the property of Squeamish Graphics and may be used in the future as they deem appropriate.

Terms: Approximately one third of this estimate ($3,000) to be billed upon acceptance; approximately one third ($3,000) upon acceptance of final layouts; the balance upon completion of the project. If any phase of the project is delayed for longer than sixty days, we will bill for work completed.

All invoices are net, payable within 30 days of receipt. Interest of 1.5 percent per month may be charged on past-due accounts.

As I have previously indicated, I believe my firm's experience handling similar projects provides Squeamish Graphics with the expertise necessary to do an outstanding job for Breakthrough.

more . . .

SQUEAMISH TO PROSPECT—3

If this proposal meets with your approval, please indicate by signing and returning one copy to me. A purchase order should be initiated as soon as possible.

If you have any questions, please call.

Thanks for the opportunity to submit this proposal. I'm looking forward to working with you.

Sincerely,

I. M. Squeamish
Principal

Print proposal. Most projects exceeding $12,000 will need a multi-page proposal detailing the process, its schedule, and its price in a format similar to this (continued on following pages). (Referenced in Chapter 13.)

(letterhead)

A Proposal
To Produce A
Capability Brochure
For Security Financial Services

Prepared for
Sally D. Client
Director of Marketing Support
(date)

2

Assignment Background

Security Financial Services, a division of Security National Bank, provides personal investment counseling and special banking services for individuals whose net worth exceeds one million dollars. The division was founded in 1983 to provide both a broader range of custom products and services and more personal attention to high-deposit customers. Security was the first bank in South Florida to provide this service. Since that time, all banks in Security's market area have offered similar programs and most have promoted them aggressively.

To date, the three-hundred-plus customers of the division have been acquired solely through referrals by officers of the bank's fifteen retail outlets. There has been no advertising and there is no literature to explain the division's products and services, or how they differ from that offered by other, competitive banks.

3

Assignment Objectives

1) To broadly support a marketing campaign that will seek to double Security Financial Service's customer base within the next twelve months.

2) To fulfill the estimated 5,000 literature requests that will result from Security's "Talk to a Specialist" advertising campaign due to begin in December 0000 and run through April 0000. The material produced must key off the ad that will be producing the requests, primarily through Security's website, www.securityflorida.com.

3) To provide literature that introduces the full-range of the division's many services to its existing customers who may know of only one Security product or service.

4) To help educate and enthuse all bank personnel about the "state of the art" nature of the products and services provided by Security Financial Services.

Creative/Scheduling Requirements

To design, write and oversee production of a brochure that explains the immediate and long-term benefits of using Security Financial Services to handle a wealthy individual's financial and estate planning.

The brochure produced can be up to 20 pages (16 text plus cover) and utilize full color. Quantity will be 25,000. There are no restrictions on style, but it is desired that the brochure focus on the higher quality personal service provided by Security.
Due to the lack of any literature at present, and the formal announcement of the division's marketing campaign at a sales meeting starting on November 12, the brochure must be delivered by November 25, 0000.

4

Freelance Associates' Experience

Freelance Associates is a Miami firm specializing in communications and graphic design services for businesses throughout the Southeast. Our firm was founded in 1995 by John J. Creative and Sarah S. Smart who combined over twenty years of corporate communications experience. Previously Mr. Creative was Vice President and Creative Director for Outstanding Advertising of Fort Lauderdale, Ms Smart was Vice President of Marketing and Strategic Planning for Swamp Land Development Corporation of Hialeah.

Since its founding in 1995, Freelance Associates has built an impressive reputation for producing materials and programs that are strongly market-focused, yet are also tasteful and contemporary. Our work has been prominently represented in every major marketing communications and graphic design competition in the Southeast.

We have worked for small firms and large, startups and those well established. Some of our more prominent clients have been: Cuba Libre Airlines… Belle Glade Jai Alai Fronton… Delectable Ugly Fruit… Berry Island Bahamas Spa & Resort… Columbian Flower Producers, Inc… and HelpingHand Medical Centers. Projects have included advertisements, corporate brochures, product sales literature, package design, store displays and corporate identity programs.

Of more specific interest to Security National Bank, our extensive financial services experience includes working with South Florida Savings & Loan, Coral Gables Municipal Savings Bank, and Retirement Funds Investments. Assignments for these and other institutions have included the production of annual reports, product sales literature, and identity and signage programs, and Internet sites. We are not currently working for any other financial services institution.

Freelance Associates currently has a staff of ten who encompass a wide range of design and marketing skills.

If we are granted this assignment, strategic planning and account service will be handled by company principal Sarah S. Smart, creative development and project management will be handled by company principal John J. Creative.

5

Freelance Associates' Process

Phase I — Information Gathering

First Meeting
The Freelance Associates account team of Sarah S. Smart and John J. Creative will meet with Security Financial Services to clarify objectives, identify subjective preferences, discuss possble thematic approaches, and uncover potential marketing problems.
In addition to Sally Client, we suggest this meeting include Laurie Jameson, Vice President of Marketing; Craig Heritage, Group Vice President; Vicki Montenegro, Account Supervisor, Florida; and any other bank personnel who can contribute to the overview of opportunities, concerns and potential problems.

In addition, we suggest that representatives of Bamboozle & Bamboozle provide a briefing of their "Talk to a Specialist" advertising campaign strategy, creative approach, website tie in, and fulfillment requirements.

We also suggest that any previously-developed materials or information on the division and its competition be made available to us.

Second Meeting
Based upon the overview obtained in the first meeting, John J. Creative will interview Sally Client and Craig Heritage to gather the specific detail and information needed to write and art direct the brochure.

Schedule
To ensure meeting your deadline of having brochures for the sales meeting on November 25th, we suggest that the first meeting be scheduled the week of September 7. The second meeting should happen a week or so later, ideally during the week of September 14.

Phase II — Idea Development

Concepts
Based on the input from the two meetings with your staff, Freelance Associates will develop up to three conceptual, or rough, approaches to the brochure. A cover treatment and one spread from one of these approaches, our recommendation, will be rendered in full size, in color, along with a quarter size dummy (mock up) of the entire brochure. Also developed will be an outline of the copy.

6

Third meeting
At this meeting we will present our approaches to Sally Client and Craig Heritage. Input from this meeting will be used to set the final direction for the brochure.

Schedule
We anticipate that the third meeting (conceptual presentation) will take place approximately two weeks after the second (detailed input), ideally the week of September 28.

Phase III — Development & Approval

Photography
We will select the photographer and supervise the taking of photographs. We will ask Security to help us in making arrangements and providing technical supervision during each photographic session.

Writing
We will develop copy in keeping with the direction provided at the third meeting and submit drafts to Sally Client for approval.

Design
We will execute the design approved at the third meeting and will coordinate and integrate the copy when it is approved. We will prepare final production materials for the approval of Sally Client.

Schedule
We anticipate that first copy draft will be completed approximately one week after the third meeting, ideally the week of October 5. Final draft will be completed approximately one week later, ideally the week of October 12.

We anticipate photography to be done during the week of October 12. We anticipate that final production materials will be available for review three weeks after the third meeting, ideally the week of October 19. Final approval of all materials will be necessary by October 27.

Phase IV — Printing & Delivery

Printer selection
Freelance Associates will ask for bids from three printers and recommend one of the three based on a combination of cost and quality factors. Selection will be made by Security Financial Services.

7

Print supervision
Freelance Associates will oversee printing of the brochure, giving instructions to the printer, supervising color separations and corrections, and checking proofs. However, Security Financial Services will have ultimate responsibility for the accuracy of the brochure as indicated by a signed approval of the pre-production laser and printer press proofs.

Schedule
Printing and binding of 25,000 four-color, 20 page brochures will take approximately two weeks from the time final, approved materials are turned over to the printer. Assuming that pre-production laser proofs are approved by October 27, delivery by November 9 is feasible.

Project Timing
Note: the delivery of this brochure by the required date requires close adherence to the schedule outline above. Delivery cannot be guaranteed unless critical dates are met.

8

Page 9

Freelance Associates' Cost Estimate

Phases I & II — Information Gathering and Idea Development

For three meetings, up to three conceptual
approaches, one quarter size dummy of
complete brochure, full-size rendering of
cover and one spread, copy outline, typography
sample. $ 5,600

Phase III — Development & Approval

Copywriting	$ 4,000	
Photo supervision/editing	2,800	
Design evaluation	3,000	
Design and typography	7,000	
Dummies and copies	400	

17,200

Phase IV — Printing & Delivery
Instructions to printer,
checking separations,
on-press supervision.   2,400

Miscellaneous expenses — our costs +20% markup
Deliveries   200

Total of Freelance Associates' estimated costs $26,200
(Estimated costs do not include taxes.)

9

Page 10

Estimate Of Other Costs

Photography

4 days @$1,000 day	$ 4,000	
Expenses and supplies	750	

$ 4,750

Printing
25,000, 8.5x11," 16-pages plus cover,
4-color process plus spot varnish on cover,
12 color separations, saddlewire bind.   19,000

Total $23,750

Note: this is an estimate for planning purposes only based on our past
experience. Actual photography and printing prices will be determined
from competitive bids.

All photography and printing will be billed directly to Security Financial
Services.

Estimates do not include shipping or taxes.

10

Page 11

Working Agreement

Estimates:
The costs and expenses cited in this proposal are our best estimates
given the information provided. If additional information is forthcoming,
the project specifications change, or the scheduling changes, cost and
expense estimates may change.

Cost and expense estimates are appropriate for 30 days from the date of
this proposal.
Taxes are not included in cost and expense estimates.

Revisions & Alterations:
Work not described in this proposal, including but not limited to revisions (AAs), corrections, alterations and additional proofs, will be billed
as an additional cost at the hourly labor rate of $150 per hour, or at our
cost plus 20% markup.

Terms:
One third of the total estimated costs in advance; one third upon acceptance of the design concept; the balance upon delivery.

If any phase of the assignment is delayed longer than sixty days, we will
bill for work completed to date.

Responsibility:
We will make every reasonable effort to assure the accuracy of the material produced, but are not responsible for the correctness of copy, illustrations, photographs, trademarks, nor for obtaining clearances or
approvals.

We will take normal measures to safeguard any materials entrusted to
us. However, we are not responsible for the loss, damage or unauthorized use of such materials, nor are we responsible for the actions of the
vendors and suppliers we utilize.

Ownership:
This proposal is for the purchase of one creative approach (concept) to
be selected by [client]. All other ideas, concepts or designs described or
exhibited remain the property of [creative firm].

Copyright to the selected creative approach and completed project will
be transferred to [client] upon payment in full for services rendered.
However, copyright transfer might not apply to artwork, photographs, or
type fonts licensed or not owned by [creative firm].

11

Page 12

[creative firm] retains the rights to display the completed project in its
print and online portfolios as examples of its work.

All materials used in the execution of this project—including artwork
and compter-generated instructions and formats (electronic files)—
remain the property of [creative firm].

Purchase Order:
If this proposal is acceptable, a Security purchase order in the amount of
$27,000 should be initiated. All invoices submitted against the purchase
order will be net, payable within 30 days of receipt. Interest may be
charged on past due invoices.

We shall be pleased to begin work upon receipt of your purchase order.

Submitted by   Approved by

Sarah S. Smart   Sally Client
Principal   Director of Marketing Support
Freelance Associates   Security Financial Services

12

Web site proposal. The format for interactive work is somewhat different from that of print proposals. (Continued on the following pages. Referenced in Chapter 13.)

(letterhead)

July 21, 0000

Ms Sally Client
Director of Marketing
The Wagging Tail Dog Care Centres, Inc.
88 Fido Circle
Any City, XX, 12345

Dear Sally:

It was a pleasure meeting again with you and your staff last Thursday.

Ever since our presentation last spring, I have been waiting to hear the good news that The Wagging Tail has secured venture funding. Congratulations!

We are excited about the opportunity JustDoit Design can play in making The Wagging Tail a local success initially, and ultimately a national franchising success.

In Thursday's meeting we discussed your need to have a Web site up and running a week before the first location opens. This will be approximately a month after the first lease is signed, which you indicated could be as early as next week. As you will see on page 3 of the attached proposal, it will take us approximately six weeks to build your site, so this should be no problem. In fact, most of the work in Phase 1 and 2 of site development can be started before your locations are known. So we can start at your earliest convenience.

The first page of the following proposal summarizes the information we received at the meeting regarding The Wagging Tail's market niche (Project Background), Target Market Individuals, and Web Site Objectives. Please review this material carefully for our accuracy in interpretation as it is the basis for the way we will approach developing your site.

After the meeting, our staff met to rough out a preliminary approach. Our initial thoughts are presented on page 2 in the proposal sections Site Style and Appearance, Site Features, and Site References. Here, too, check to make sure that we are on the right track at this early stage.

JustDoit's Development Process on page 3 will provide a rough guide to various project functions and stages. It also provides cost estimates based on the information provided so far. The range reflects the fact that some site features have yet to be determined. Other factors that can effect the final cost are explained in Estimate Options and Additions on page 4.

More > > > >

Doit to Client—2

Although I have tried to anticipate most factors that will affect cost, a final estimate can only be given after the site direction and design has been finalized.

Lastly, please familiarize yourself with the Working Agreement text on pages 5 and 6. These are our regular procedures, which also closely follow standard industry practices.

I'll call you early next week to answer any questions that the proposal might raise, and to discuss a schedule for moving forward.

Again, thanks for the confidence you have shown in JustDoit Design. My staff and I are excited about the opportunity. We look forward to starting what will be a rewarding project for our team and for yours

Sincerely,

Justin Doit
Principal
JustDoit Design

Web Site Proposal For
The Wagging Tail Dog Care Centres

Project Background

The number of dogs in urban areas continues to grow, especially among young professionals. While these individuals desire the love and companionship of man's best friend, they often lack the time or accessibility to space required to provide proper exercise, care, and grooming. Many dogs spend all day sleeping and get only an inadequate walk on city streets in the evening.

The Wagging Tail (TWT) Dog Care Centres, Inc. is a new corporation founded to provide owners with attractive and affordable short-term daycare, including occasional boarding when their owners travel. It will offer the dog equivalent of child daycare for urban professionals—a safe, healthy, educational, and socializing atmosphere in which dogs can spend the day.

Three initial company-owned locations are planned in the metropolitan area—MetroNorth, MetroSouth, and MetroCentral.

Locations in other markets will be considered on a franchise basis later.

Target Market Individuals (from meeting of July 14th)

• Single or married males, 25 to 40 without children (primary).
• Single or married females 25 to 40 without children (secondary).
• Care as much about their dogs as parents do about their children.
• Often feel guilty, conflicted between career and pet needs.
• Reside in multi-unit buildings in densely populated areas.
• Cost is not a major factor, but must not appear excessive.
• Convenience, including pickup, is crucial factor in appealing to them.

Web Site Objectives (from meeting of July 14th)

• Promote that TWT is a new concept focused around customer ease and convenience.
• Show loving care, happy pets, appreciative owners.
• Create awareness in the "non-kennel" home-like atmosphere.
• Indicate availability of veterinarian care when needed.
• Show each of the three locations and facilities and list its staff biographies.
• Provide employment information for each location.
• Solicit interest among possible franchisees.
• Make sure the creative approach is also applicable to later printed material.

-1-

Site Style and Appearance

• Warm, friendly, and comfortable—like one dog owner talking to another.
• Urban male style/color palette but with recognition that many viewers will be female.
• Inviting, non-serious, humorous—quip of day, cartoons, and animation are all appropriate.
• Easy accessibility—fast, well organized, navigation ease, no need for special plug-ins.
• Must also appear professional, trustworthy, stable.

Site Features

• 15 to 20 pages as appropriate.
• To be built using up to five different, original page templates.
• One quarter of pages (25%) devoted to each of the three locations' facilities and staff.
• On-line registration to accommodate complete owner and dog data, including services requested.
• Registration data to be automatically entered into TWT FileMaker Pro database. (Automatic updating by customers will not be available initially, but may later.)
• E-commerce gateway to allow charging registration fees to MasterCard, VISA, American Express, or Discover. (Back-end arrangements to be handled by TWT.)
• Routine maintenance possible by TWT using GoLive.
• JustDoit Design will be available to help with non-routine maintenance.
• Site hosting to be determined by TWT prior to first location opening.

Site References

It is helpful when developing a new site to look at what competitors and others have done. Although there are no direct competitors, and the site we develop will be stylistically and operationally unique, the following have some of the features and style we believe should be in the TWT site.

www.xxxxx.com—has the humorous, yet professional approach we feel is suitable.
www.yyyyyy.com—has the ease of navigation and use we feel works particularly well.

Other sites we like, and the reasons why are:

www.zzzzz.com—has online registration for services similar TWT's needs.
www.uuuuu.com—its treatment of facilities and staff biographies is very informative.
www.tttt.com—a professional services site that uses a novel approach to humor.
www.sssss.com—shows franchise potential and opportunities well.

-2-

JustDoit's Development Process

Phase 1—Orientation and development of strategic concept (approximately two weeks).
- Confirm and refine objectives with TWT marketing staff.
- Confirm and refine target market with TWT marketing staff.
- Establish success criteria with TWT marketing staff.
- Establish preliminary site and page hierarchy.
- Develop three strategies/concepts.
- Develop one or more graphic options for each strategy/concept.
- Present options for evaluation (color prints & electronic files) to Sally Client.

Estimate   *$13,000*

Phase 2—Concept approval and initial development (approximately two weeks).
- Sally Client to select concept for refinement.
- Incorporation of feedback and revisions.
- Create site breakdown—site map, layout, style sheets, color palette, navigation, and copy, illustration and photography needs.
- Review site in light of programming expectations and limitations.
- Develop site artwork.
- Present artwork for approval to Sally Client.

Estimate   *$4,500/$6,500*

Phase 3—Revisions, final development, and programming (approximately two weeks).
- Incorporate artwork feedbacks and revisions.
- Finalize illustration, photography, and animation.
- Program a 15-20 page editable site including: template based for global editing, cascading style sheets (CSS), multi-platform Mac and Windows testing on several browsers, key words and meta tags for page indexing.
- Off-line preview to Sally Client.
- Revise site as necessary.
- Installation and testing on designated server.
- Go live (date to be determined).

Estimate   *$11,000/$13,000*

Estimate total   *$28,500/$32,500*

Please see the following page for estimate options and additions.

-3-

Estimate Options and Additions

Copy strategy is included in Phase 1. Copy development is not included in Phase 2. Copy can be provided by TWT or JustDoit Design will provide it at an estimated cost of $6,000 to $8,000.

Miscellaneous expenses, such as deliveries, prints, messengers, and travel are not included, and will be billed at cost. We estimate them to be between $250 and $500.

Royalty-free stock photography and illustration will be used where appropriate. These costs will be estimated at the end of Phase 1. Original photography and any original illustration or animation will also be estimated at that time. Original photography is $2,500 to $3,000 a day plus expenses, models, and location fees. Usage for original photography or illustration beyond the Web site might be additional. (See Ownership on page 6.) Photo art direction is $1,200 per day plus expenses. Photoshop retouching, if necessary, is extra and is billed at $150 per hour. Illustrations are $400 to $1,800 depending on complexity. Animation costs are $500 to $2,000 depending on complexity. As proposed the site does not require complex Flash programming. If it is later required, it is available at $150 per hour.

-4-

Working Agreement

Estimates

The costs and expenses cited in this proposal are our best estimates given the information provided. They include meetings, consultation time, design, programming, and production time, and a reasonable amount of revisions. If additional information is forthcoming, project specifications change, or the scheduling changes, cost and expense estimates may also change.

The effect of major changes, additional services, and delays cannot be determined until a final design direction has been established. If requirements arise for additional work or scheduling changes not reflected in this estimate, we will provide an updated estimate when the final design direction has been approved.

Cost and expense estimates are appropriate for 30 days from the date of this proposal. Taxes are not included in cost and expense estimates.

Revisions & Alterations

Work not described in this proposal, including but not limited to revisions (AAs), corrections, alterations, and additional proofs, will be billed as an additional cost at the hourly labor rate of $150 per hour, or at our cost plus 25% markup.

Terms

Unless otherwise arranged in advance, a retainer fee of 50% of the design, production, and expense estimates is required upon initiation of each project phase. The remainder of the costs for each phase will be invoiced upon its completion. Invoice terms are net 30 days. Invoices remaining unpaid after 30 days will be assessed interest at 1.5% per month (18% annually). If any phase of this project is delayed longer than 60 days, we will bill for work completed to date.

Should TWT elect to terminate this project, JustDoit Design will invoice 50% of the lowest total estimate figure, or for actual work performed, which is greater, plus expenses.

Should JustDoit Design find it necessary to refer past due accounts to an attorney for collection, then TWT shall reimburse JustDoit Design for all attorney's fees and collection costs incurred. Any such fees incurred in the collection process will be added to the amount due, and the account shall not be considered paid in full until the entire debt has been settled.

Responsibility

JustDoit Design will make every reasonable effort to ensure the accuracy of what is produced, but is not responsible for the correctness of copy, illustrations, photographs, nor for obtaining clearances or approvals.

TWT shall assume full responsibility for any accepted graphic recommendations from JustDoit Design including but not limited to trademark and patent searches, registrations, feasibility

-5-

testing, and legal compliance responsibilities. TWT shall indemnify JustDoit Design and hold it harmless from any damages, costs, or losses that might arise as the result of any action against either party regarding products and/or services performed with regards to this project.

JustDoit Design will take normal measures to safeguard any materials entrusted to us. However, we are not responsible for the loss, damage, or unauthorized use of such materials, nor are we responsible for the actions of the vendors and suppliers we utilize.

Ownership

This proposal is for the development and implementation of one strategic idea or concept. All preliminary concepts, ideas, approaches, plans, reports, recommendations, designs, artwork, and electronic files remain the sole property of JustDoit Design, and may be used in the future at their discretion.

All materials used in the production of this assignment—including original artwork and computer generated artwork, formats, and electronic code—remains the property of JustDoit Design.

Unless otherwise agreed upon, all original photography and illustration are for the sole purpose of the Web site and may not be used in other applications. If TWT wishes to purchase unlimited rights to the use of original photography or illustration (ownership of copyright), please inform JustDoit Design and this will be a consideration in the selection of and negotiation with photographers or illustrators.

Copyright to the Web site design will be considered transferred and reproduction rights granted upon receipt of payment in full.

Purchase Order

If this proposal is acceptable, please sign as indicated below and initiate a purchase order in the amount of $28,500.

We shall be pleased to begin work on the schedule you determine after receipt of the TWT purchase order.

Submitted by: _____   Date:_____
              Justin Doit
              Principal
              JustDoit Design

Approved by: _____   Date:_____
             Sally Client
             Director of Marketing
             The Wagging Tail Dog Care Centres

-6-

Web surveying forms. Assessing client satisfaction anonymously after the fact is easy and inexpensive using e-mail and an Internet surveying service. (Referenced in Chapter 15.)

To: jprospectiva@prospect.com
From: president@agrowingcompany.com
Subject: Satisfaction survey
Cc:
Bcc:

Dear John:

Occasionally we survey our clients regarding how well we've met their expectations.

We do this because we recognize that you have a choice of suppliers, many of whom offer services of similar quality. What has always set us apart, and where our surveys come in, is our unusual ability to listen and adjust to our clients' needs. And by so doing provide the best value in the (city) area.

So I would like to ask if you would help us by responding to our Client Satisfaction Survey. All it takes is a couple minutes to click on the below link and answer ten questions. The survey is anonymous. Your name or e-mail address will not be recorded (unless you tell us otherwise).

Use this link to take the survey:
http://www.somesurveysoftware.com/EndUser.aspx?E0XA8BHE0A4BDB7

Thanks for your help, and for being one of our valued clients.

Sally Striver
President

(signature block)

A Growing Company
Client Satisfaction Survey (Date)

1. **How would you rate our style/creativity?**
   O Superb   O Excellent   O Sufficient   O Somewhat lacking

2. **How well have we helped you define your objectives?**
   O N/A   O Very   O Moderately   O Not well

3. **How well have we met the objectives for what we've handled?**
   O Very   O Moderately   O Not well

4. **How quickly did we produce a strong creative concept?**
   O One try   O Couple tries   O Several tries

5. **How efficiently have we handled scheduling and production?**
   O Very   O Moderately   O Not well

6. **How knowledgeable and professional are we to work with?**
   O Very   O Average   O Not very

7. **How have you found the value (price+results) of our services?**
   O High   O Average   O Low

8. **What would you like us to do better or differently?**

9. **Overall, how do we rate compared to your experience with similar firms?**
   O N/A   O Very well   O Average   O Low

10. **Any experiences you would like to share with us?**

If we may use any of your responses, please provide your e-mail address so we can get in touch with you.

Submit

APPENDIX IV

A SHORT MARKETING LEXICON

Like any specialty, marketing has its own language. Recognizing some important terms (and being able to use them in conversation) enables you to both understand and impress clients. Below are some of the more common, non-obvious, and important terms that a creative firm is likely to encounter, with an emphasis on branding terms.

80/20 principle—refers to the notion that 80 percent of many clients' business (or profit) comes from the top 20 percent of their customers. It is, however, an inappropriate principle for creative firms to follow. (Sometimes also called "The Pareto Principle.")

AIDA model—the pattern according to which all promotional activities should create one of more of these four outcomes: Attention, Interest, Desire, and Action.

Brand

> *architecture*—the ways in which an organization structures and organizes its portfolio of brands. There are three main systems: parent, which identifies an organization ("Kodak"); linked, whereby a parent brand is linked to a product brand ("Apple iPad"); and independent, whereby products are individually branded without any parent brand (Proctor & Gamble's "Bounty").

> *concept*—the dominant idea or image that a brand's sponsor (owner) wants to have register with customers. (Similar to "brand essence.")

> *conviction or commitment*—the strength of attitude or attachment that customers feel toward a brand. (Similar to, but not as strong as, "brand preference.")

> *development index (BDI)*—the percentage of a brand's sales in a specific market (geographic, demographic, or other) compared to the percentage of the national population in that market. For example,

if 5 percent of a brand's sales come from a market that has 5 percent of the national population, the BDI is 100.

earnings—(1) a brand's net income; (2) the share of total earnings that can be attributed to a specific brand.

equity—(1) the monetary value of a brand to an organization; (2) the sum of all the qualities that make a brand distinctive.

essence—(1) a brand's indispensible elements expressed in the simplest terms; (2) its positioning statement or unique selling proposition (USP). (Similar to "brand concept.")

extension—the application of an established brand to a new product, usually in an unrelated category or market. (Sometimes also referred to as franchise extension or line extension.)

franchise—the customer loyalty that attaches to a brand. (Not to be confused with business franchising.)

harmonization—the process of ensuring that all products in a particular brand range have a consistent name, visual identity, and, ideally, positioning across several geographic or product markets.

harvesting—the process of decreasing a brand's marketing expenditures and relying on customer loyalty to sustain its sales.

image—a combination of the visual recognition, emotions, and connotations evoked by the brand.

insistence—the condition under which customers will accept no substitute and will search extensively for the preferred brand. (Also see "brand loyalty" and "brand preference.")

leveraging—the broadening of a company's product range by introducing additional types of products under a brand name that is already successful in another category.

life cycle—the theory that every brand will go through at least four distinct phases—introduction, growth, maturity, and decline. Specific management strategies are applied at each stage to maximize brand effectiveness.

loyalists—those who repeatedly purchase a brand with little external motivation.

loyalty—a measure of the degree to which a buyer recognizes, prefers, and insists on a particular brand. (Also see "brand preference" and "brand insistence.")

mapping—a research technique that attempts to determine a brand's specific strengths and weaknesses versus those of competitive brands.

mark—the visual part of a brand—a design, logo, or other symbol; often a registered trademark. (Also see "brand name.")

name—the spoken part of a brand. (Also see "brand mark.")

parity—the extent of differences that customers perceive among brands. High parity equates to high differentiation; low parity to low differentiation. In the latter case, one brand is essentially the same as another.

Pareto principle. (See "80/20 principle.")

personality—(1) perceptions that customers have about a brand as distinct from what the product actually does; (2) the attribution of human personality traits (seriousness, warmth, imagination, etc.) to a brand as a way of achieving differentiation.

positioning—the distinctive, non-visual strategies a firm uses to ensure that customers can easily differentiate its brand from competitors' brands.

power—the ability of a brand to strongly influence its market.

preference—the stage of brand loyalty at which a buyer will select a particular brand but will choose a competitor's brand if the preferred brand is unavailable. (Also see "brand conviction," "brand loyalty," "brand insistence.")

promiscuity—an environment or market in which there is little or no loyalty to brands (the opposite of "brand loyalty").

recognition—a state wherein customers are aware of the existence of a brand but have not developed a preference for it.

reinforcement—activity that seeks to get customers who have tried a particular brand to become repeat purchasers.

repositioning—(1) the process of modifying one or more of a product's elements in an attempt to attract more customers; (2) the process of modifying a product so that it becomes more attractively branded.

revitalization—the attempt to breathe life into a mature or dying product through new branding efforts.

revival—a way to gain market visibility and penetration faster and with less cost than by introducing a new brand.

sponsor—the owner of a brand.

switching—the migration of customer support from one brand to another.

tone of voice—the specific emotional appeal (friendly, knowledgeable, wise, etc.) that a brand uses to speak to its audiences.

tribe—a group of customers who share common values, experiences, and preferences.

valuing—the process of identifying and measuring the economic benefit that derives from brand ownership.

values—the basic attributes that are crucial to a brand's continuing differentiation and success, and that must not be changed or compromised. (Also see "brand essence.")

Commodity—an item with features that are indistinguishable from its competitors' features.

Demand curve—the relationship between price and quantity; as the former goes up, the latter goes down. (Compare to "supply curve.")

Demographics—statistical data about a given population. (Compare to "psychographics.")

Early adopters—customers who will take a chance on a new product; often, important trendsetters (sometimes called pioneer buyers).

Elasticity/inelasticity—characteristics of a product or market: when small changes significantly affect demand, the product or market is said to be elastic; when they won't, it is said to be inelastic.

Equilibrium price—the going market price for an item or service.

Equity protection or strategies—plans to reduce the erosion of market share through inattention or brand misuse, counterfeiting, and theft.

Facilitators—a catchall term for advertising agencies, design firms, product testing labs, wholesalers, retailers, and the like.

Generic market—customers with only broadly similar needs for which products can be easily substituted. (Compare to "product market.")

Law of diminishing demand—the observation that as price is raised, demand falls. The law of increasing demand is the opposite.

Marketing concept—the idea that all activities, from product research to after-sale service, are focused entirely on the wishes of customers. (Compare to "production concept.")

Micromarketing—the process of catering to the specific needs of small populations (sometimes called niche marketing or segmentation marketing).

MSA (Metropolitan Statistical Area)—an economic area or unit with a fairly large city at its center.

PLC (Product Life Cycle)—the concept that expenses are usually highest right after a product's introduction and that profits are highest at maturity.

Positioning—placing a product in its best environment for selling.

Prestige pricing—setting a high price to imply a product's exceptional quality or high status.

Primary data—a research term that denotes newly discovered information. (Compare to "secondary data.")

Primary demand—interest in a product category, not a specific brand.

Product market—customers with very specific needs and little latitude for substitutions. (Compare to "generic market.")

Production concept/orientation—the making of products without prior marketing input.

Psychographics—the lifestyle data of individuals; normally the term comprises Activities, Interests, and Opinions (AIO). (Compare to "demographics.")

Pulsing—a strategically uneven distribution of promotional activity (sometimes called flighting).

Pure market/competition—a situation in which there are similar products, knowledgeable customers, and affordable prices.

Sales promotion—activity that stimulates sales at the point-of-purchase.

Scale economies—the savings that accrue from mass volume and repetitive tasks: the more items that are produced, the lower the costs of production become and the more prices should drop.

Secondary data—a research term that denotes already published information. (Compare to "primary data.")

Segmentation—the breaking down of an activity or product into several relevant categories.

SKU (Stock Keeping Unit)—the specific inventory number assigned to each product by a retailer.

Stimulus response model—a pattern that describes circumstances in which individuals respond in the same way to stimuli.

Supply curve—the relationship between price and supply; as the latter goes up, the former goes down. (Compare to "demand curve.")

Threshold effect—the point at which a marketing effort becomes productive.

Turn rate—the length of time that an item sits on a retailer's shelf. A short turn rate is key to profitability.

Utility—the power to satisfy customers' needs.

INDEX

Graphic Artists Guild, 138
gross margin, 73
growth, strategic significance, 23

H
hiring a salesperson
    affordability calculations, 72–74
    alternatives to full-time hire, 71, 74–76
    compensation considerations, 76–77
    consideration of business mix in, 78
    consideration of business plan in, 76
    determining need for, 72, 180–181
    getting applications, 78–79
    individual assessment, 78
    non-compete agreement as condition
        for, 79–80
    risks, 77–78
    screening applicants, 79
    staff involvement in, 79
    see also salespeople

I
image creation
    benefits of marketing, 14
    generalist versus specialist, 18
    marketing strategy objectives, 17–18
Internet and online marketing
    advantages of, in promotions, 52–53
    blogs and podcasts, 56–57
    business networking, 55–56
    client satisfaction surveys, 169, 209
    e-mail promotions, 52–53, 54–55
    freelance job listings, 55
    keyword advertising, 55
    social media and networking, 21, 44, 56,
        69
    traditional media and, 50–51
    see also Web sites

J
Jaycees, 44

K
Kiwanis, 44

L
law of diminishing demand, 213

legal issues
    agent agreements, 138, 201
    in branding of products and services,
        186–187
    copyright and intellectual property
        rights, 162
    pre-project paperwork, 138–139
    sales non-compete agreements, 198
    standard contracts, 139–140
letter of agency, 138
letter of introduction, 62, 63, 197
letters of agreement, 140–141, 203
LinkedIn.com, 44
location, 18–19
loss of client, reasons for, 161–164
lowest real cost, 32

M
mail lists, 52, 59
    for e-mail, 54
    generating leads from, 180
marketing, generally
    control of business image by, 14
    in corporate cultures, 37–38
    in current technological environment,
        49, 50–51
    evolution of small creative firms, 33–34
    importance of, 11–12, 13, 34
    misconceptions, 12–13
    negative perception of, by creative and
        artistic individuals, 11, 13
    post-presentation, 136
    responsibilities for, 36–37
    selling and, 13
    supplementary benefits, 13–14
    tactics, 33
    see also after-marketing; consistent and
        ongoing marketing efforts; costs of
        marketing; marketing plan; strate-
        gies, marketing
marketing plan
    development process, 41–43
    efficiency of, 178
    employee participation in creation of,
        42–43
    expectations of results from, 178–180
    formalization, 39–40

team for, 122–123, 124
zero-based approach, 123
procurement function of organizations, 12
commoditization trends, 27
production concept/orientation, 214
production function of organization, 12
product life cycle, 213
product market, 213
profitability
benefits of marketing, 14–15
defense of pricing, 92–93
promotion
in current technological environment, 49–51
direct mail, 51–52
as element of marketing strategy, 19–20
frequency, 20
ineffective approaches, 50
printed materials, 50–51, 70
purpose, 49
short term and long term objectives, 19–20
threshold effect, 50
unique demands of service marketing, 21
proposals and estimates
detailed proposals, 141, 204–206
following-up after unsuccessful bids, 146–147
legal protection in, 138–139
letters of agreement, 140–141, 203
negotiations, 145–146
objectives, 138–139
personal presentations, 144–146
preparation costs, 138
psychology of pricing in, 91
rationale for written agreements, 137–138
responding to request for quote/proposal, 142–143
simple estimates, 140, 202
standard legal contracts, 139–140
success rate, 146
for Web site design, 207–208
worksheets, 140, 202
prospecting
client background information, 196

contact mining, 66–67
follow-up, 67–68
Internet use, 56
record keeping, 67, 196, 197
responding to unsolicited inquiries, 68–70, 85
sending samples, 68
turning down unsuitable clients, 70
see also cold-calling
psychographics, 214
publicity, 21, 38
pulsing, 214
pure markets, 214

Q
quality of client base
benefits of consistent marketing, 16, 29
differentiation of firm by, 111
marketing objectives, 22
strategic considerations, 21–22
quality of firm's work, differentiation by, 109–111

R
referrals
advantages of, as source of business, 43–44, 175, 176
client feedback to encourage, 167
client mix resulting from, 14, 16
common approach of creative services suppliers, 13
expectations of referring client, 16
implications for profitability, 16, 176
in marketing plan, 44
negative effects of reliance on, 14, 15–16, 175–176
paying for, 45, 75
percentage of business from, 44, 176–177
reliability, 16, 175–176
requesting, 44–45, 196
strategies for generating, 44–45
refinement presentations, 149–150, 155–157
reliability, 165
request for quote/proposal, 142–143
return on investment, 146

threshold effect, 50, 214
turn rate, 214

U
utility, 214

V
value propositions, 108–109, 199
volume strategy, 28–29

W
Web sites, 68–69
    content and style, 53–54, 68–69
    contract proposal for designing,
        207–208
    portfolio presentations on, 117
    posting prices on, 68–69
    promotional significance, 49, 53
workflow management
    benefits of marketing, 14–15, 160,
        177–178
    marketing plan rationale, 41
    stability goals, 24
    unreliability of referrals, 16, 175–176